BART SIMPSON™
TO THE RESCUE!

HARPER

NEW YORK · LONDON · TORONTO · SYDNEY

BART SIMPSON TO THE RESCUE!

Collects Bart Simpson *53-54 and 56-58*

Copyright © 2014 by
Bongo Entertainment, Inc. All rights reserved.
No part of this book may be used or reproduced in any manner whatsoever
without written permission except in the case of brief quotations
embodied in critical articles and reviews. For information address
HarperCollins Publishers,
10 East 53rd Street, New York, NY 10022.

FIRST EDITION

ISBN 978-0-06-230183-3

14 15 16 17 18 TC 10 9 8 7 6 5 4 3 2 1

Publisher: Matt Groening
Creative Director: Nathan Kane
Managing Editor: Terry Delegeane
Director of Operations: Robert Zaugh
Art Director: Chia-Hsien Jason Ho
Art Director Special Projects: Serban Cristescu
Assistant Art Director: Mike Rote
Production Manager: Christopher Ungar
Assistant Editor: Karen Bates
Production: Nathan Hamill, Art Villanueva
Administration: Ruth Waytz, Pete Benson
Editorial Assistant: Max Davison
Legal Guardian: Susan A. Grode

Printed by TC Transcontinental, Beauceville, QC, Canada. 02/05/14

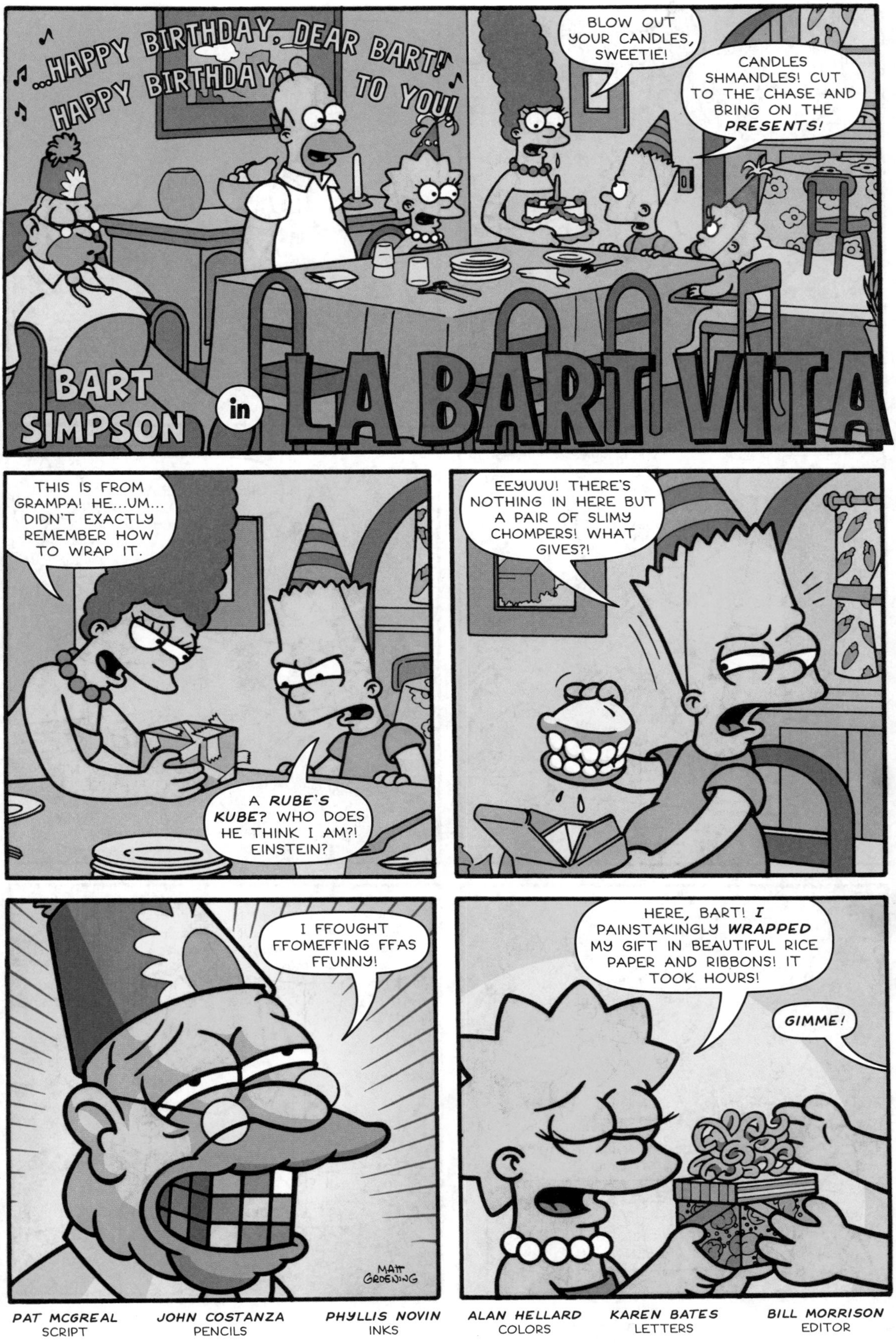
...HAPPY BIRTHDAY, DEAR BART! HAPPY BIRTHDAY TO YOU!
BLOW OUT YOUR CANDLES, SWEETIE!
CANDLES SHMANDLES! CUT TO THE CHASE AND BRING ON THE *PRESENTS!*
BART SIMPSON in LA BART VITA
THIS IS FROM GRAMPA! HE...UM... DIDN'T EXACTLY REMEMBER HOW TO WRAP IT.
A *RUBE'S KUBE*? WHO DOES HE THINK I AM?! EINSTEIN?
EEYUUU! THERE'S NOTHING IN HERE BUT A PAIR OF SLIMY CHOMPERS! WHAT GIVES?!
I FFOUGHT FFOMEFFING FFAS FFUNNY!
MATT GROENING
HERE, BART! *I* PAINSTAKINGLY ***WRAPPED*** MY GIFT IN BEAUTIFUL RICE PAPER AND RIBBONS! IT TOOK HOURS!
GIMME!

PAT MCGREAL SCRIPT | ***JOHN COSTANZA*** PENCILS | ***PHYLLIS NOVIN*** INKS | ***ALAN HELLARD*** COLORS | ***KAREN BATES*** LETTERS | ***BILL MORRISON*** EDITOR

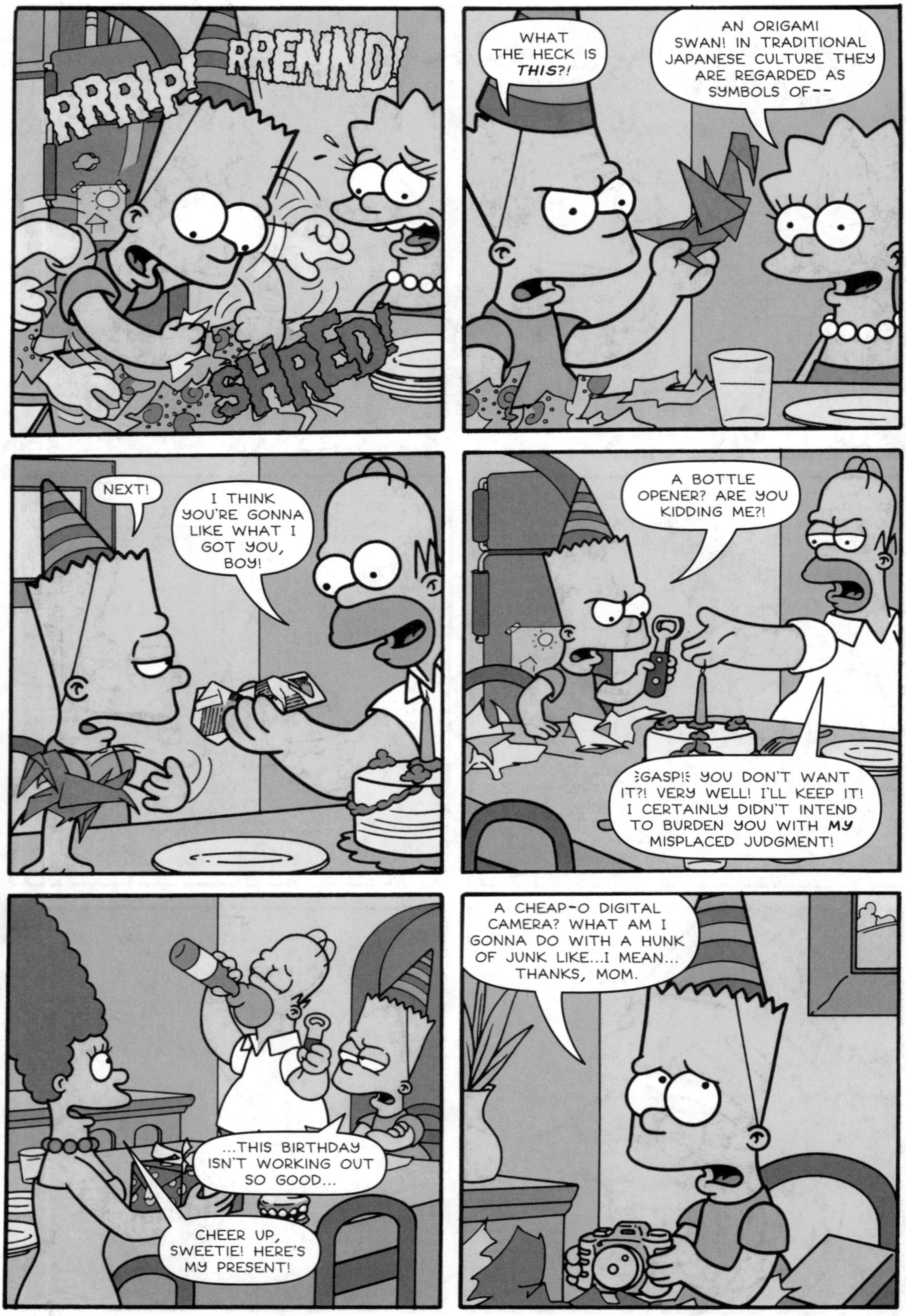
RRRIP!
RRENND!
SHRED!
WHAT THE HECK IS THIS?!
AN ORIGAMI SWAN! IN TRADITIONAL JAPANESE CULTURE THEY ARE REGARDED AS SYMBOLS OF--
NEXT!
I THINK YOU'RE GONNA LIKE WHAT I GOT YOU, BOY!
A BOTTLE OPENER? ARE YOU KIDDING ME?!
:GASP!: YOU DON'T WANT IT?! VERY WELL! I'LL KEEP IT! I CERTAINLY DIDN'T INTEND TO BURDEN YOU WITH MY MISPLACED JUDGMENT!
...THIS BIRTHDAY ISN'T WORKING OUT SO GOOD...
CHEER UP, SWEETIE! HERE'S MY PRESENT!
A CHEAP-O DIGITAL CAMERA? WHAT AM I GONNA DO WITH A HUNK OF JUNK LIKE...I MEAN... THANKS, MOM.

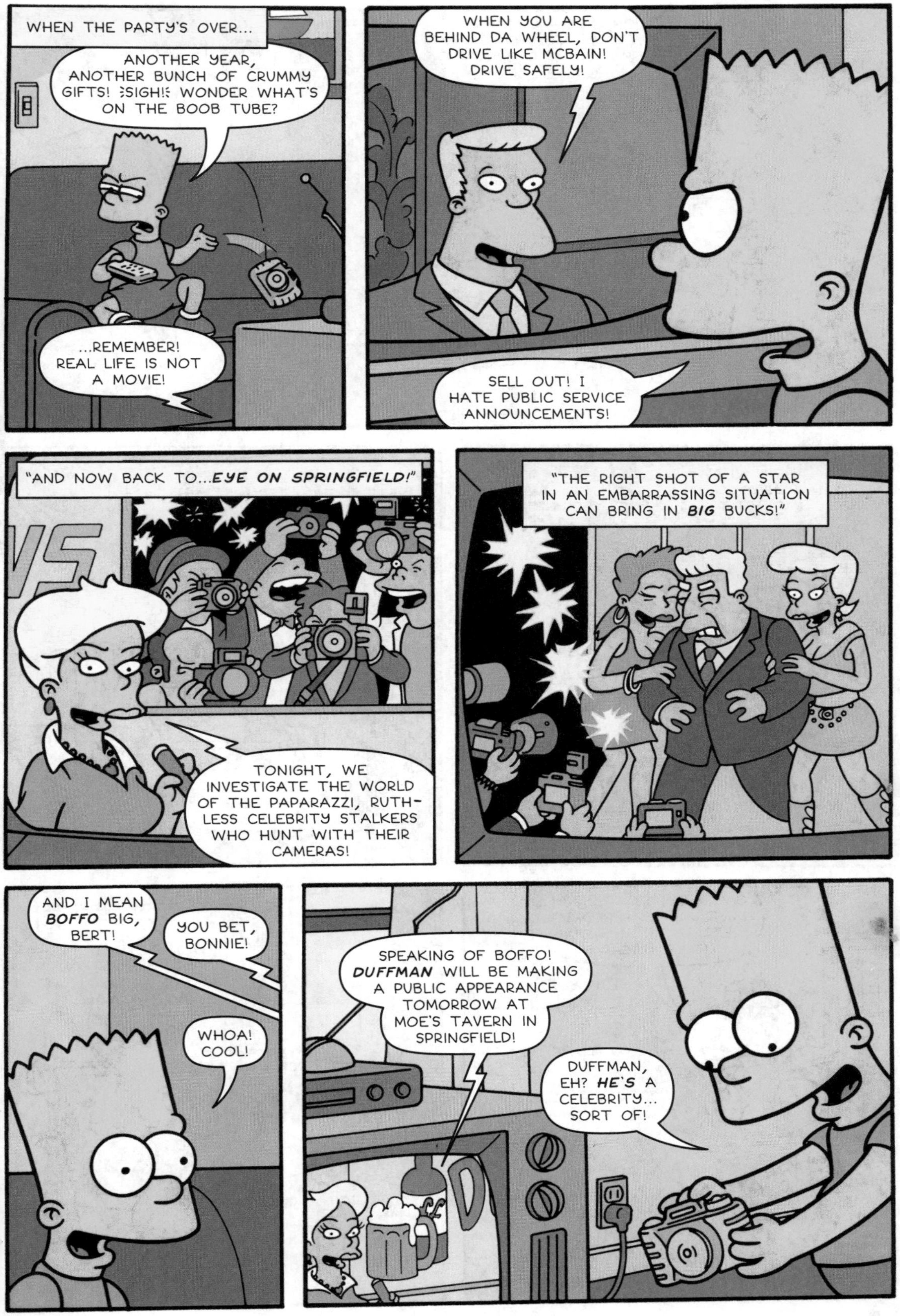
WHEN THE PARTY'S OVER...
ANOTHER YEAR, ANOTHER BUNCH OF CRUMMY GIFTS! SIGH! WONDER WHAT'S ON THE BOOB TUBE?
...REMEMBER! REAL LIFE IS NOT A MOVIE!
WHEN YOU ARE BEHIND DA WHEEL, DON'T DRIVE LIKE MCBAIN! DRIVE SAFELY!
SELL OUT! I HATE PUBLIC SERVICE ANNOUNCEMENTS!
"AND NOW BACK TO...EYE ON SPRINGFIELD!"
TONIGHT, WE INVESTIGATE THE WORLD OF THE PAPARAZZI, RUTH-LESS CELEBRITY STALKERS WHO HUNT WITH THEIR CAMERAS!
"THE RIGHT SHOT OF A STAR IN AN EMBARRASSING SITUATION CAN BRING IN BIG BUCKS!"
AND I MEAN BOFFO BIG, BERT!
YOU BET, BONNIE!
WHOA! COOL!
SPEAKING OF BOFFO! DUFFMAN WILL BE MAKING A PUBLIC APPEARANCE TOMORROW AT MOE'S TAVERN IN SPRINGFIELD!
DUFFMAN, EH? HE'S A CELEBRITY... SORT OF!

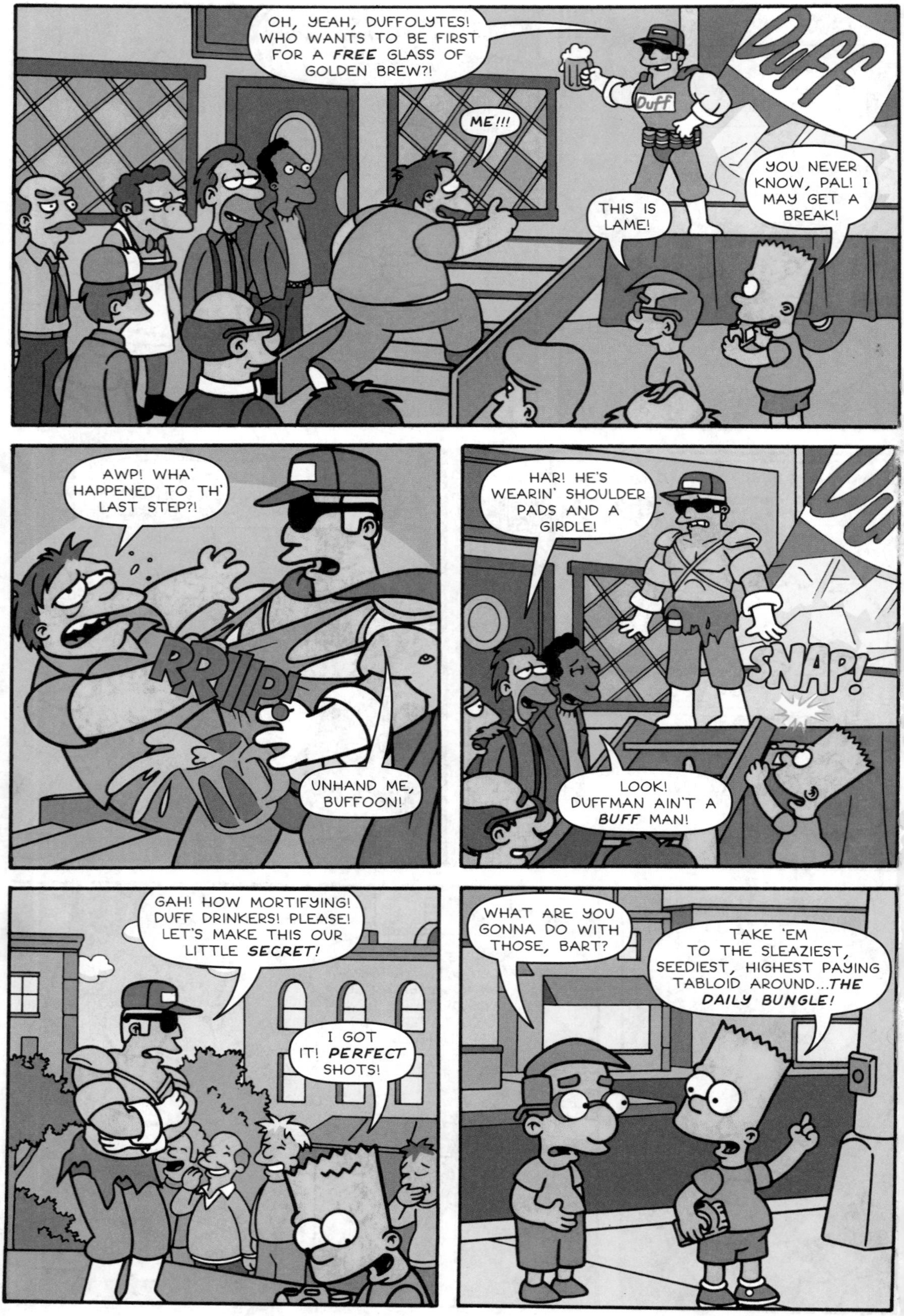

OH, YEAH, DUFFOLYTES! WHO WANTS TO BE FIRST FOR A FREE GLASS OF GOLDEN BREW?!
Duff
Duff
ME!!!
THIS IS LAME!
YOU NEVER KNOW, PAL! I MAY GET A BREAK!
AWP! WHA' HAPPENED TO TH' LAST STEP?!
RRIIP!
UNHAND ME, BUFFOON!
HAR! HE'S WEARIN' SHOULDER PADS AND A GIRDLE!
SNAP!
LOOK! DUFFMAN AIN'T A BUFF MAN!
GAH! HOW MORTIFYING! DUFF DRINKERS! PLEASE! LET'S MAKE THIS OUR LITTLE SECRET!
I GOT IT! PERFECT SHOTS!
WHAT ARE YOU GONNA DO WITH THOSE, BART?
TAKE 'EM TO THE SLEAZIEST, SEEDIEST, HIGHEST PAYING TABLOID AROUND...THE DAILY BUNGLE!

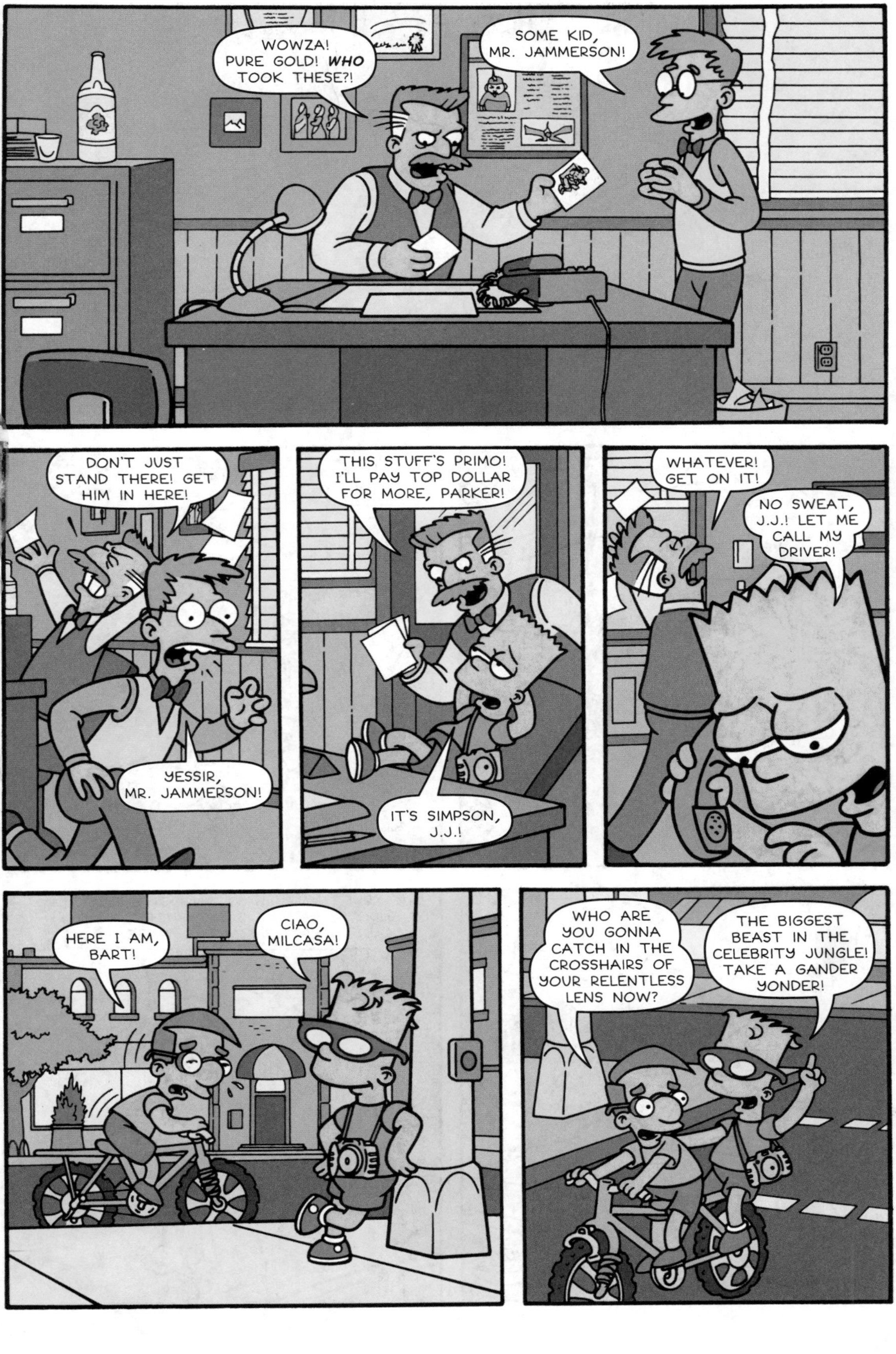
WOWZA! PURE GOLD! ***WHO*** TOOK THESE?!
SOME KID, MR. JAMMERSON!
DON'T JUST STAND THERE! GET HIM IN HERE!
YESSIR, MR. JAMMERSON!
THIS STUFF'S PRIMO! I'LL PAY TOP DOLLAR FOR MORE, PARKER!
IT'S SIMPSON, J.J.!
WHATEVER! GET ON IT!
NO SWEAT, J.J.! LET ME CALL MY DRIVER!
HERE I AM, BART!
CIAO, MILCASA!
WHO ARE YOU GONNA CATCH IN THE CROSSHAIRS OF YOUR RELENTLESS LENS NOW?
THE BIGGEST BEAST IN THE CELEBRITY JUNGLE! TAKE A GANDER YONDER!

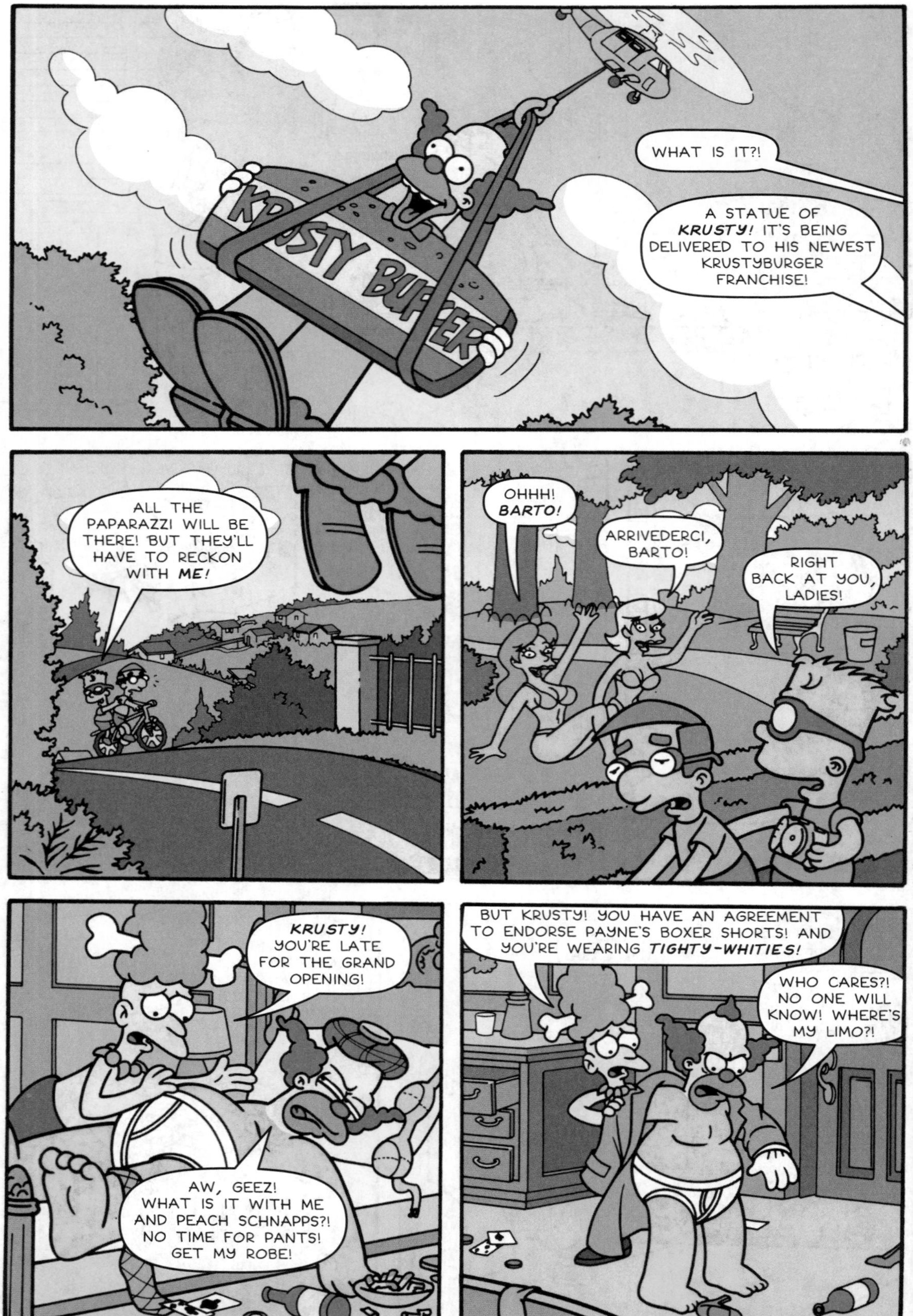
KRUSTY BURGER
WHAT IS IT?!
A STATUE OF KRUSTY! IT'S BEING DELIVERED TO HIS NEWEST KRUSTYBURGER FRANCHISE!
ALL THE PAPARAZZI WILL BE THERE! BUT THEY'LL HAVE TO RECKON WITH ME!
OHHH! BARTO!
ARRIVEDERCI, BARTO!
RIGHT BACK AT YOU, LADIES!
KRUSTY! YOU'RE LATE FOR THE GRAND OPENING!
AW, GEEZ! WHAT IS IT WITH ME AND PEACH SCHNAPPS?! NO TIME FOR PANTS! GET MY ROBE!
BUT KRUSTY! YOU HAVE AN AGREEMENT TO ENDORSE PAYNE'S BOXER SHORTS! AND YOU'RE WEARING TIGHTY-WHITIES!
WHO CARES?! NO ONE WILL KNOW! WHERE'S MY LIMO?!

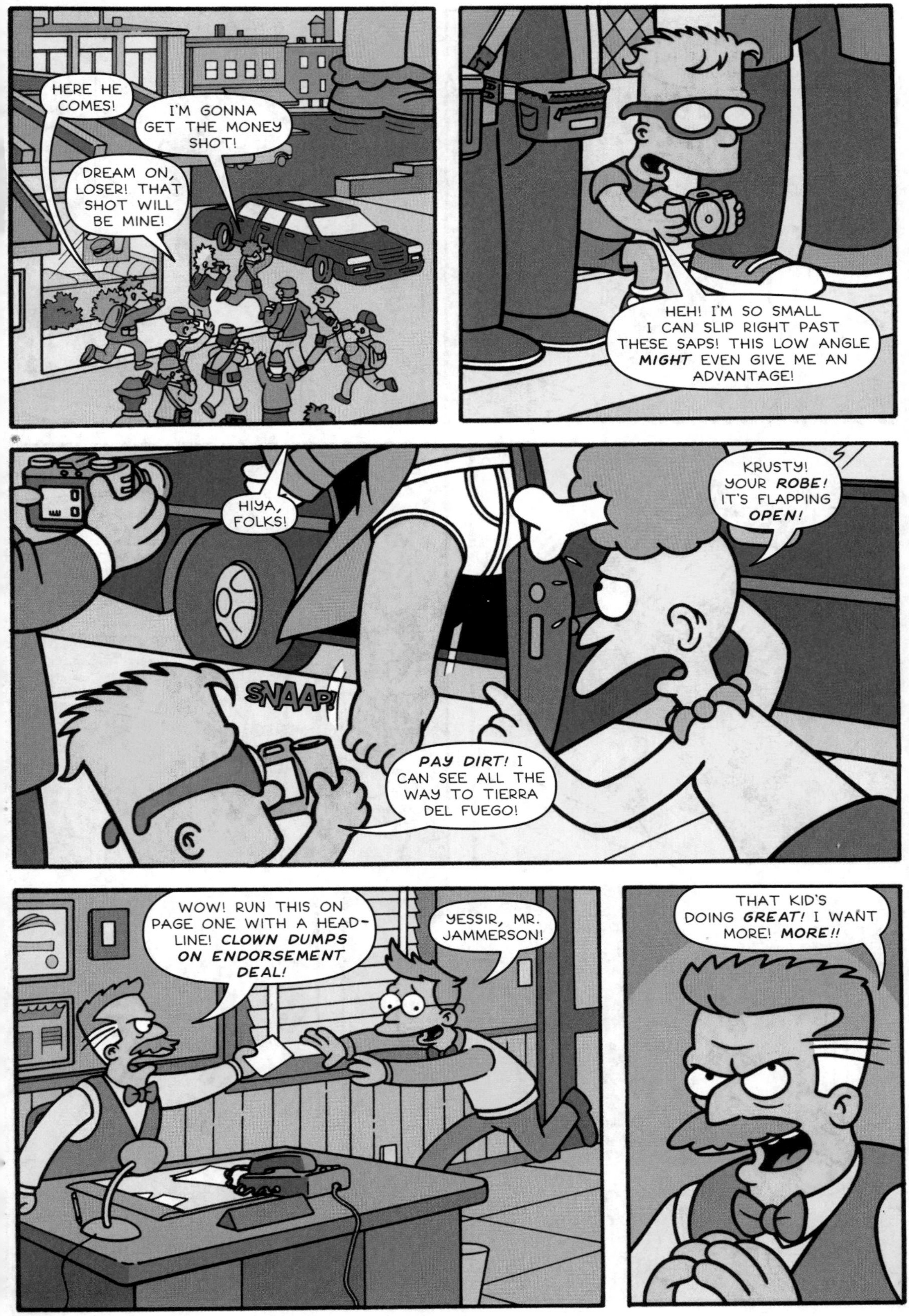
HERE HE COMES!
I'M GONNA GET THE MONEY SHOT!
DREAM ON, LOSER! THAT SHOT WILL BE MINE!
HEH! I'M SO SMALL I CAN SLIP RIGHT PAST THESE SAPS! THIS LOW ANGLE MIGHT EVEN GIVE ME AN ADVANTAGE!
HIYA, FOLKS!
KRUSTY! YOUR ROBE! IT'S FLAPPING OPEN!
SNAAP!
PAY DIRT! I CAN SEE ALL THE WAY TO TIERRA DEL FUEGO!
WOW! RUN THIS ON PAGE ONE WITH A HEAD-LINE! CLOWN DUMPS ON ENDORSEMENT DEAL!
YESSIR, MR. JAMMERSON!
THAT KID'S DOING GREAT! I WANT MORE! MORE!!

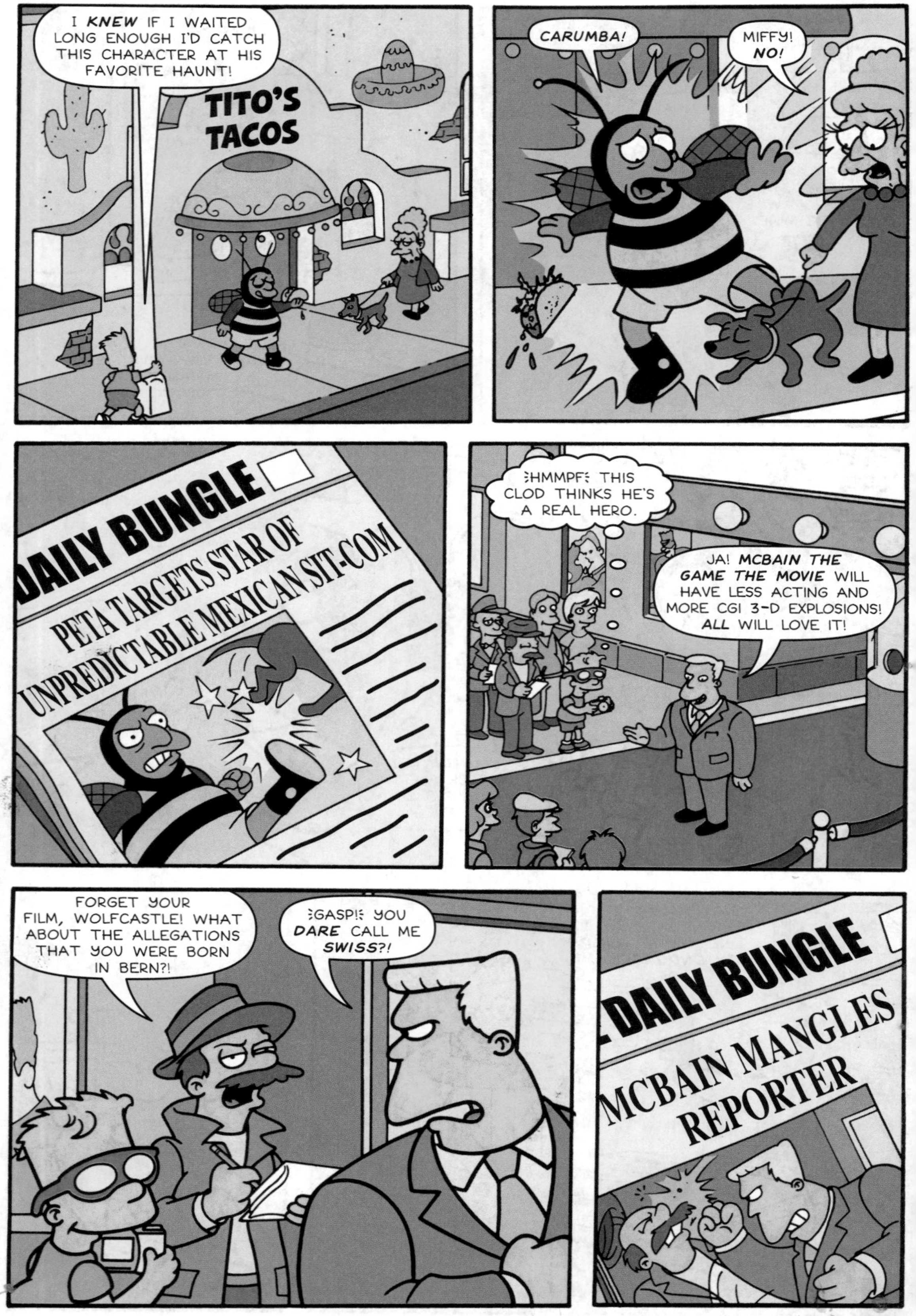
I KNEW IF I WAITED LONG ENOUGH I'D CATCH THIS CHARACTER AT HIS FAVORITE HAUNT!
TITO'S TACOS
CARUMBA!
MIFFY! NO!
DAILY BUNGLE
PETA TARGETS STAR OF UNPREDICTABLE MEXICAN SIT-COM
⁝HMMPF⁝ THIS CLOD THINKS HE'S A REAL HERO.
JA! MCBAIN THE GAME THE MOVIE WILL HAVE LESS ACTING AND MORE CGI 3-D EXPLOSIONS! ALL WILL LOVE IT!
FORGET YOUR FILM, WOLFCASTLE! WHAT ABOUT THE ALLEGATIONS THAT YOU WERE BORN IN BERN?!
⁝GASP!⁝ YOU DARE CALL ME SWISS?!
DAILY BUNGLE
MCBAIN MANGLES REPORTER

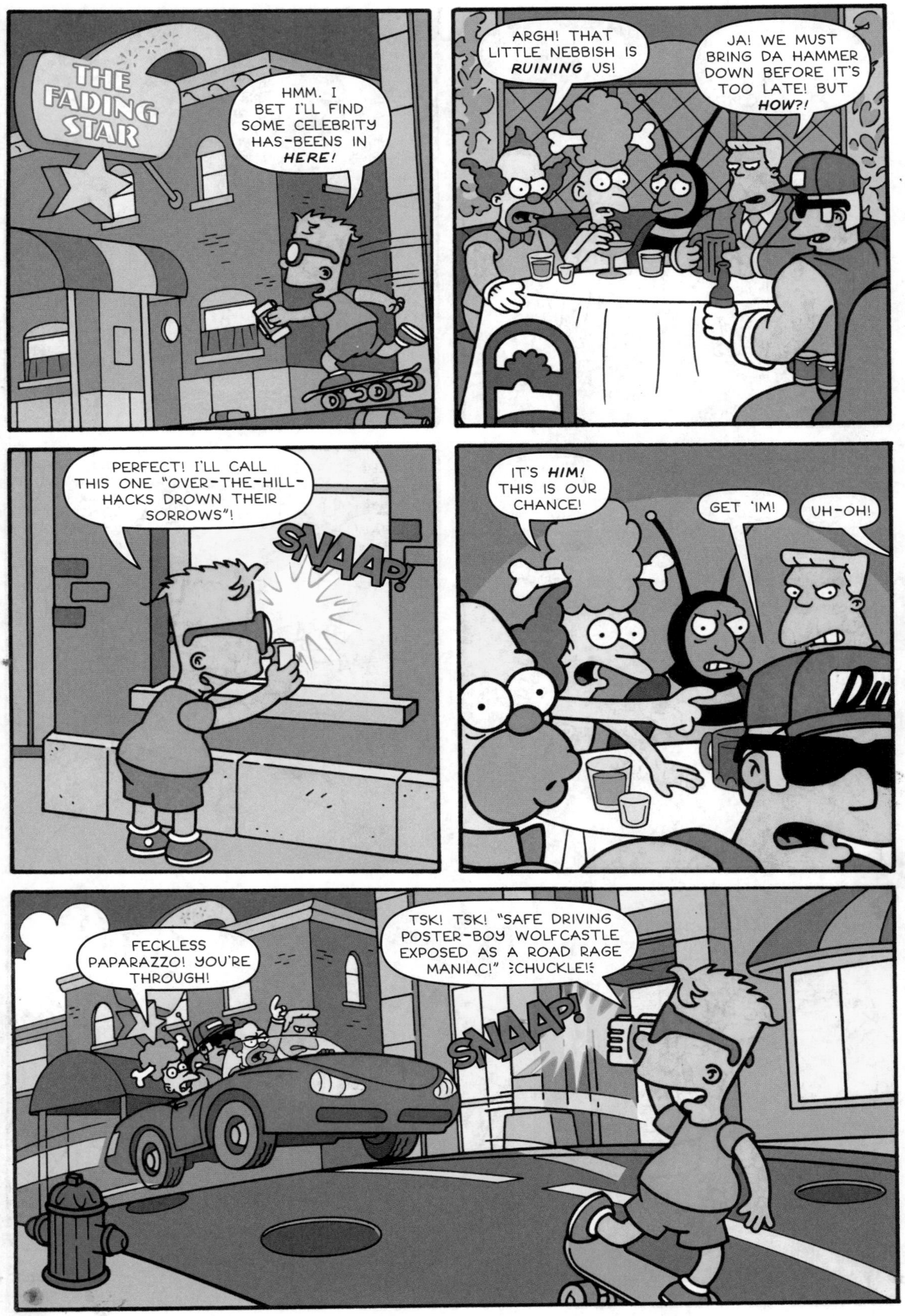
THE FADING STAR
HMM. I BET I'LL FIND SOME CELEBRITY HAS-BEENS IN HERE!
ARGH! THAT LITTLE NEBBISH IS RUINING US!
JA! WE MUST BRING DA HAMMER DOWN BEFORE IT'S TOO LATE! BUT HOW?!
PERFECT! I'LL CALL THIS ONE "OVER-THE-HILL-HACKS DROWN THEIR SORROWS"!
SNAAP!
IT'S HIM! THIS IS OUR CHANCE!
GET 'IM!
UH-OH!
FECKLESS PAPARAZZO! YOU'RE THROUGH!
TSK! TSK! "SAFE DRIVING POSTER-BOY WOLFCASTLE EXPOSED AS A ROAD RAGE MANIAC!" CHUCKLE!
SNAAP!

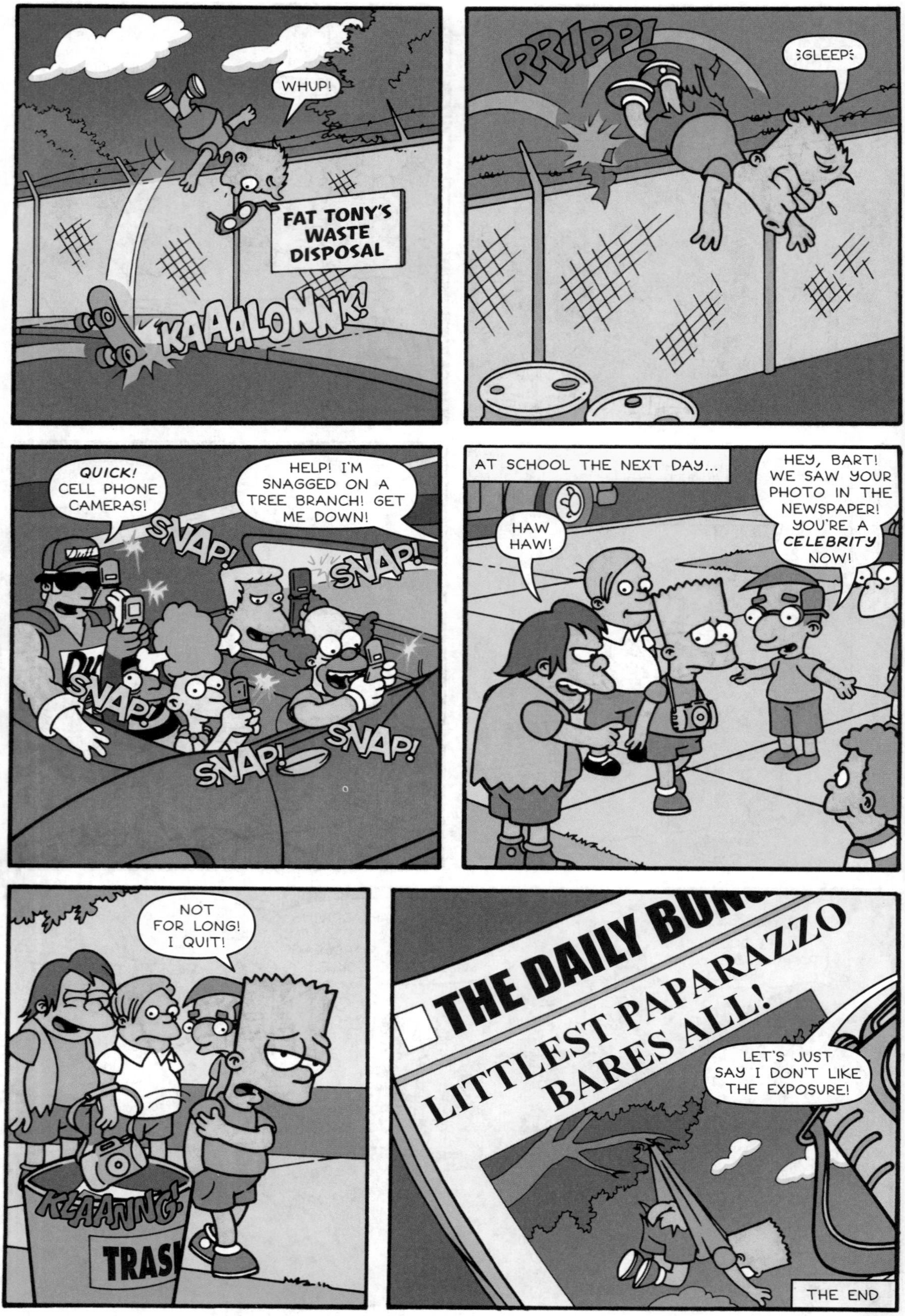
WHUP!
FAT TONY'S WASTE DISPOSAL
KAAALONNK!
RRIPP!
GLEEP
QUICK! CELL PHONE CAMERAS!
HELP! I'M SNAGGED ON A TREE BRANCH! GET ME DOWN!
SNAP!
SNAP!
SNAP!
SNAP!
SNAP!
AT SCHOOL THE NEXT DAY...
HAW HAW!
HEY, BART! WE SAW YOUR PHOTO IN THE NEWSPAPER! YOU'RE A CELEBRITY NOW!
NOT FOR LONG! I QUIT!
KLAANNG!
TRAS
THE DAILY BUN
LITTLEST PAPARAZZO BARES ALL!
LET'S JUST SAY I DON'T LIKE THE EXPOSURE!
THE END

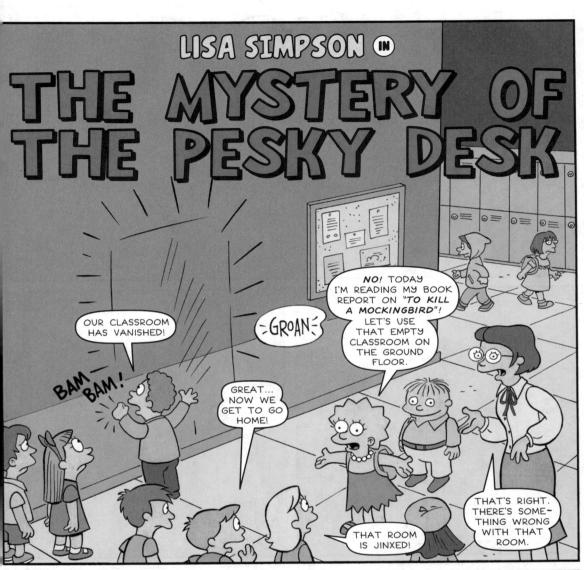

LISA SIMPSON IN
THE MYSTERY OF THE PESKY DESK

OUR CLASSROOM HAS VANISHED!

-GROAN-

NO! TODAY I'M READING MY BOOK REPORT ON *"TO KILL A MOCKINGBIRD"*! LET'S USE THAT EMPTY CLASSROOM ON THE GROUND FLOOR.

BAM BAM!

GREAT... NOW WE GET TO GO HOME!

THAT'S RIGHT. THERE'S SOMETHING WRONG WITH THAT ROOM.

THAT ROOM IS JINXED!

JINXES ARE JUST SUPERSTITION...THAT ABANDONED ROOM WILL BE FINE.

BUT I WONDER WHAT HAPPENED TO OUR BELOVED CLASSROOM?

PING!

IT'S AMAZING WHAT YOU CAN DO WITH A LITTLE WALLBOARD AND HOMER'S TOOLS.

CAROL LAY
STORY & ART

ALAN HELLARD
COLORS

KAREN BATES
LETTERS

BILL MORRISON
EDITOR

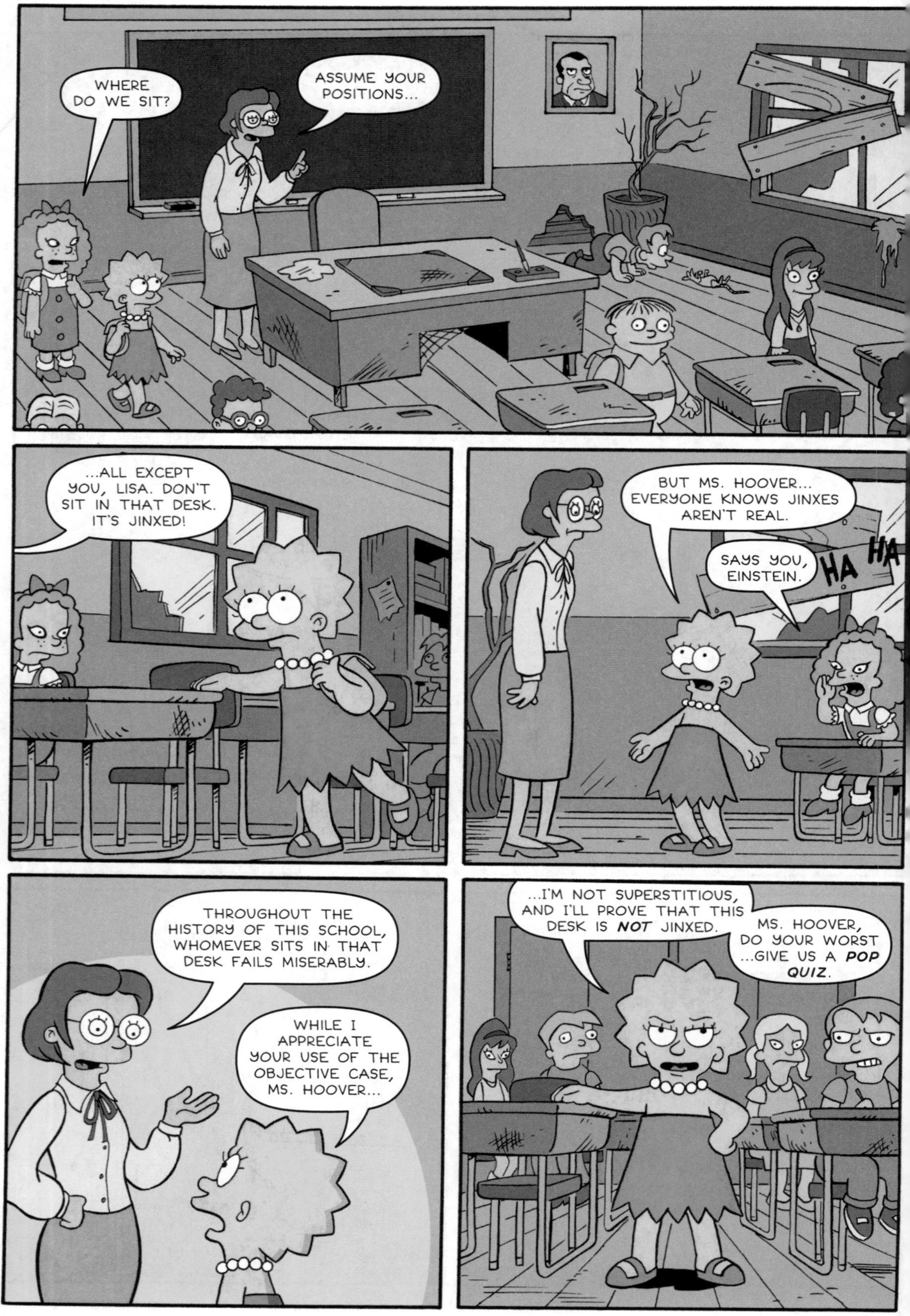
WHERE DO WE SIT?
ASSUME YOUR POSITIONS...
...ALL EXCEPT YOU, LISA. DON'T SIT IN THAT DESK. IT'S JINXED!
BUT MS. HOOVER... EVERYONE KNOWS JINXES AREN'T REAL.
SAYS YOU, EINSTEIN.
HA HA
THROUGHOUT THE HISTORY OF THIS SCHOOL, WHOMEVER SITS IN THAT DESK FAILS MISERABLY.
WHILE I APPRECIATE YOUR USE OF THE OBJECTIVE CASE, MS. HOOVER...
...I'M NOT SUPERSTITIOUS, AND I'LL PROVE THAT THIS DESK IS **NOT** JINXED.
MS. HOOVER, DO YOUR WORST ...GIVE US A **POP QUIZ**.

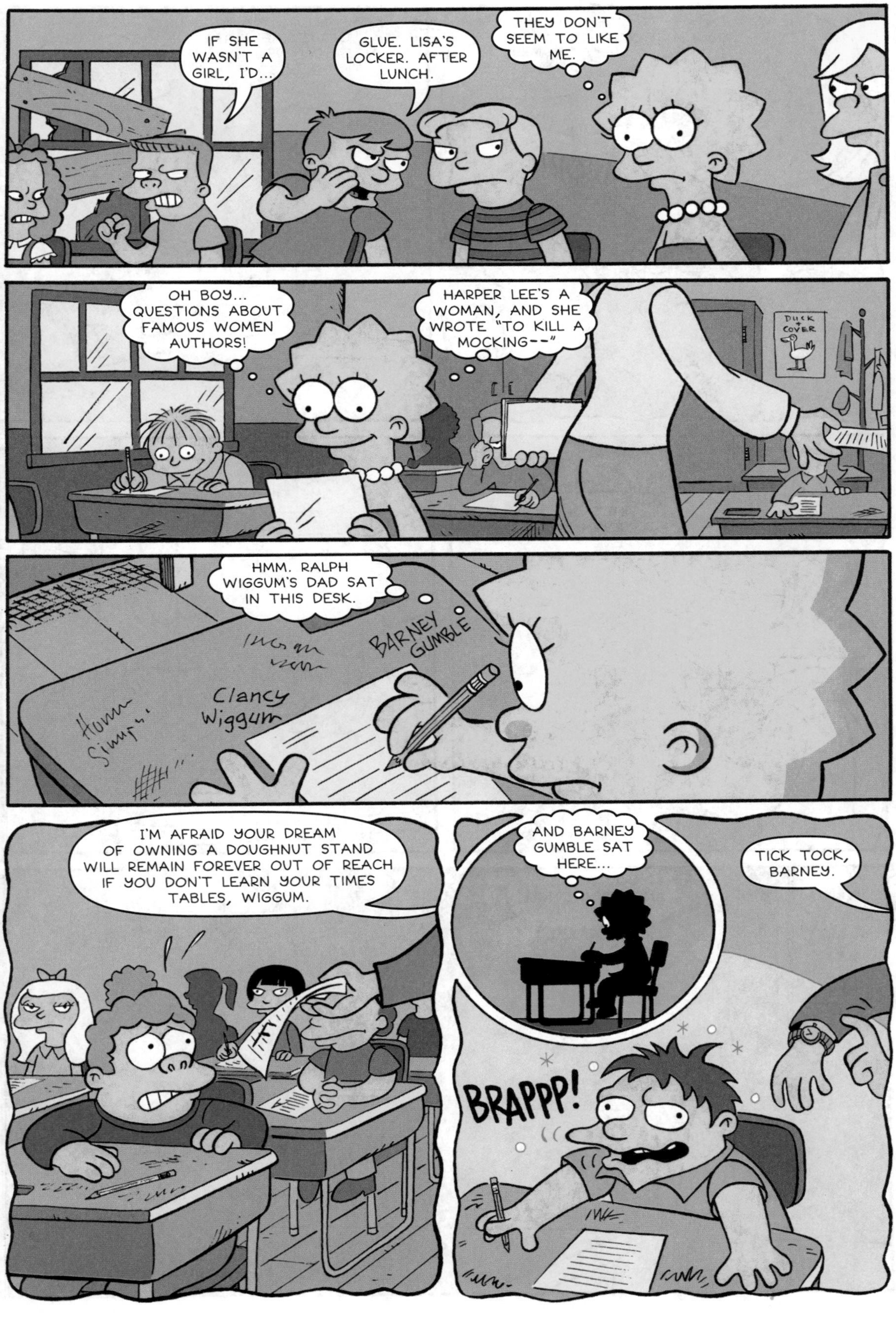
IF SHE WASN'T A GIRL, I'D...
GLUE. LISA'S LOCKER. AFTER LUNCH.
THEY DON'T SEEM TO LIKE ME.
OH BOY... QUESTIONS ABOUT FAMOUS WOMEN AUTHORS!
HARPER LEE'S A WOMAN, AND SHE WROTE "TO KILL A MOCKING--"
DUCK + COVER
HMM. RALPH WIGGUM'S DAD SAT IN THIS DESK.
BARNEY GUMBLE
Clancy Wiggum
I'M AFRAID YOUR DREAM OF OWNING A DOUGHNUT STAND WILL REMAIN FOREVER OUT OF REACH IF YOU DON'T LEARN YOUR TIMES TABLES, WIGGUM.
AND BARNEY GUMBLE SAT HERE...
TICK TOCK, BARNEY.
BRAPPP!

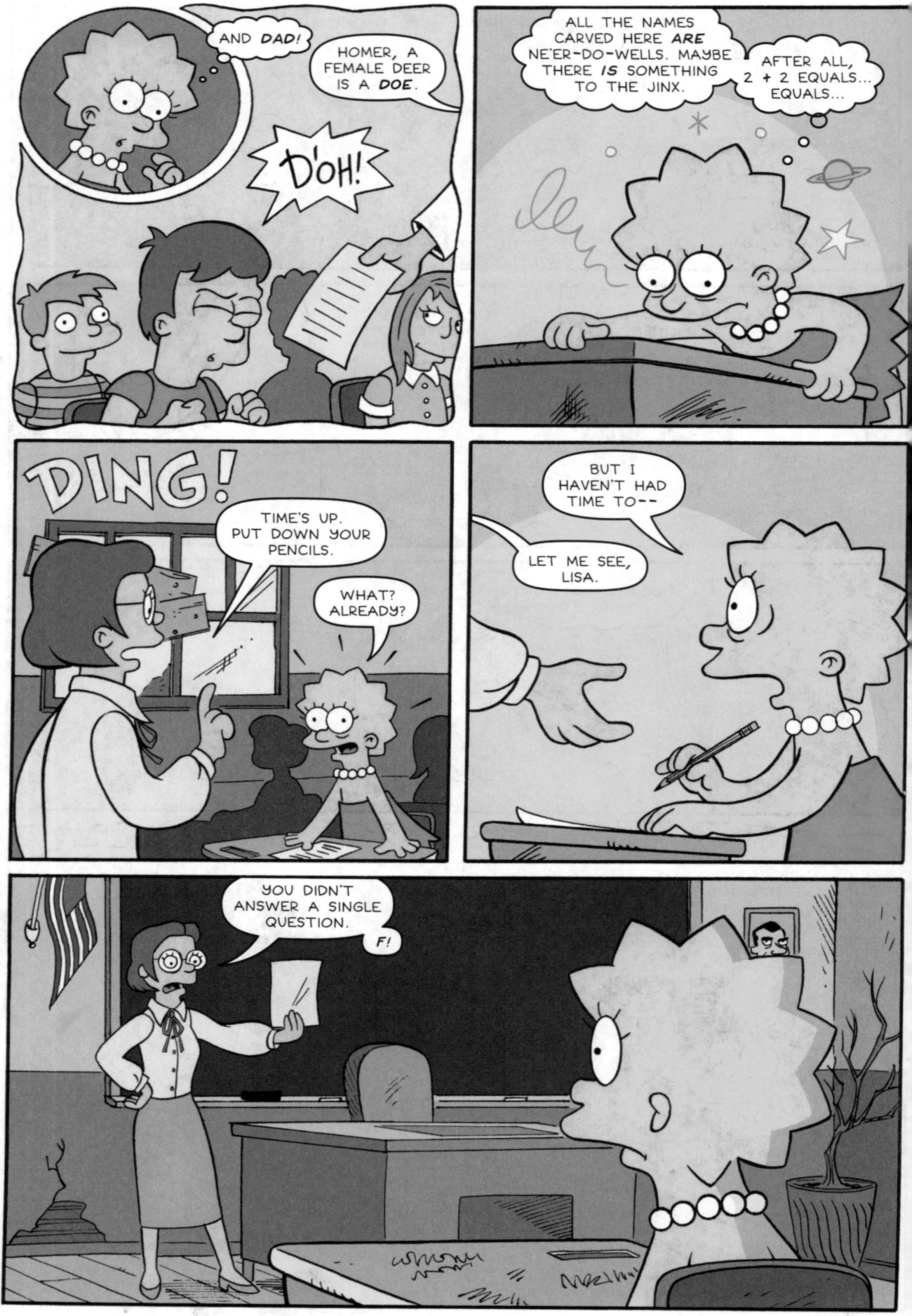
AND DAD!
HOMER, A FEMALE DEER IS A DOE.
D'OH!
ALL THE NAMES CARVED HERE ARE NE'ER-DO-WELLS. MAYBE THERE IS SOMETHING TO THE JINX.
AFTER ALL, 2 + 2 EQUALS... EQUALS...
DING!
TIME'S UP. PUT DOWN YOUR PENCILS.
WHAT? ALREADY?
BUT I HAVEN'T HAD TIME TO--
LET ME SEE, LISA.
YOU DIDN'T ANSWER A SINGLE QUESTION.
F!

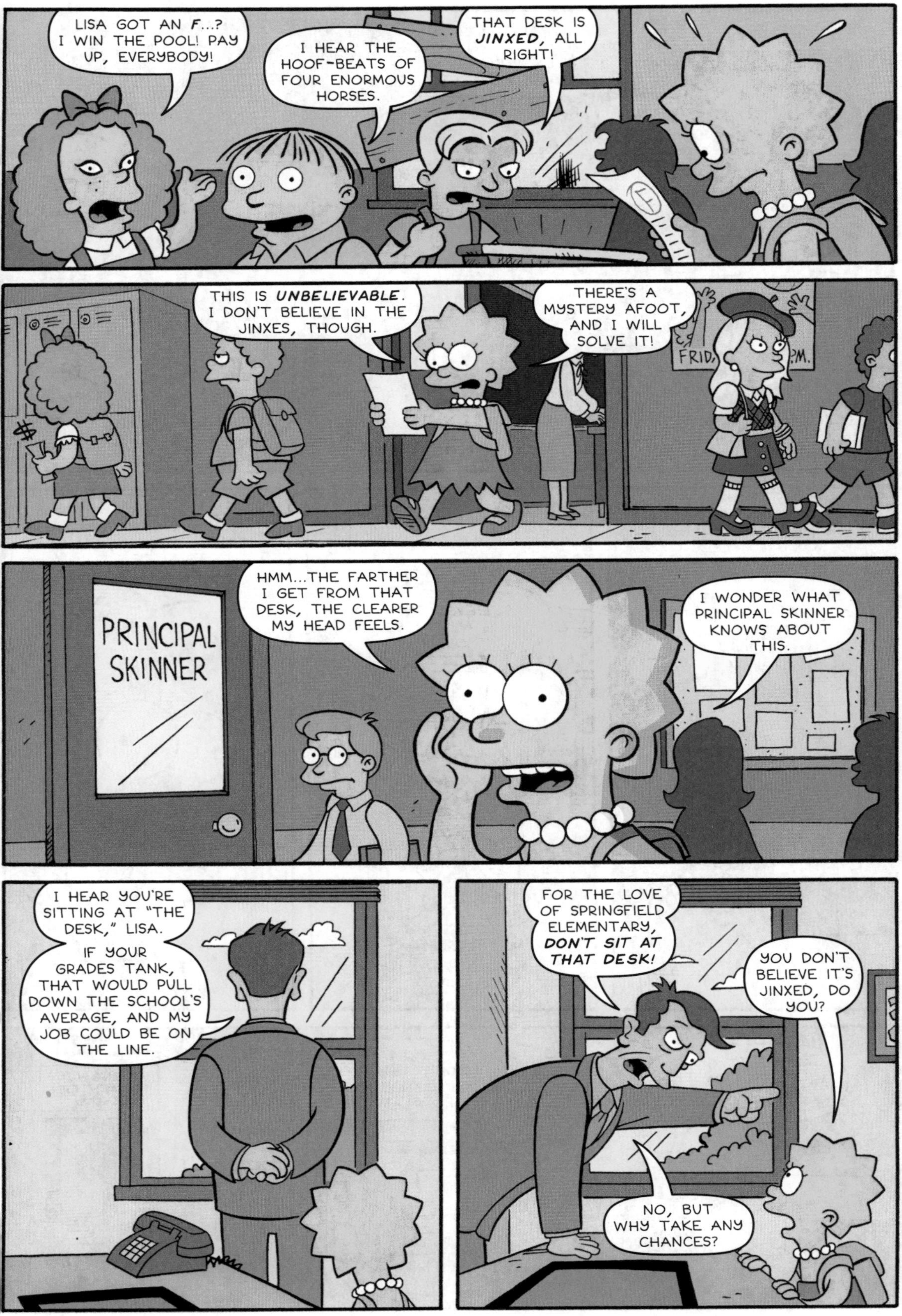
LISA GOT AN F...? I WIN THE POOL! PAY UP, EVERYBODY!
I HEAR THE HOOF-BEATS OF FOUR ENORMOUS HORSES.
THAT DESK IS JINXED, ALL RIGHT!
THIS IS UNBELIEVABLE. I DON'T BELIEVE IN THE JINXES, THOUGH.
THERE'S A MYSTERY AFOOT, AND I WILL SOLVE IT!
PRINCIPAL SKINNER
HMM...THE FARTHER I GET FROM THAT DESK, THE CLEARER MY HEAD FEELS.
I WONDER WHAT PRINCIPAL SKINNER KNOWS ABOUT THIS.
I HEAR YOU'RE SITTING AT "THE DESK," LISA.
IF YOUR GRADES TANK, THAT WOULD PULL DOWN THE SCHOOL'S AVERAGE, AND MY JOB COULD BE ON THE LINE.
FOR THE LOVE OF SPRINGFIELD ELEMENTARY, DON'T SIT AT THAT DESK!
YOU DON'T BELIEVE IT'S JINXED, DO YOU?
NO, BUT WHY TAKE ANY CHANCES?

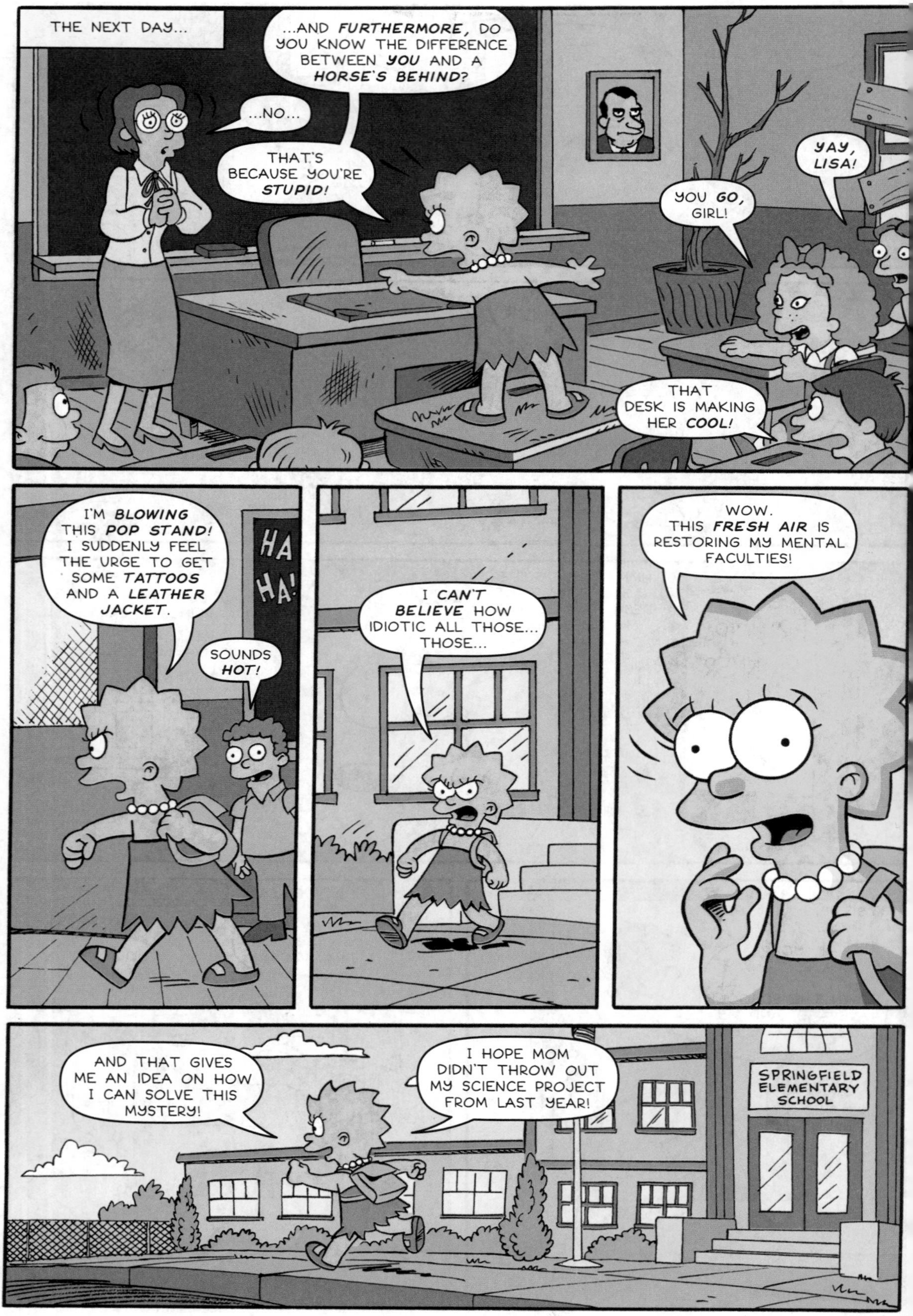
THE NEXT DAY...
...AND FURTHERMORE, DO YOU KNOW THE DIFFERENCE BETWEEN YOU AND A HORSE'S BEHIND?
...NO...
THAT'S BECAUSE YOU'RE STUPID!
YOU GO, GIRL!
YAY, LISA!
THAT DESK IS MAKING HER COOL!
I'M BLOWING THIS POP STAND! I SUDDENLY FEEL THE URGE TO GET SOME TATTOOS AND A LEATHER JACKET.
HA HA!
SOUNDS HOT!
I CAN'T BELIEVE HOW IDIOTIC ALL THOSE... THOSE...
WOW. THIS FRESH AIR IS RESTORING MY MENTAL FACULTIES!
AND THAT GIVES ME AN IDEA ON HOW I CAN SOLVE THIS MYSTERY!
I HOPE MOM DIDN'T THROW OUT MY SCIENCE PROJECT FROM LAST YEAR!
SPRINGFIELD ELEMENTARY SCHOOL

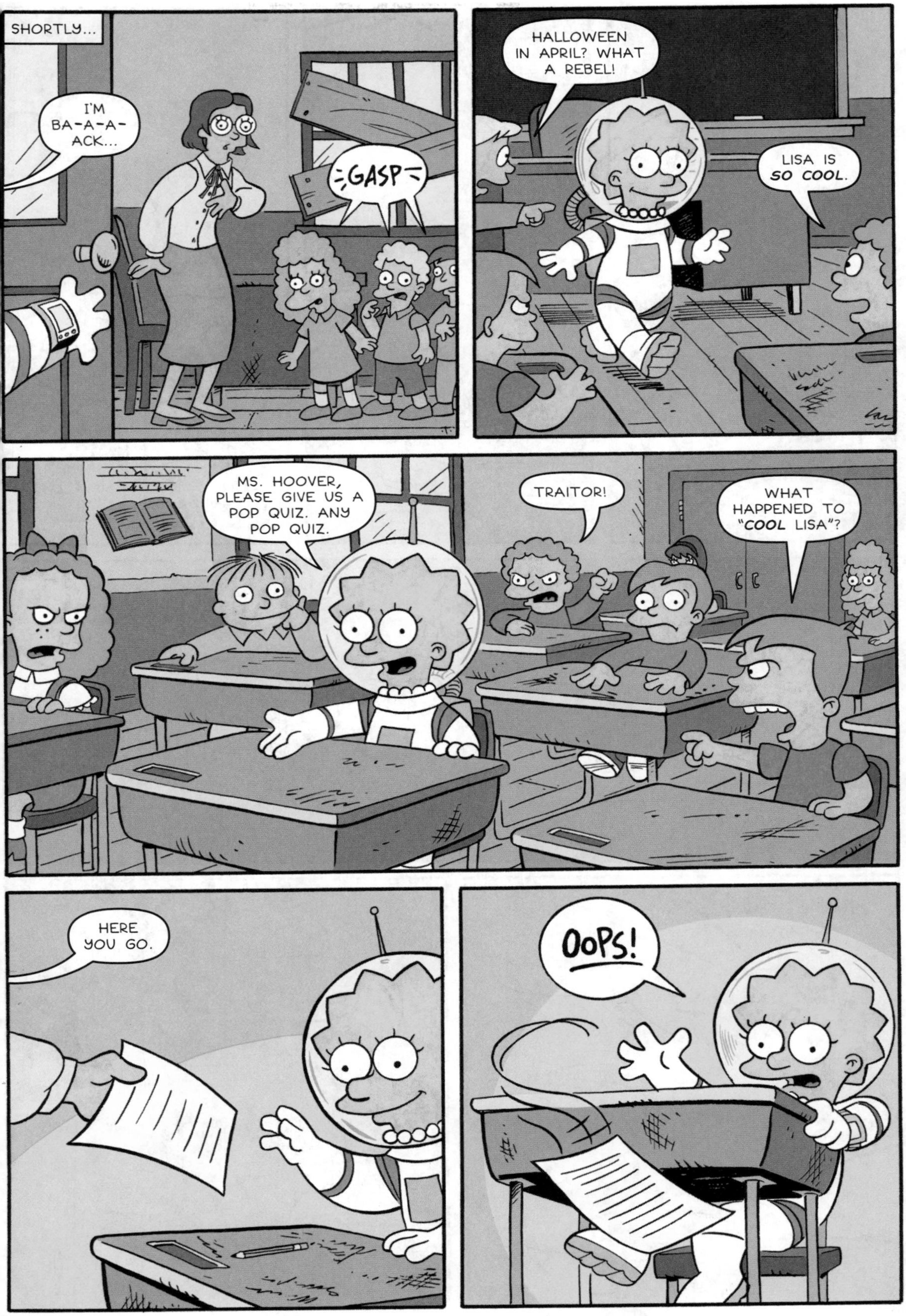
SHORTLY...
I'M BA-A-A-ACK...
GASP
HALLOWEEN IN APRIL? WHAT A REBEL!
LISA IS SO COOL.
MS. HOOVER, PLEASE GIVE US A POP QUIZ. ANY POP QUIZ.
TRAITOR!
WHAT HAPPENED TO "COOL LISA"?
HERE YOU GO.
OOPS!

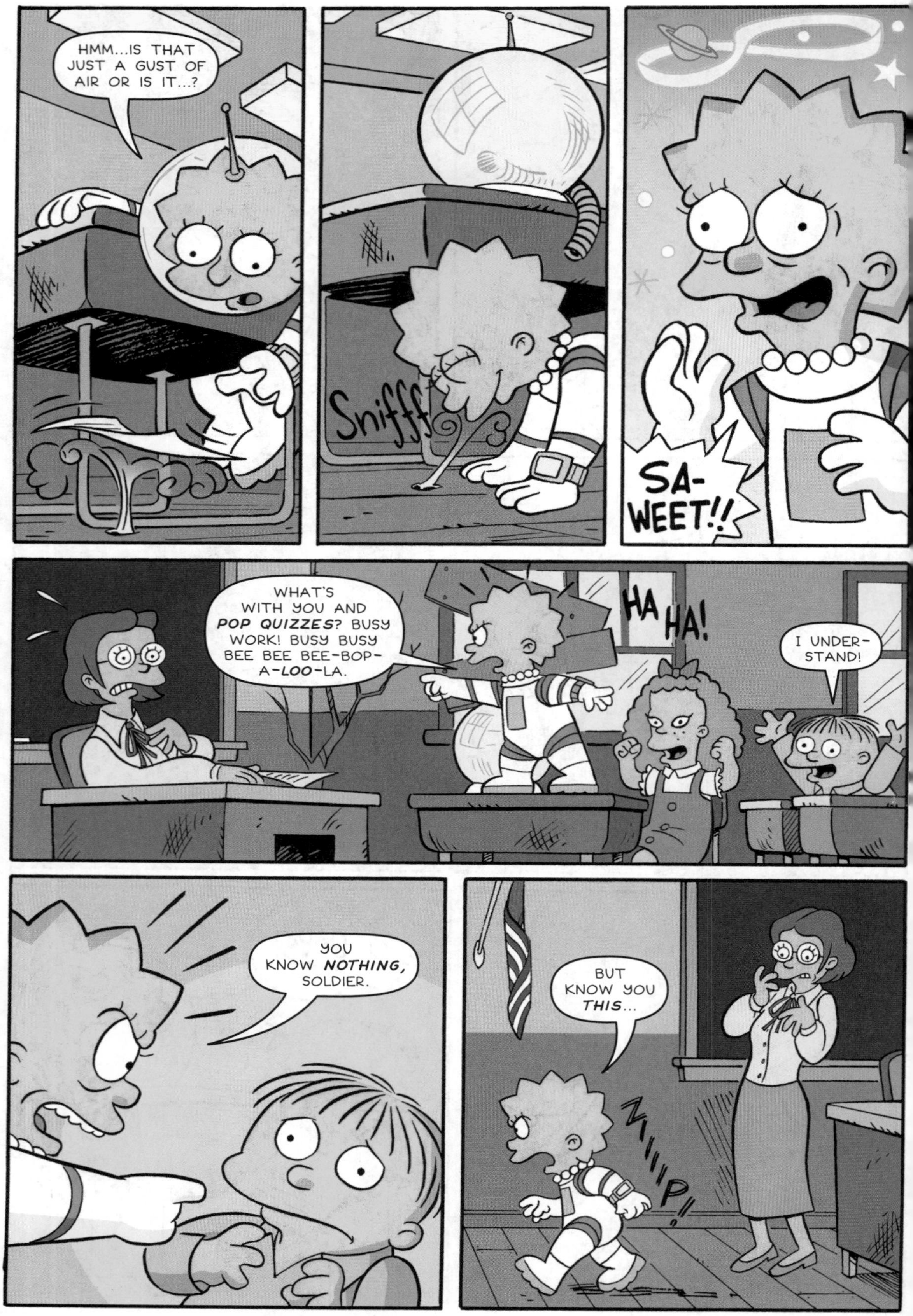
HMM...IS THAT JUST A GUST OF AIR OR IS IT...?
SNIFFF
SA-WEET!!
WHAT'S WITH YOU AND POP QUIZZES? BUSY WORK! BUSY BUSY BEE BEE BEE-BOP-A-LOO-LA.
HA HA!
I UNDER-STAND!
YOU KNOW NOTHING, SOLDIER.
BUT KNOW YOU THIS...
ZIIIP!!

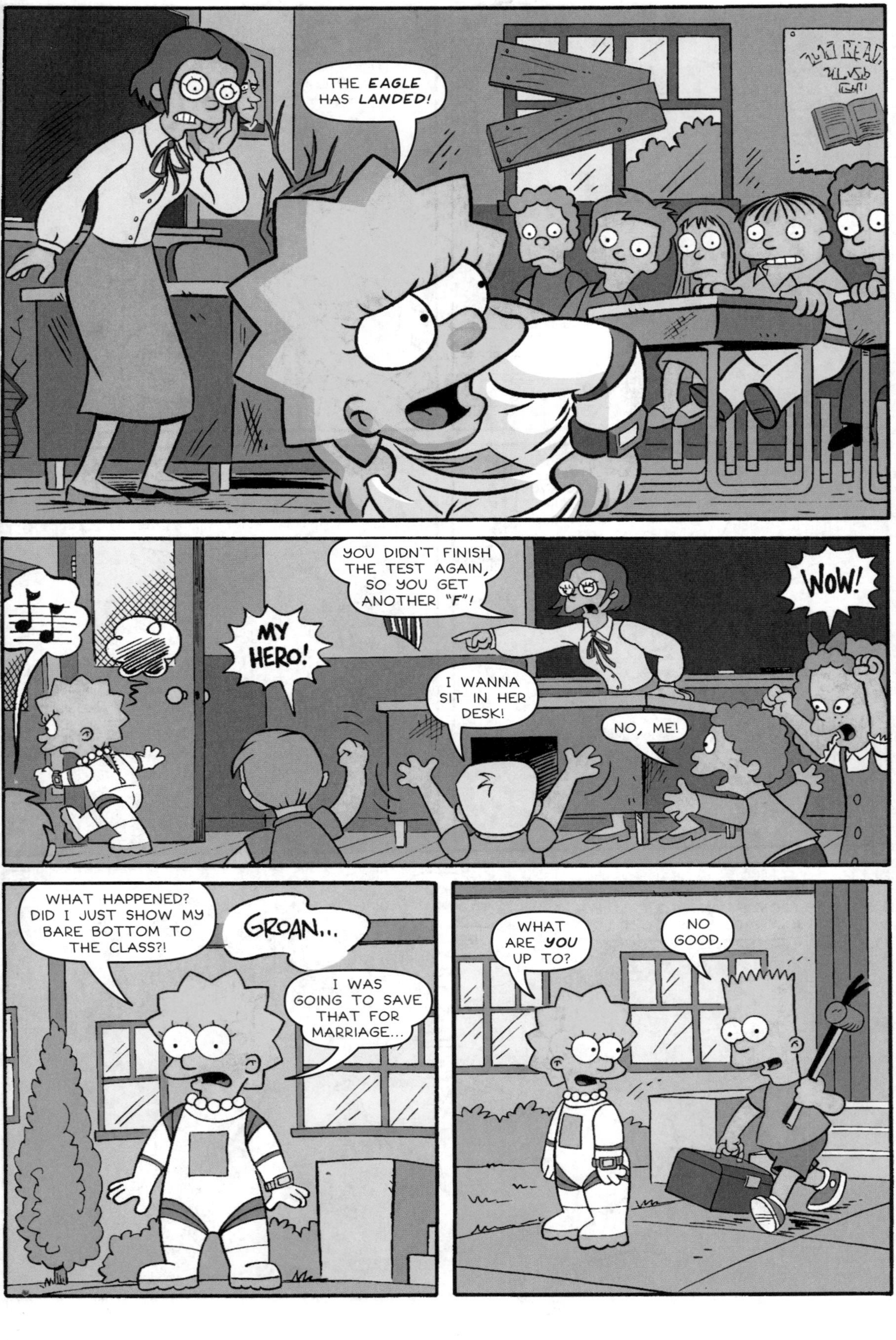
THE EAGLE HAS LANDED!
YOU DIDN'T FINISH THE TEST AGAIN, SO YOU GET ANOTHER "F"!
WOW!
MY HERO!
I WANNA SIT IN HER DESK!
NO, ME!
WHAT HAPPENED? DID I JUST SHOW MY BARE BOTTOM TO THE CLASS?!
GROAN...
I WAS GOING TO SAVE THAT FOR MARRIAGE...
WHAT ARE YOU UP TO?
NO GOOD.

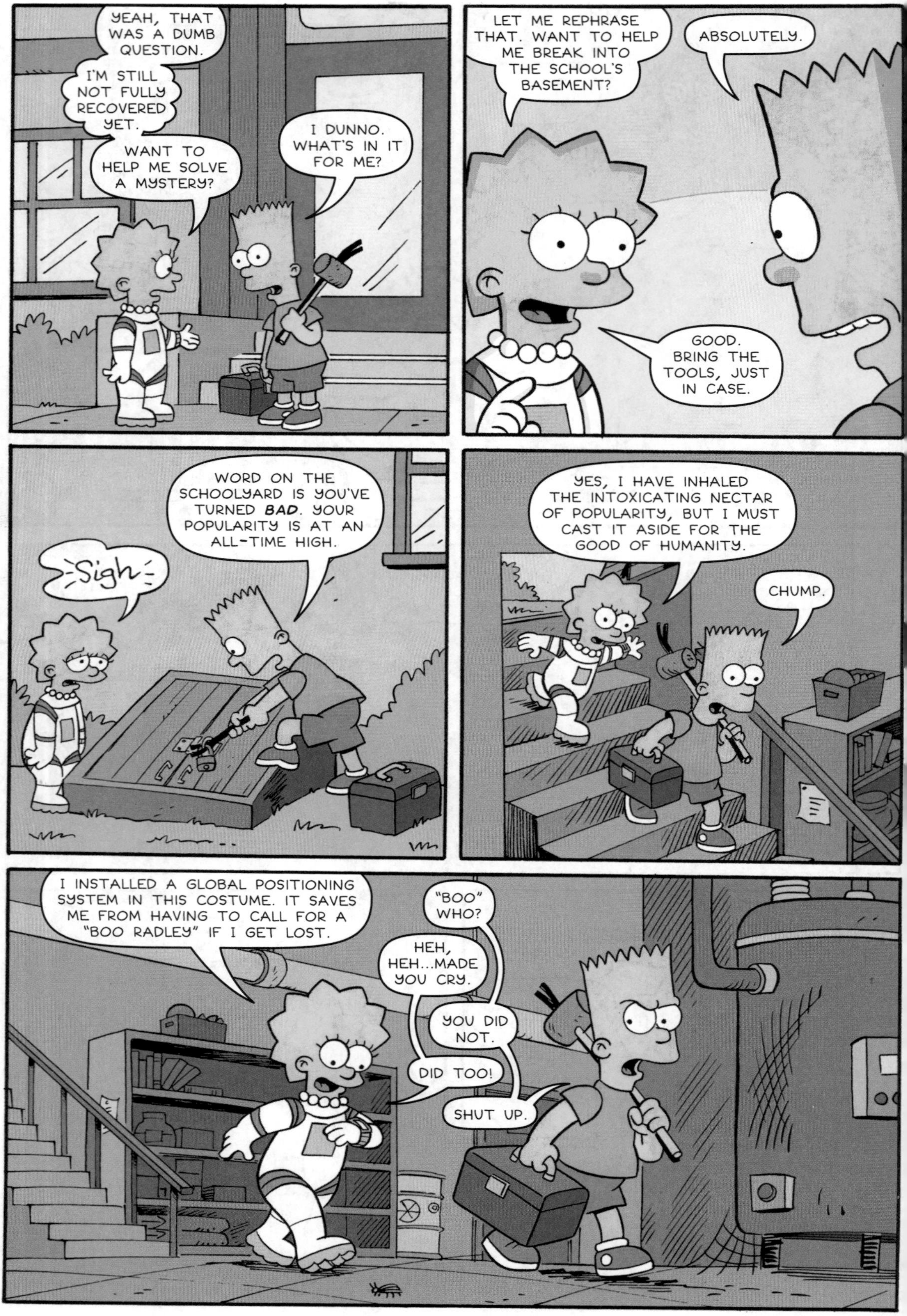
YEAH, THAT WAS A DUMB QUESTION.
I'M STILL NOT FULLY RECOVERED YET.
WANT TO HELP ME SOLVE A MYSTERY?
I DUNNO. WHAT'S IN IT FOR ME?
LET ME REPHRASE THAT. WANT TO HELP ME BREAK INTO THE SCHOOL'S BASEMENT?
ABSOLUTELY.
GOOD. BRING THE TOOLS, JUST IN CASE.
WORD ON THE SCHOOLYARD IS YOU'VE TURNED **BAD**. YOUR POPULARITY IS AT AN ALL-TIME HIGH.
Sigh
YES, I HAVE INHALED THE INTOXICATING NECTAR OF POPULARITY, BUT I MUST CAST IT ASIDE FOR THE GOOD OF HUMANITY.
CHUMP.
I INSTALLED A GLOBAL POSITIONING SYSTEM IN THIS COSTUME. IT SAVES ME FROM HAVING TO CALL FOR A "BOO RADLEY" IF I GET LOST.
"BOO" WHO?
HEH, HEH...MADE YOU CRY.
YOU DID NOT.
DID TOO!
SHUT UP.

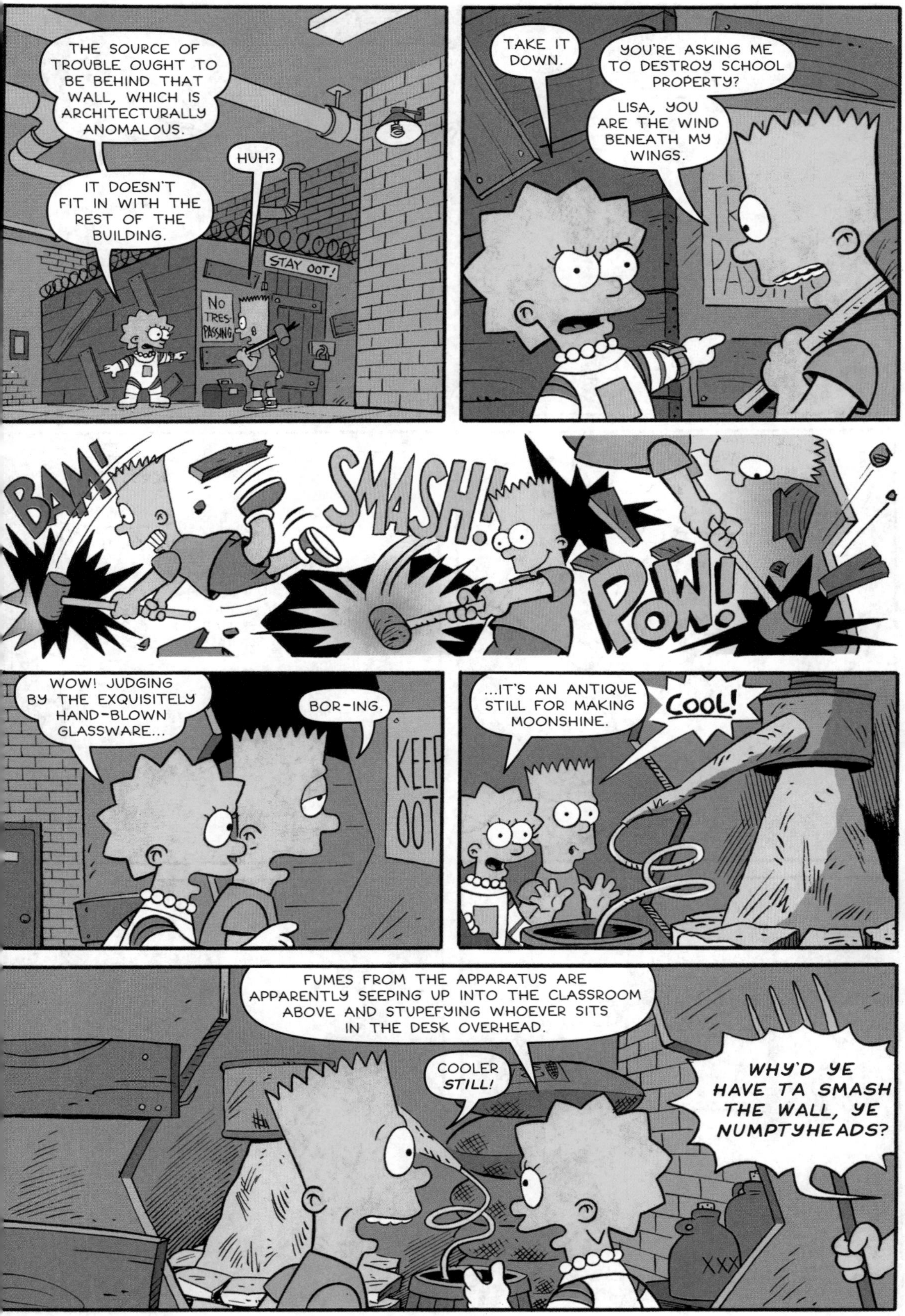
THE SOURCE OF TROUBLE OUGHT TO BE BEHIND THAT WALL, WHICH IS ARCHITECTURALLY ANOMALOUS.
HUH?
IT DOESN'T FIT IN WITH THE REST OF THE BUILDING.
STAY OOT!
NO TRES-PASSING
TAKE IT DOWN.
YOU'RE ASKING ME TO DESTROY SCHOOL PROPERTY?
LISA, YOU ARE THE WIND BENEATH MY WINGS.
BAM!
SMASH!
POW!
WOW! JUDGING BY THE EXQUISITELY HAND-BLOWN GLASSWARE...
BOR-ING.
KEEP OOT
...IT'S AN ANTIQUE STILL FOR MAKING MOONSHINE.
COOL!
FUMES FROM THE APPARATUS ARE APPARENTLY SEEPING UP INTO THE CLASSROOM ABOVE AND STUPEFYING WHOEVER SITS IN THE DESK OVERHEAD.
COOLER STILL!
WHY'D YE HAVE TA SMASH THE WALL, YE NUMPTYHEADS?
XXX

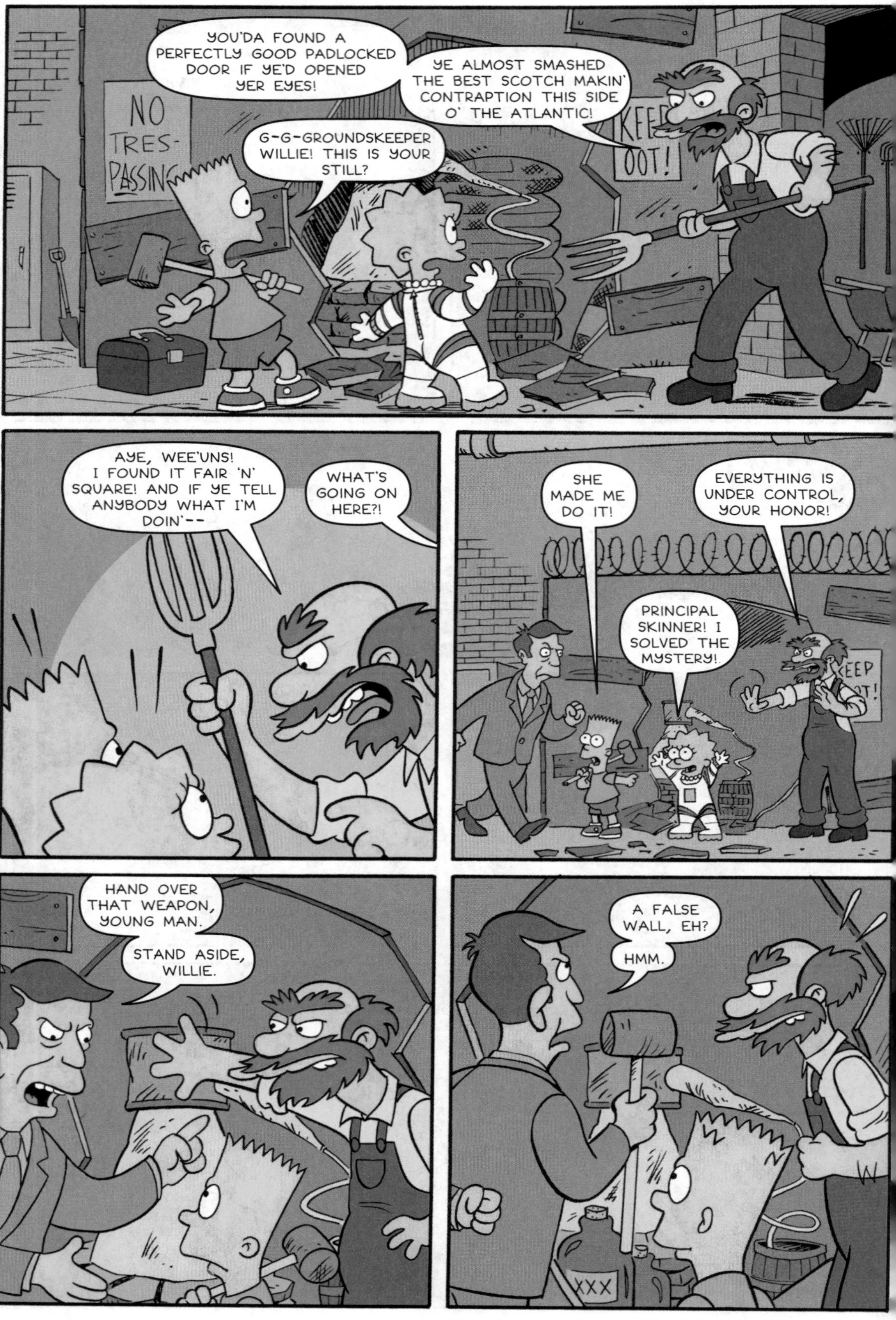
YOU'DA FOUND A PERFECTLY GOOD PADLOCKED DOOR IF YE'D OPENED YER EYES!
YE ALMOST SMASHED THE BEST SCOTCH MAKIN' CONTRAPTION THIS SIDE O' THE ATLANTIC!
NO TRES-PASSING
KEEP OOT!
G-G-GROUNDSKEEPER WILLIE! THIS IS YOUR STILL?
AYE, WEE'UNS! I FOUND IT FAIR 'N' SQUARE! AND IF YE TELL ANYBODY WHAT I'M DOIN'--
WHAT'S GOING ON HERE?!
SHE MADE ME DO IT!
EVERYTHING IS UNDER CONTROL, YOUR HONOR!
PRINCIPAL SKINNER! I SOLVED THE MYSTERY!
HAND OVER THAT WEAPON, YOUNG MAN.
STAND ASIDE, WILLIE.
A FALSE WALL, EH?
HMM.
XXX

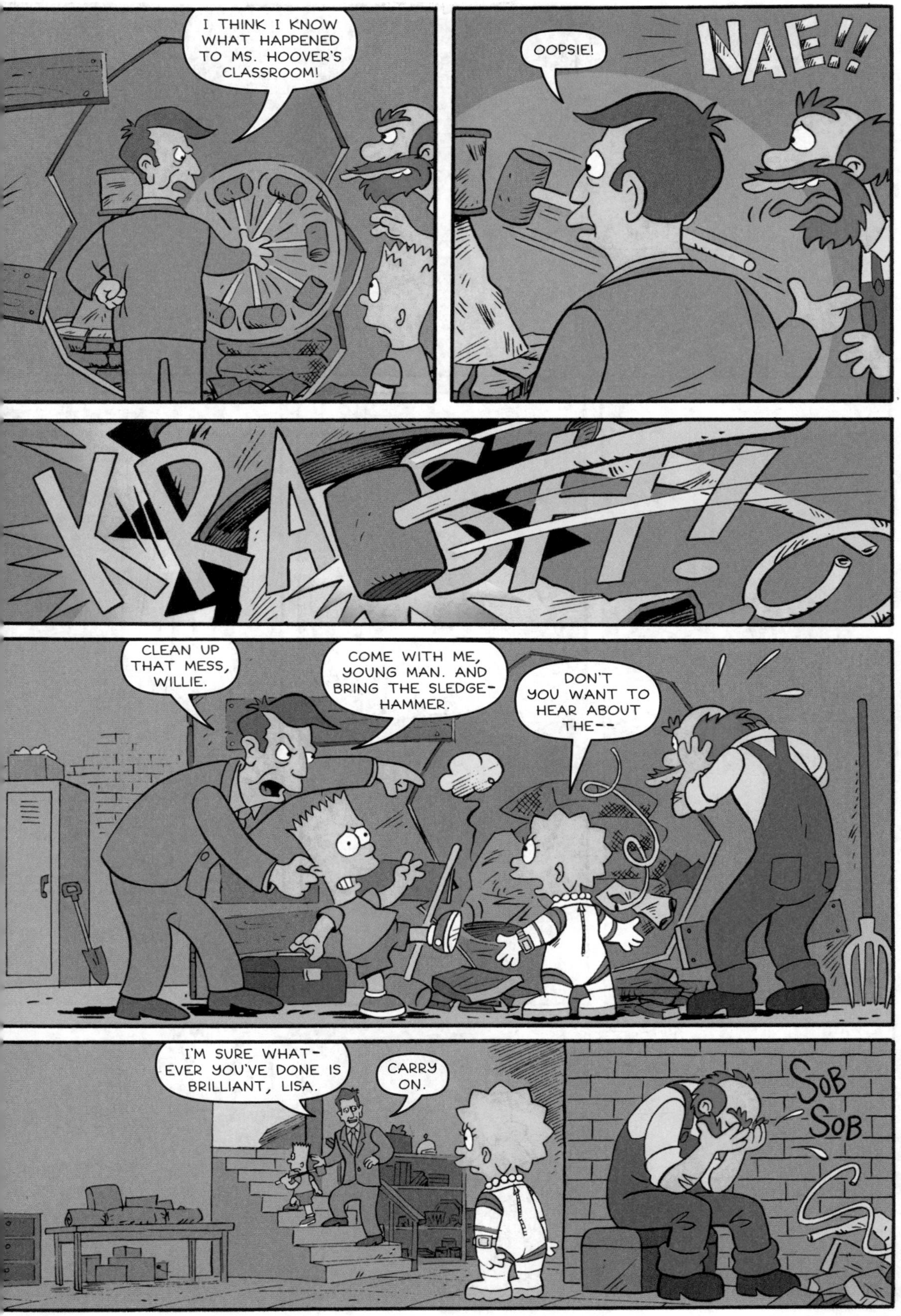
I THINK I KNOW WHAT HAPPENED TO MS. HOOVER'S CLASSROOM!
OOPSIE!
NAE!!
KRASH!
CLEAN UP THAT MESS, WILLIE.
COME WITH ME, YOUNG MAN. AND BRING THE SLEDGE-HAMMER.
DON'T YOU WANT TO HEAR ABOUT THE--
I'M SURE WHAT-EVER YOU'VE DONE IS BRILLIANT, LISA.
CARRY ON.
SOB
SOB

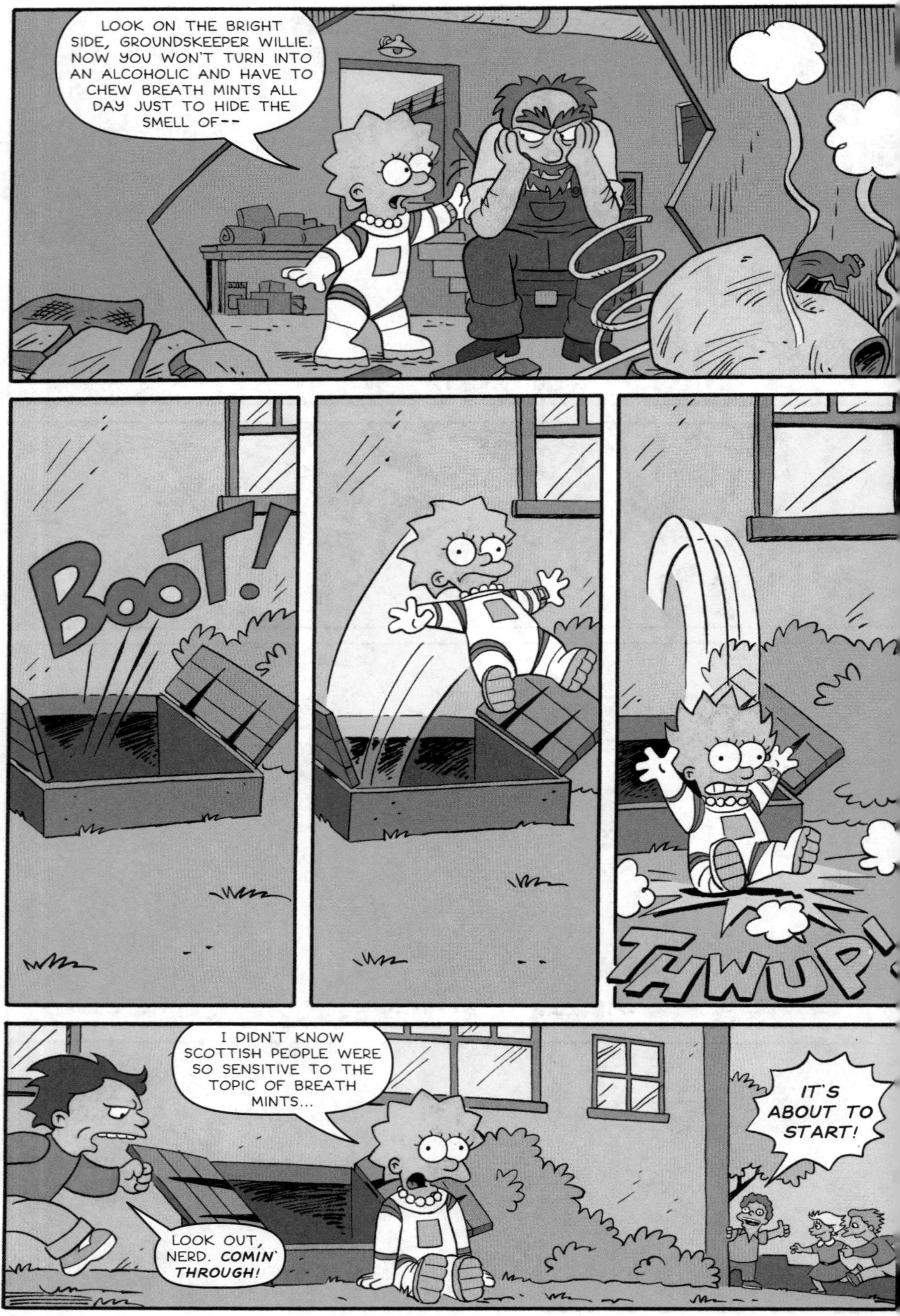
LOOK ON THE BRIGHT SIDE, GROUNDSKEEPER WILLIE. NOW YOU WON'T TURN INTO AN ALCOHOLIC AND HAVE TO CHEW BREATH MINTS ALL DAY JUST TO HIDE THE SMELL OF--
BOOT!
THWUP!
I DIDN'T KNOW SCOTTISH PEOPLE WERE SO SENSITIVE TO THE TOPIC OF BREATH MINTS...
IT'S ABOUT TO START!
LOOK OUT, NERD. COMIN' THROUGH!

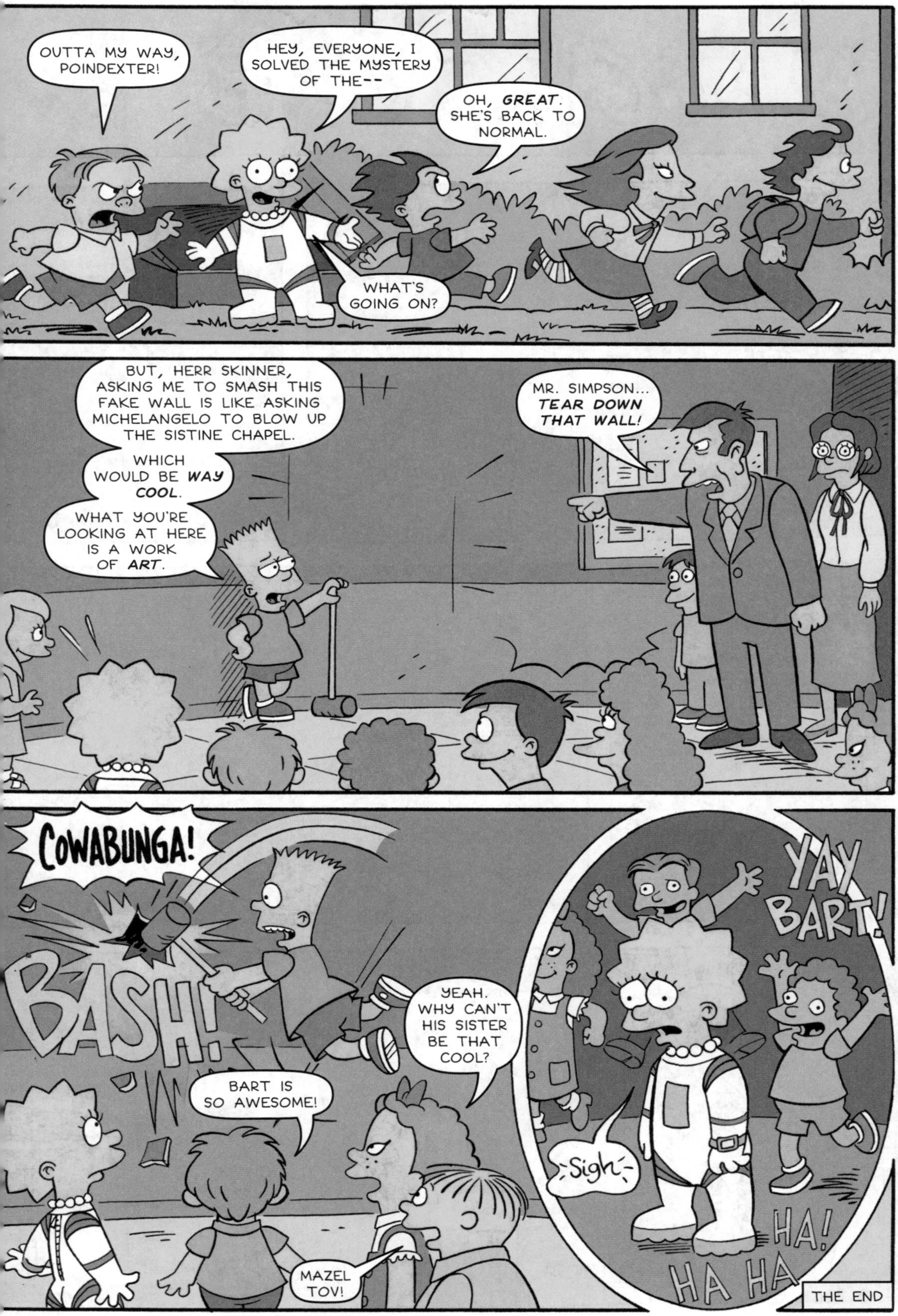
OUTTA MY WAY, POINDEXTER!
HEY, EVERYONE, I SOLVED THE MYSTERY OF THE--
OH, **GREAT**. SHE'S BACK TO NORMAL.
WHAT'S GOING ON?
BUT, HERR SKINNER, ASKING ME TO SMASH THIS FAKE WALL IS LIKE ASKING MICHELANGELO TO BLOW UP THE SISTINE CHAPEL.
WHICH WOULD BE **WAY COOL**.
WHAT YOU'RE LOOKING AT HERE IS A WORK OF **ART**.
MR. SIMPSON... ***TEAR DOWN THAT WALL!***
COWABUNGA!
BASH!
YEAH. WHY CAN'T HIS SISTER BE THAT COOL?
BART IS SO AWESOME!
MAZEL TOV!
YAY BART!
Sigh
HA! HA HA
THE END

MAGGIE'S CRIB

by ARAGONES

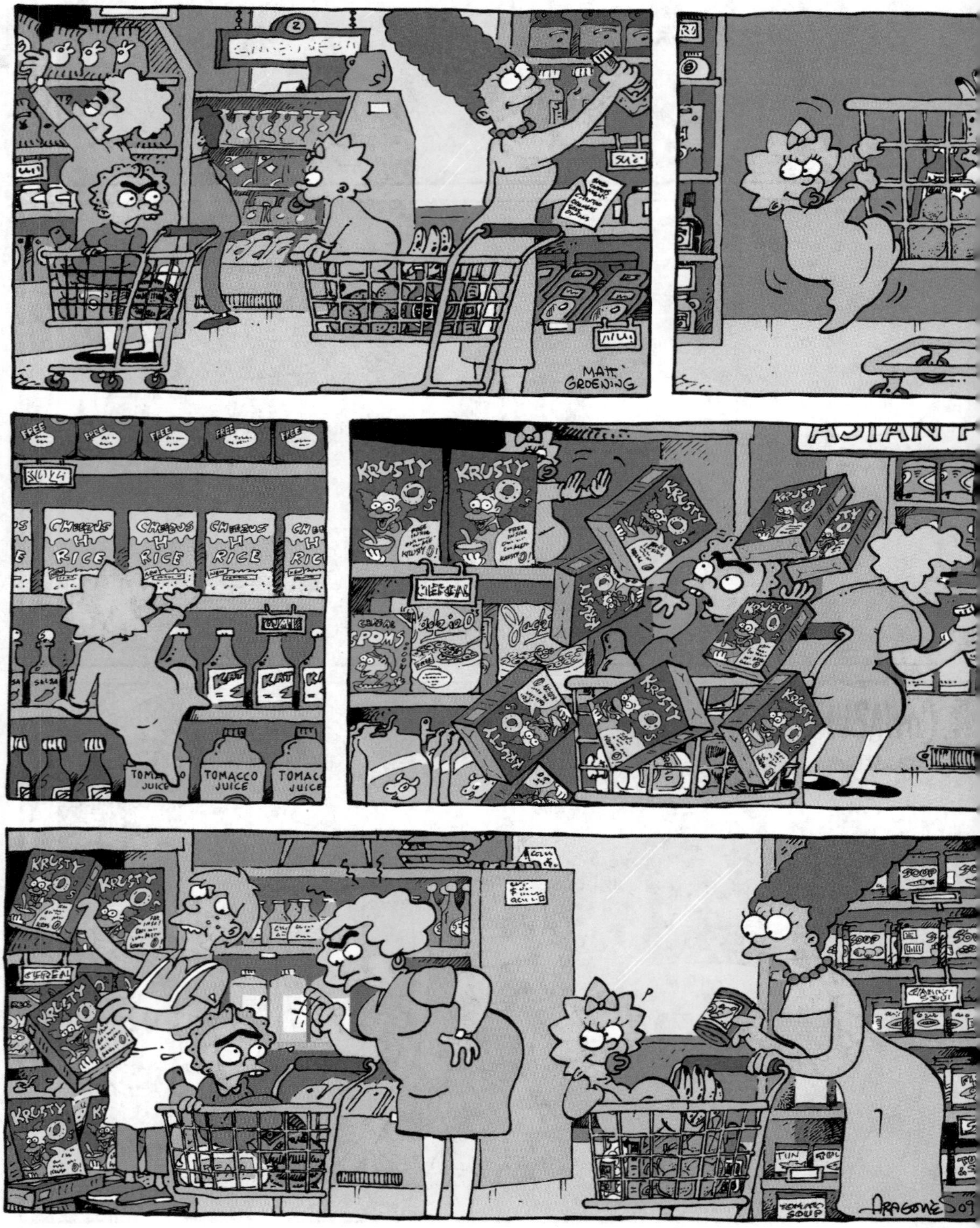
MATT GROENING
CHEEZUS H RICE
TOMACCO JUICE
KRUSTY O's
ASIAN
SOUP
TOMATO SOUP
ARAGONÉS 09

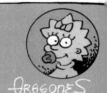

SERGIO ARAGONÉS
STORY & ART

ART VILLANUEVA
COLORS

BILL MORRISON
EDITOR

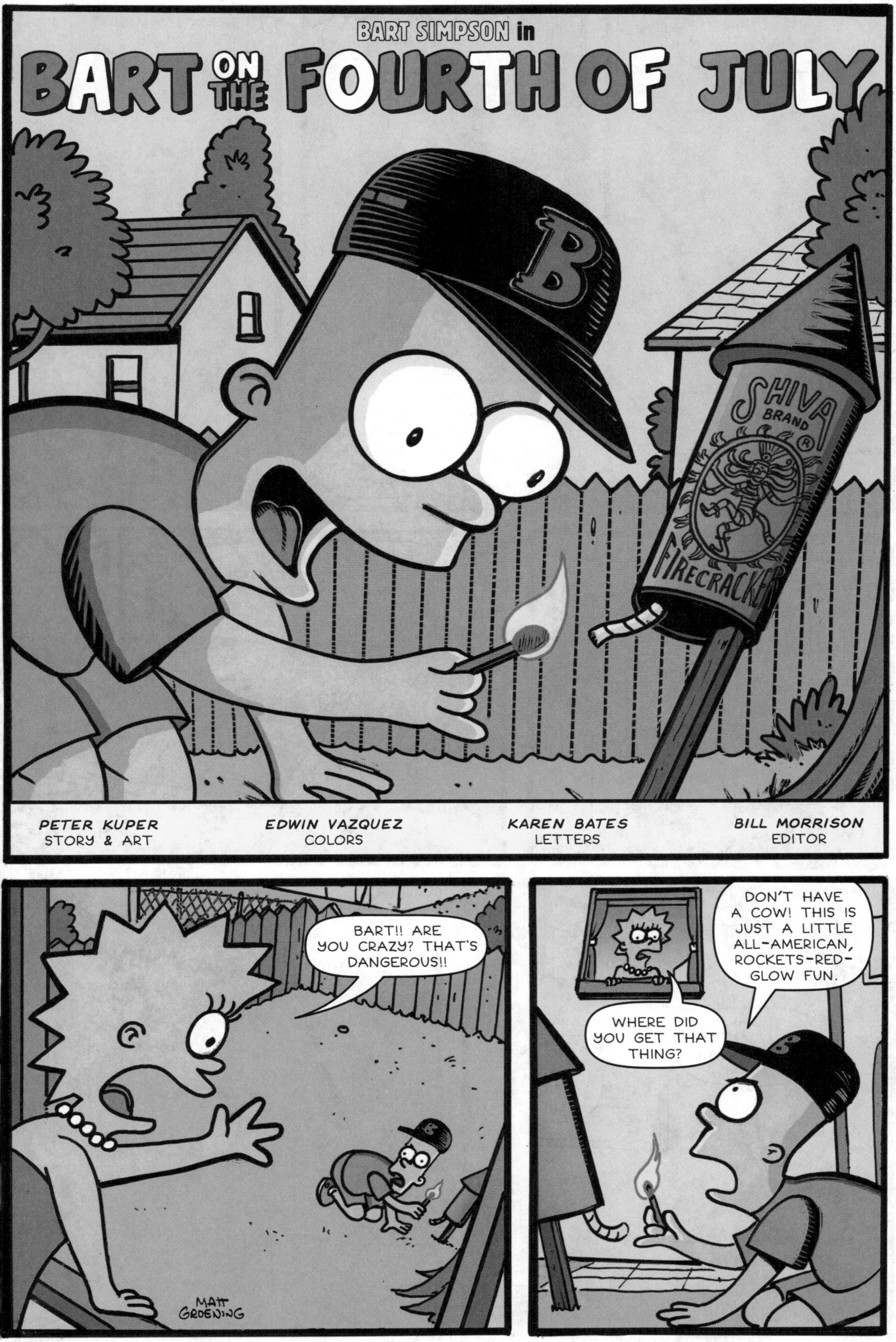
BART SIMPSON in
BART ON THE FOURTH OF JULY
SHIVA BRAND FIRECRACKER
PETER KUPER
STORY & ART
EDWIN VAZQUEZ
COLORS
KAREN BATES
LETTERS
BILL MORRISON
EDITOR
BART!! ARE YOU CRAZY? THAT'S DANGEROUS!!
MATT GROENING
WHERE DID YOU GET THAT THING?
DON'T HAVE A COW! THIS IS JUST A LITTLE ALL-AMERICAN, ROCKETS-RED-GLOW FUN.

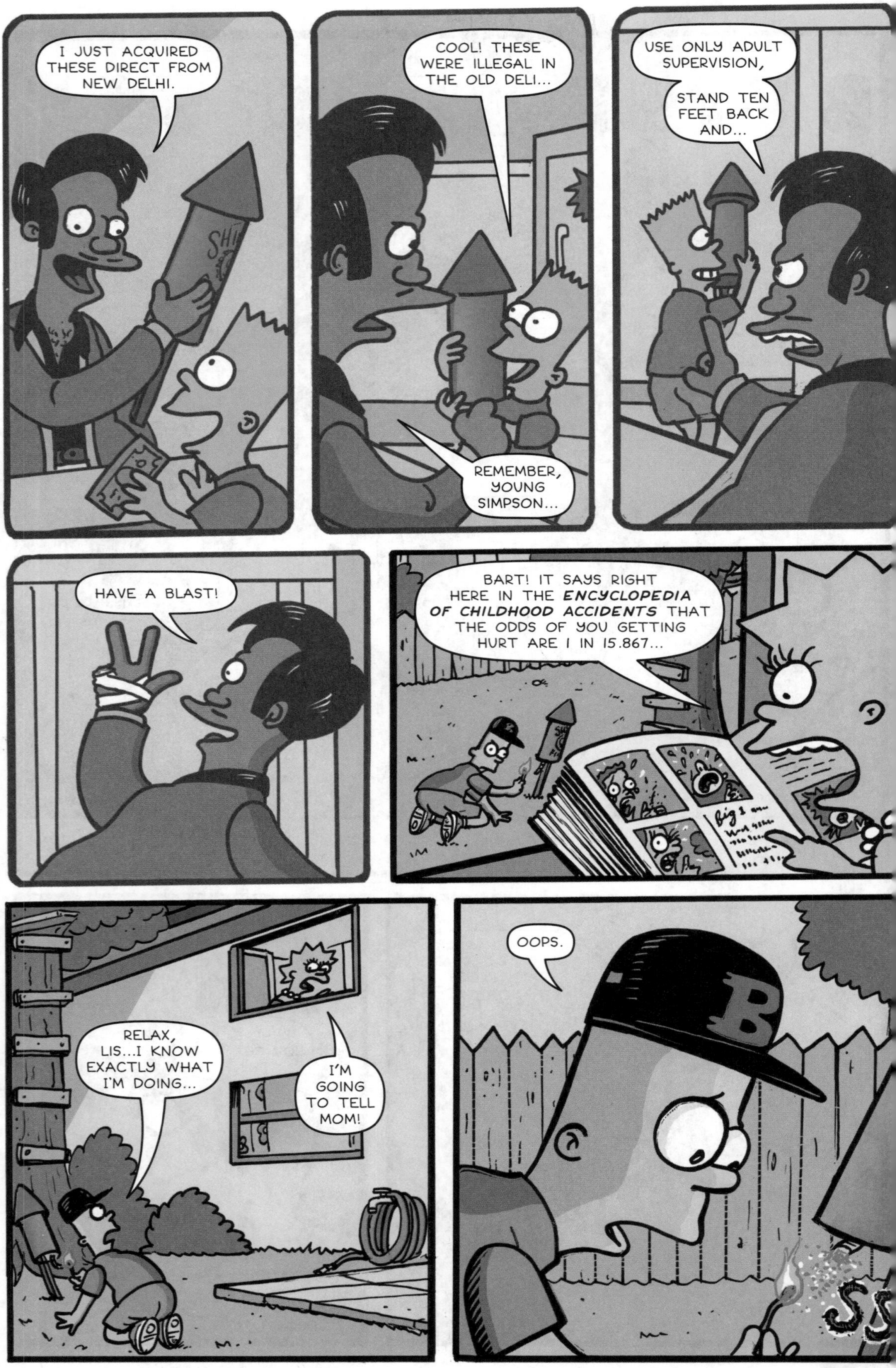
I JUST ACQUIRED THESE DIRECT FROM NEW DELHI.
COOL! THESE WERE ILLEGAL IN THE OLD DELI...
REMEMBER, YOUNG SIMPSON...
USE ONLY ADULT SUPERVISION,
STAND TEN FEET BACK AND...
HAVE A BLAST!
BART! IT SAYS RIGHT HERE IN THE ***ENCYCLOPEDIA OF CHILDHOOD ACCIDENTS*** THAT THE ODDS OF YOU GETTING HURT ARE 1 IN 15.867...
RELAX, LIS...I KNOW EXACTLY WHAT I'M DOING...
I'M GOING TO TELL MOM!
OOPS.
B

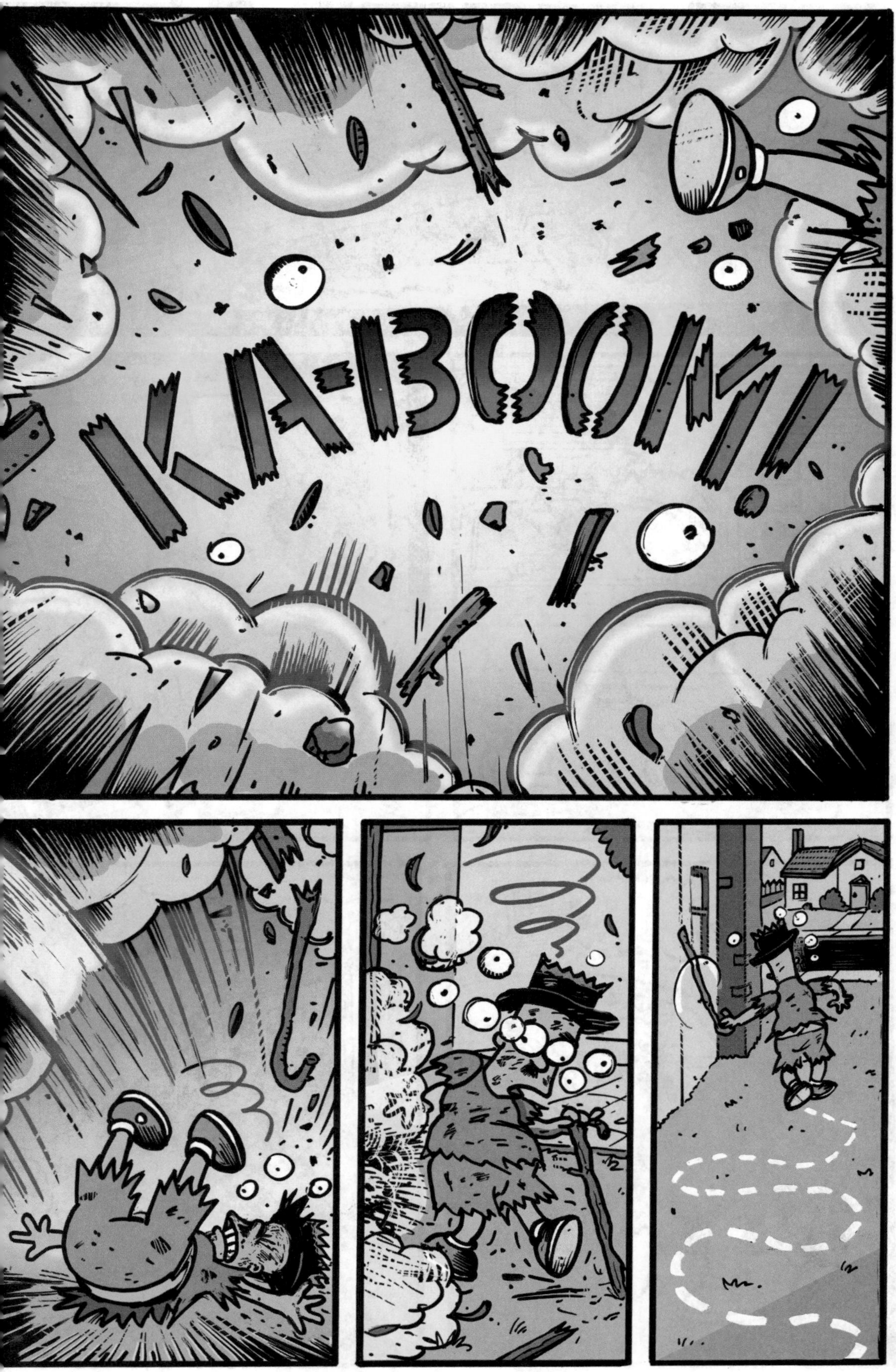
KA-BOOM!!

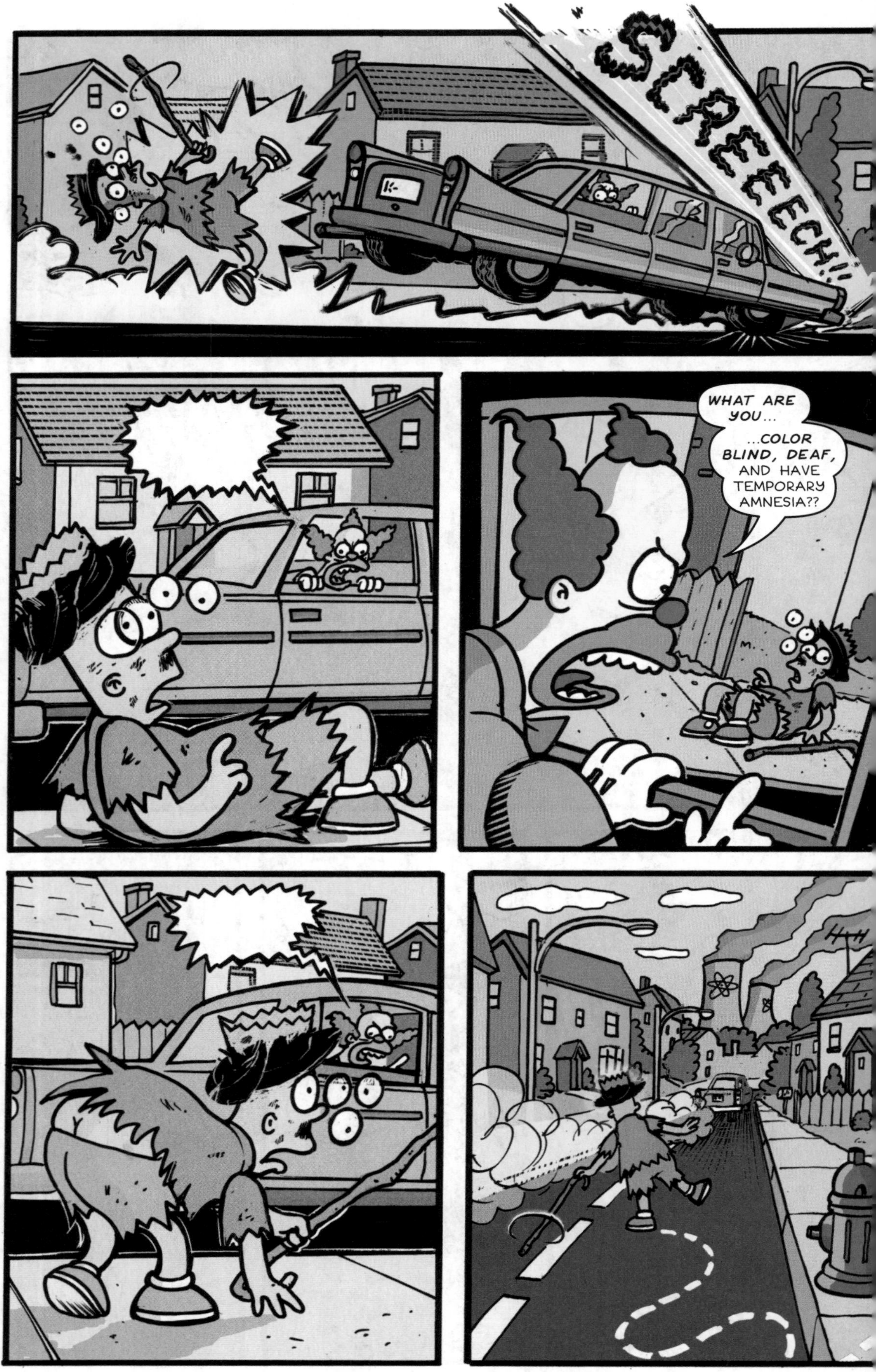
SCREEECH!!!
WHAT ARE YOU...
...COLOR BLIND, DEAF, AND HAVE TEMPORARY AMNESIA??

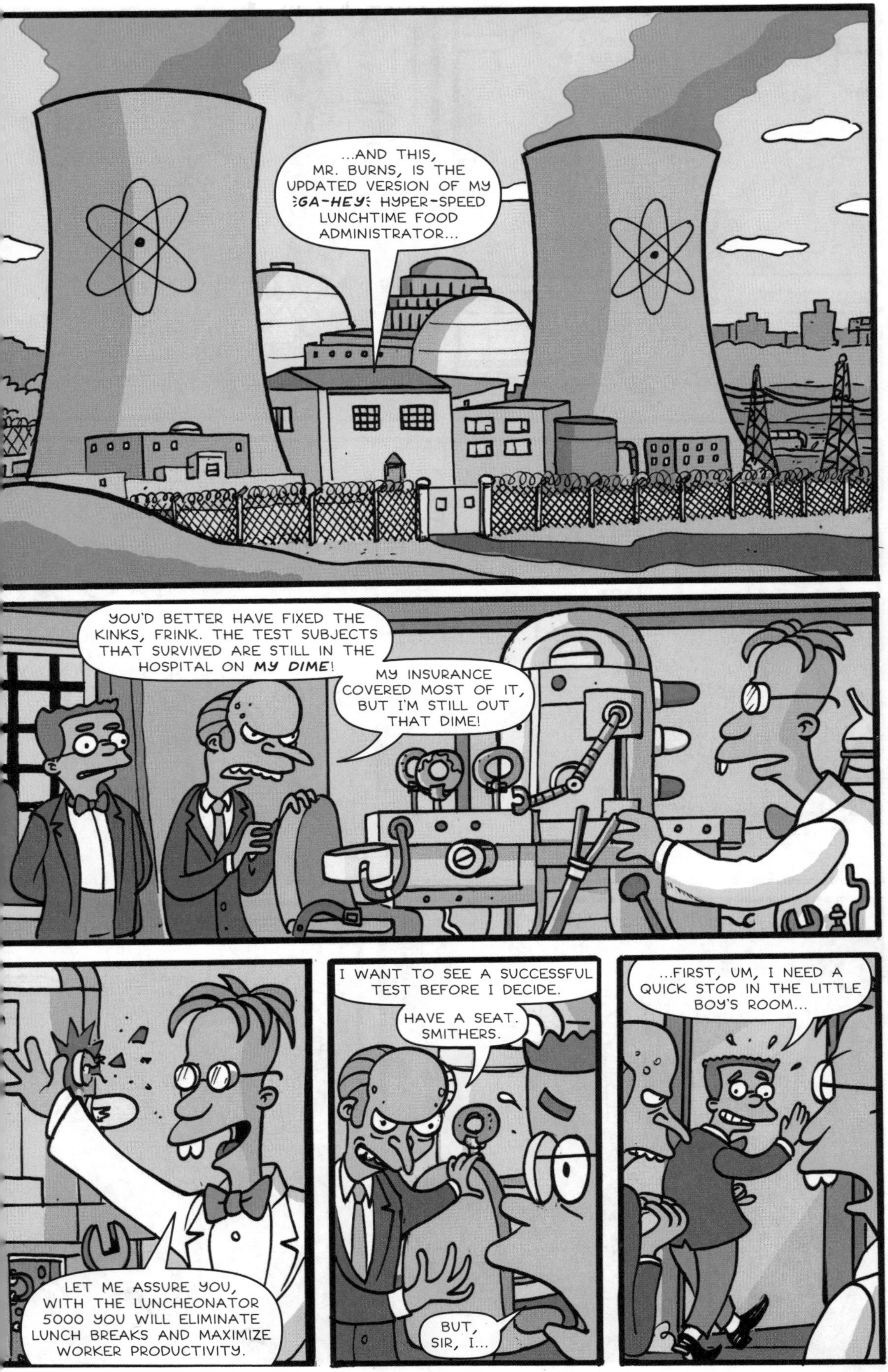
...AND THIS, MR. BURNS, IS THE UPDATED VERSION OF MY GA-HEY HYPER-SPEED LUNCHTIME FOOD ADMINISTRATOR...
YOU'D BETTER HAVE FIXED THE KINKS, FRINK. THE TEST SUBJECTS THAT SURVIVED ARE STILL IN THE HOSPITAL ON MY DIME!
MY INSURANCE COVERED MOST OF IT, BUT I'M STILL OUT THAT DIME!
LET ME ASSURE YOU, WITH THE LUNCHEONATOR 5000 YOU WILL ELIMINATE LUNCH BREAKS AND MAXIMIZE WORKER PRODUCTIVITY.
I WANT TO SEE A SUCCESSFUL TEST BEFORE I DECIDE.
HAVE A SEAT. SMITHERS.
BUT, SIR, I...
...FIRST, UM, I NEED A QUICK STOP IN THE LITTLE BOY'S ROOM...

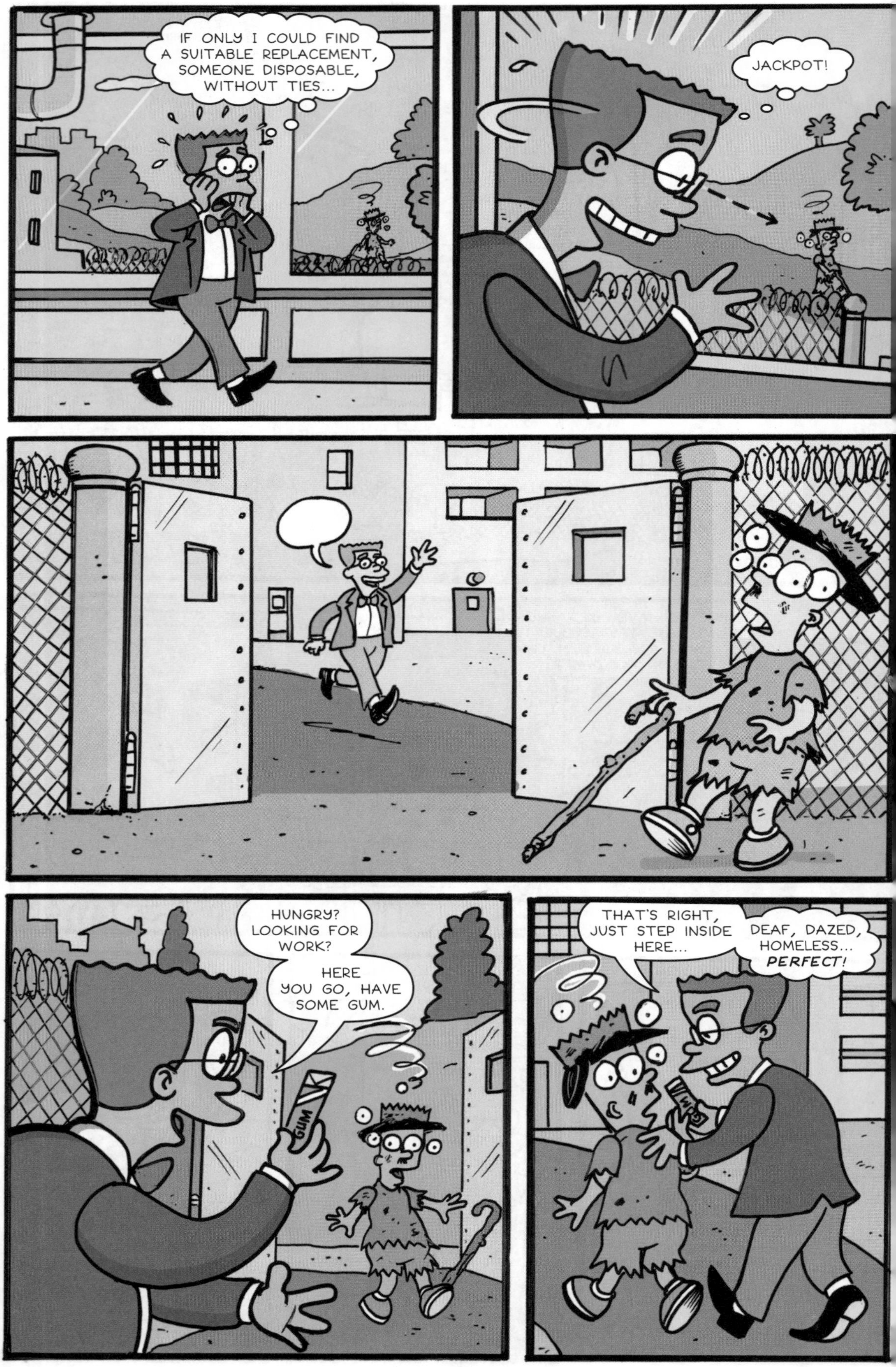
IF ONLY I COULD FIND A SUITABLE REPLACEMENT, SOMEONE DISPOSABLE, WITHOUT TIES...
JACKPOT!
HUNGRY? LOOKING FOR WORK?
HERE YOU GO, HAVE SOME GUM.
GUM
THAT'S RIGHT, JUST STEP INSIDE HERE...
DEAF, DAZED, HOMELESS... *PERFECT!*

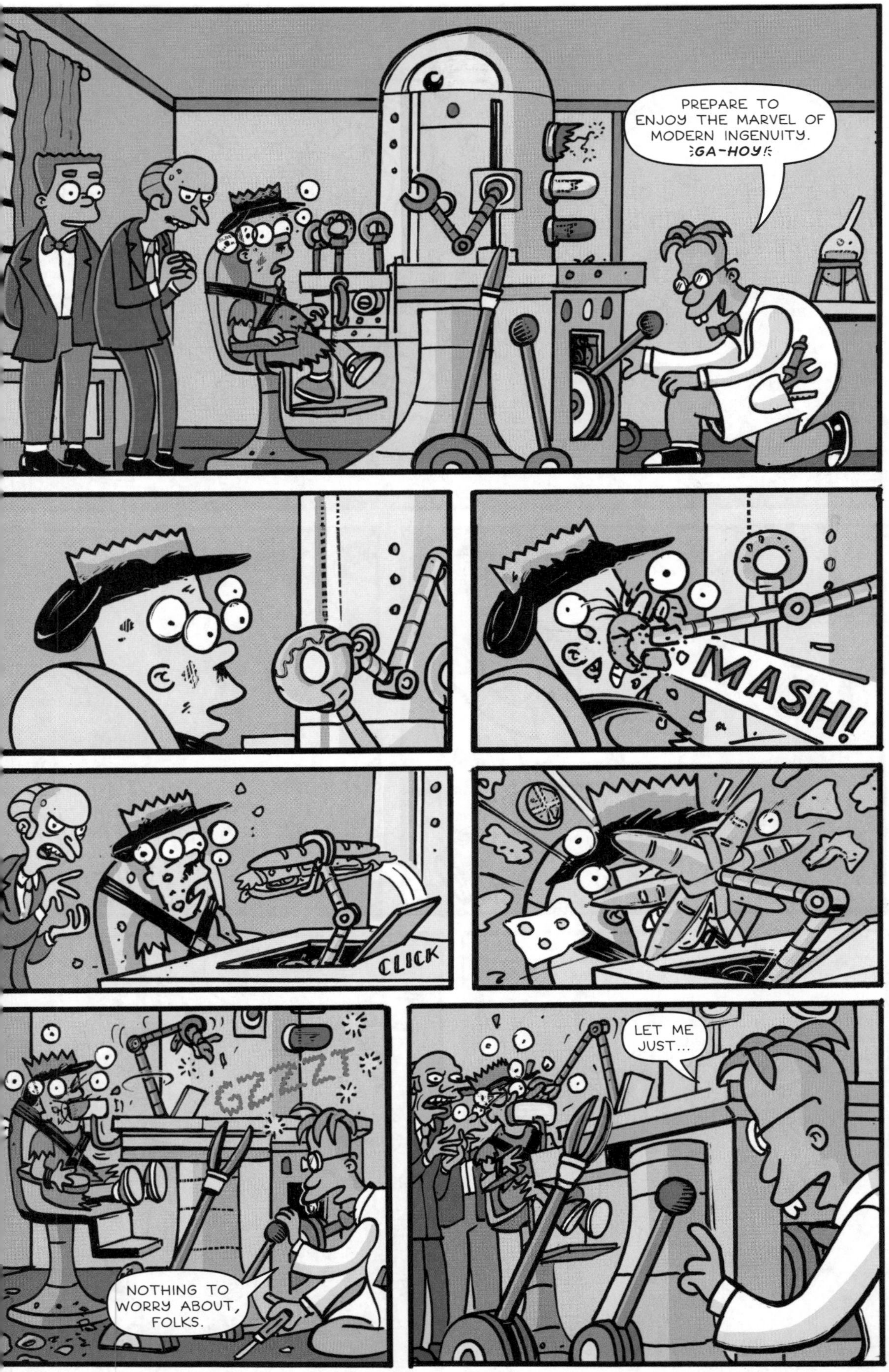
PREPARE TO ENJOY THE MARVEL OF MODERN INGENUITY. GA-HOY!
MASH!
CLICK
GZZZT
NOTHING TO WORRY ABOUT, FOLKS.
LET ME JUST...

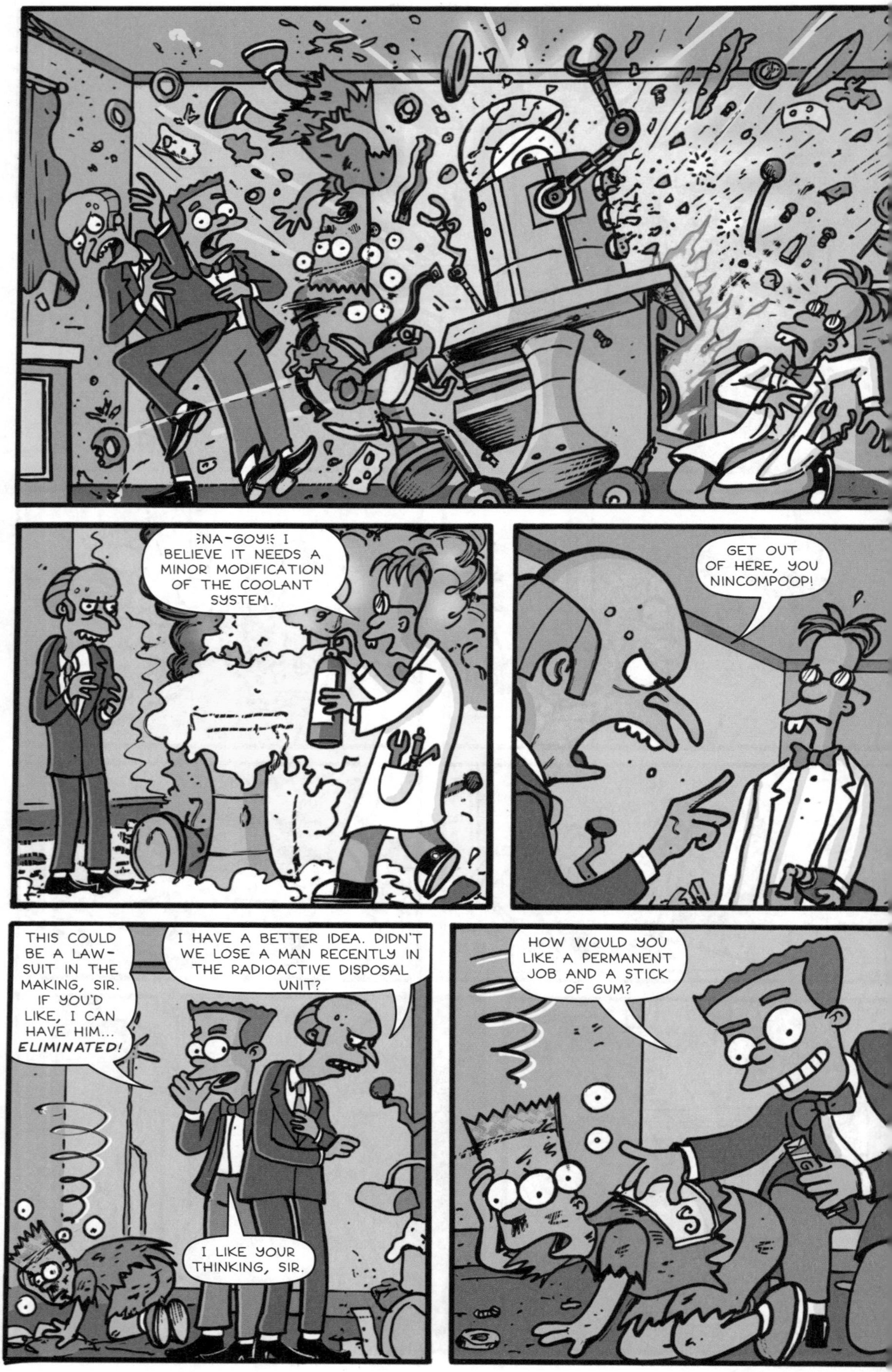

⁝NA-GOY!⁝ I BELIEVE IT NEEDS A MINOR MODIFICATION OF THE COOLANT SYSTEM.
GET OUT OF HERE, YOU NINCOMPOOP!
THIS COULD BE A LAW-SUIT IN THE MAKING, SIR. IF YOU'D LIKE, I CAN HAVE HIM... ELIMINATED!
I HAVE A BETTER IDEA. DIDN'T WE LOSE A MAN RECENTLY IN THE RADIOACTIVE DISPOSAL UNIT?
I LIKE YOUR THINKING, SIR.
HOW WOULD YOU LIKE A PERMANENT JOB AND A STICK OF GUM?

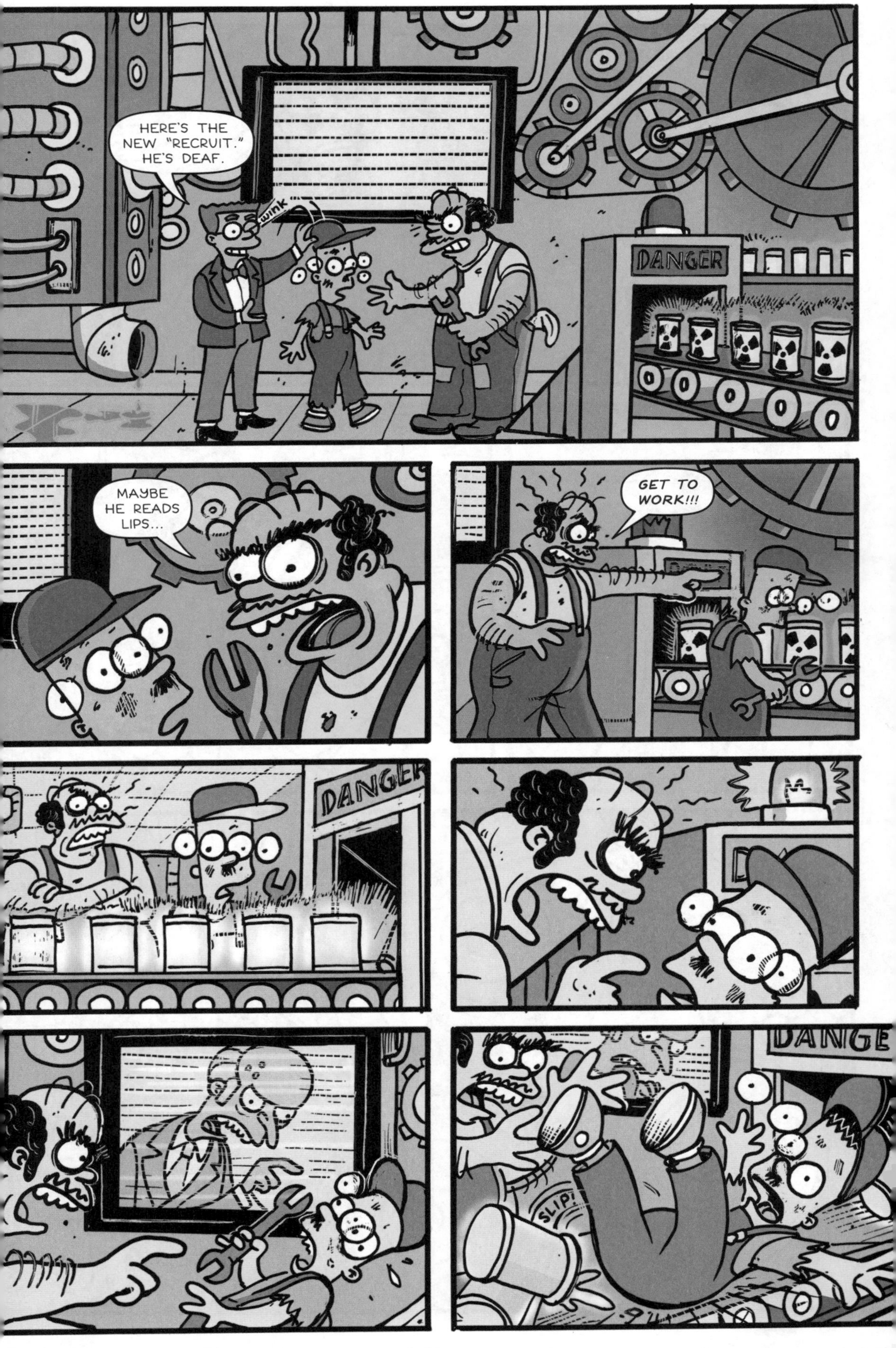
HERE'S THE NEW "RECRUIT." HE'S DEAF.
WINK
DANGER
MAYBE HE READS LIPS...
GET TO WORK!!!
DANGER
DANGE
SLIP!

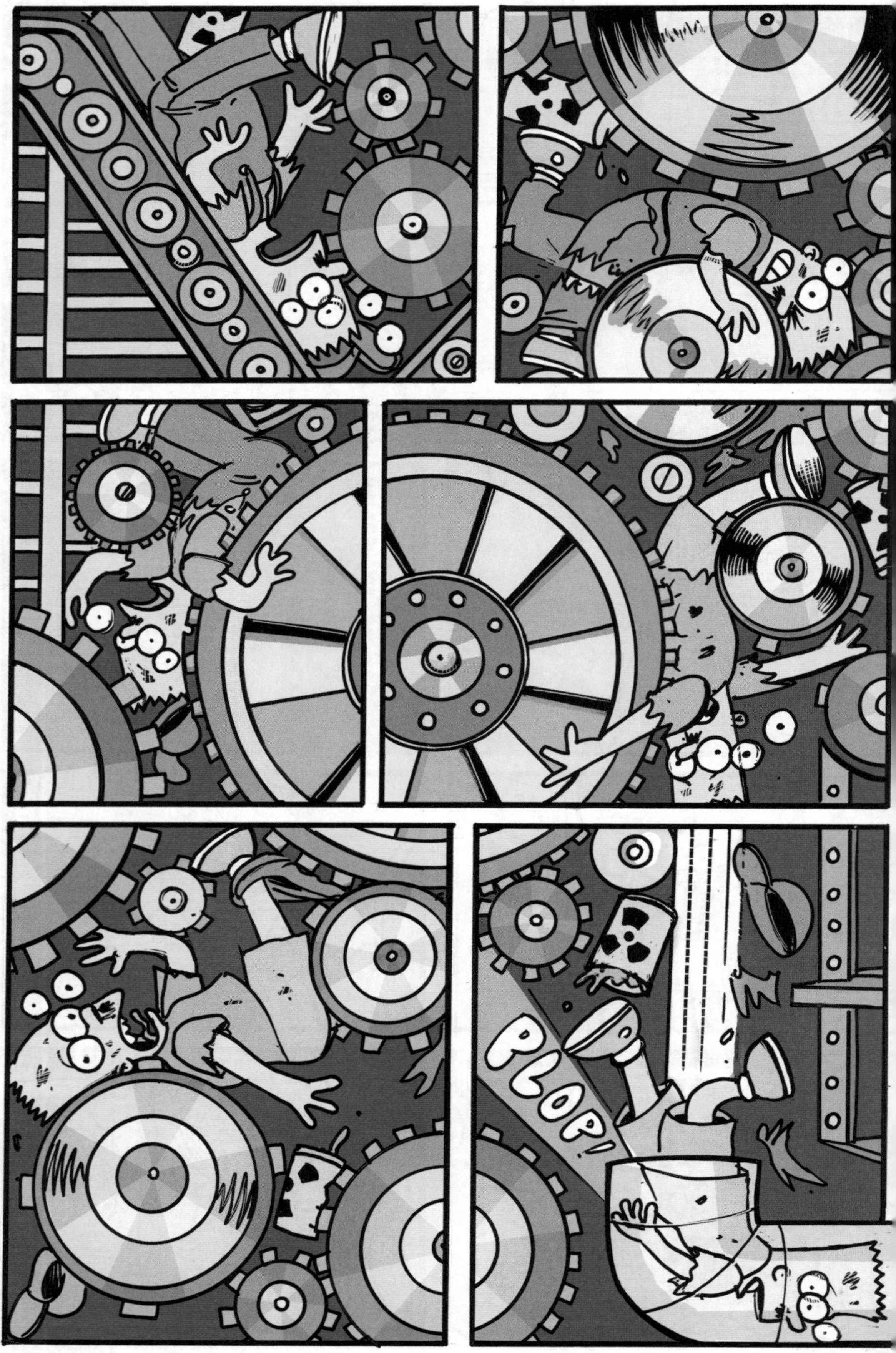
PLOP!

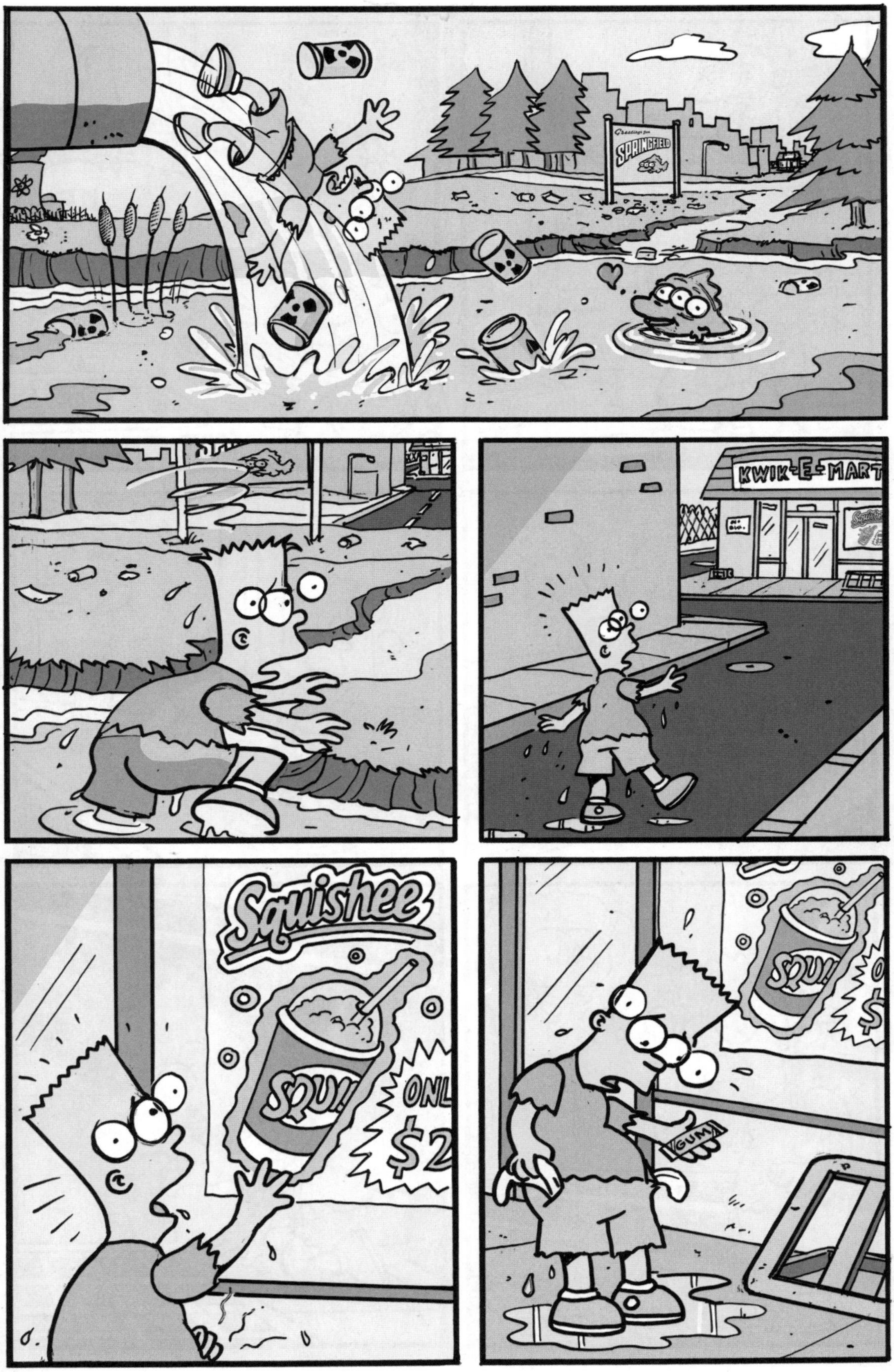
SPRINGFIELD
KWIK-E-MART
Squishee
SQUI
ONL
$2
GUM

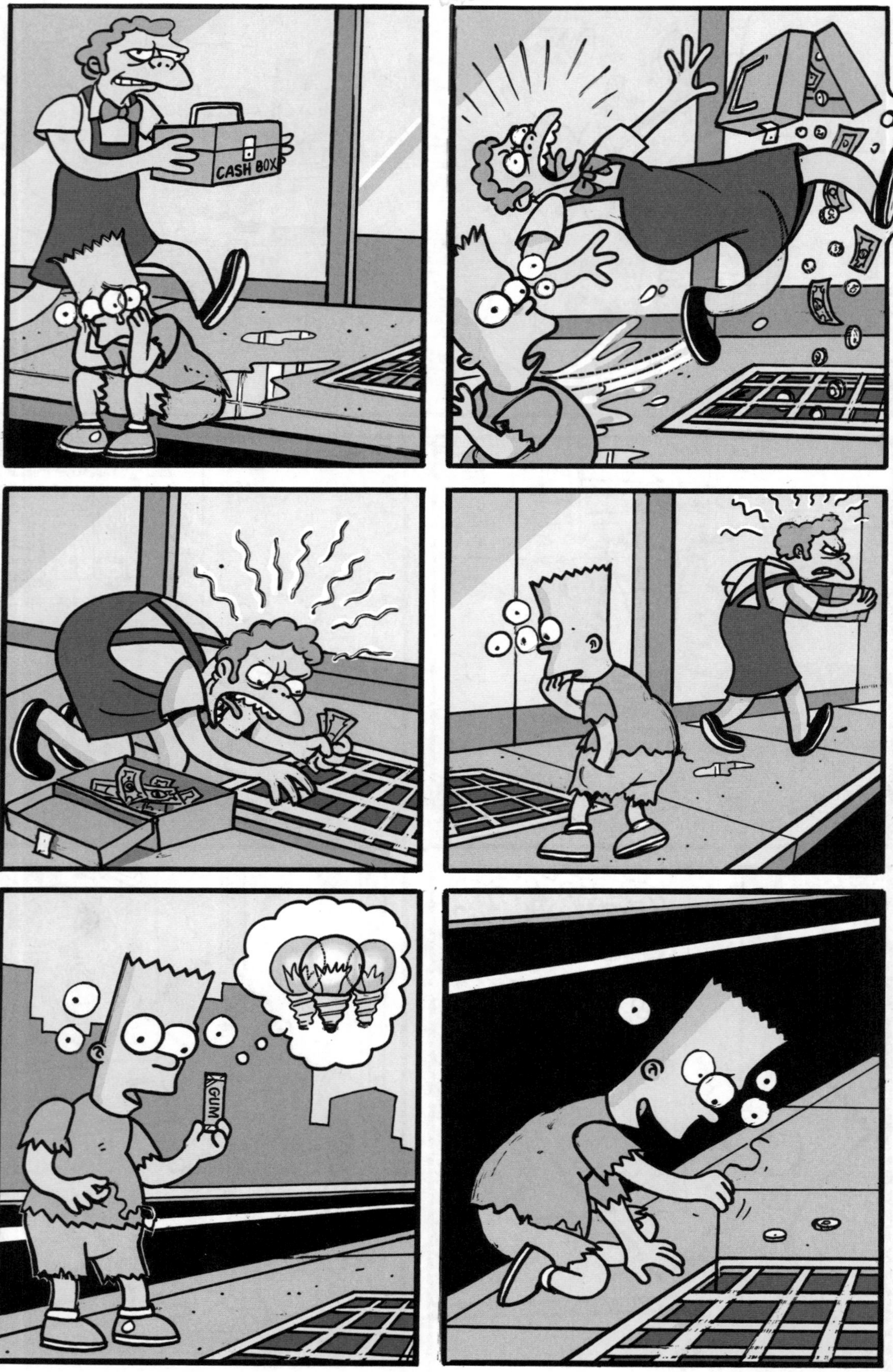
CASH BOX
GUM

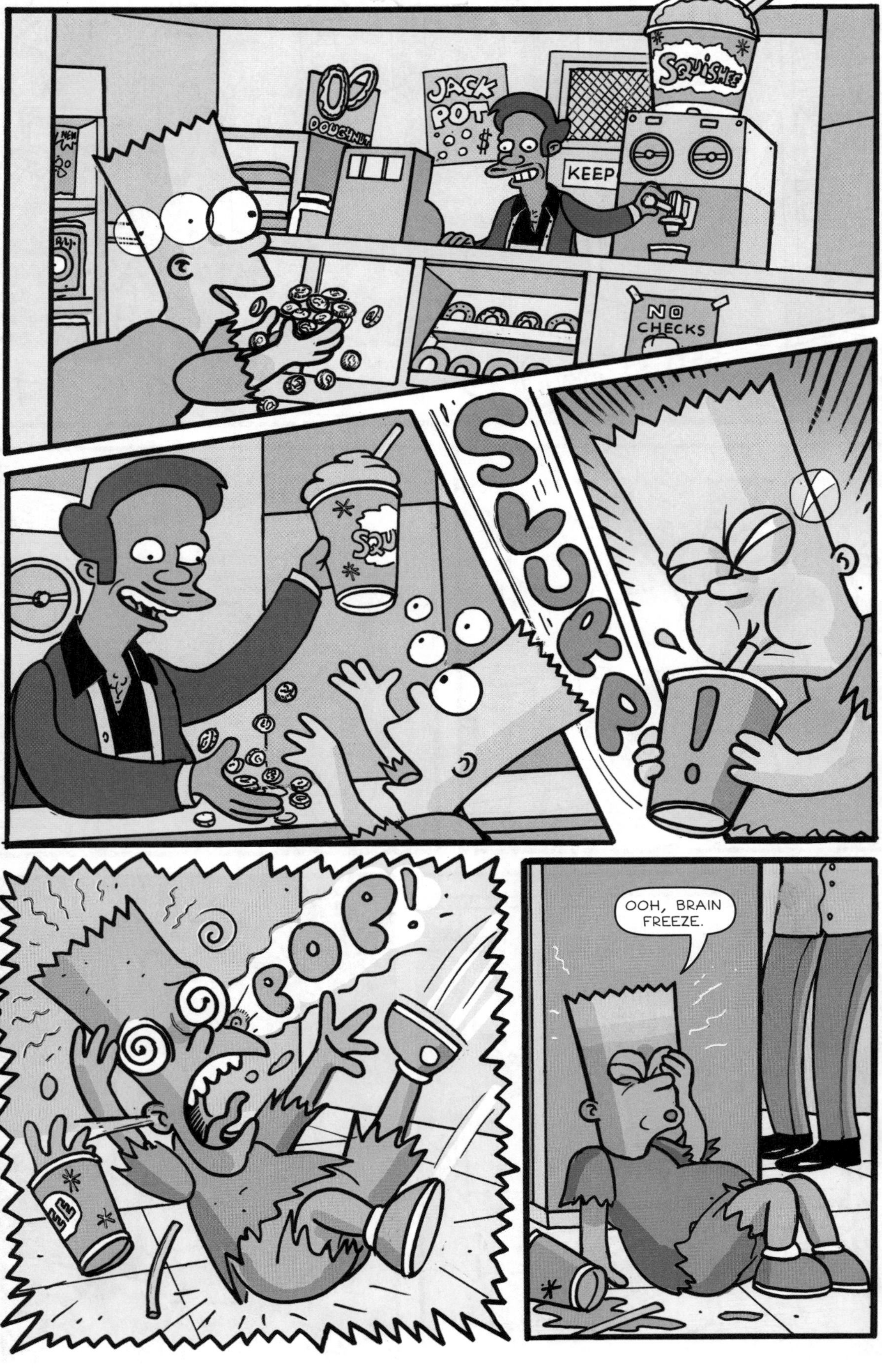
SQUISHEE
DOUGHNUTS
JACK POT $
KEEP
NO CHECKS
SQU
SLURP!
POP!
OOH, BRAIN FREEZE.

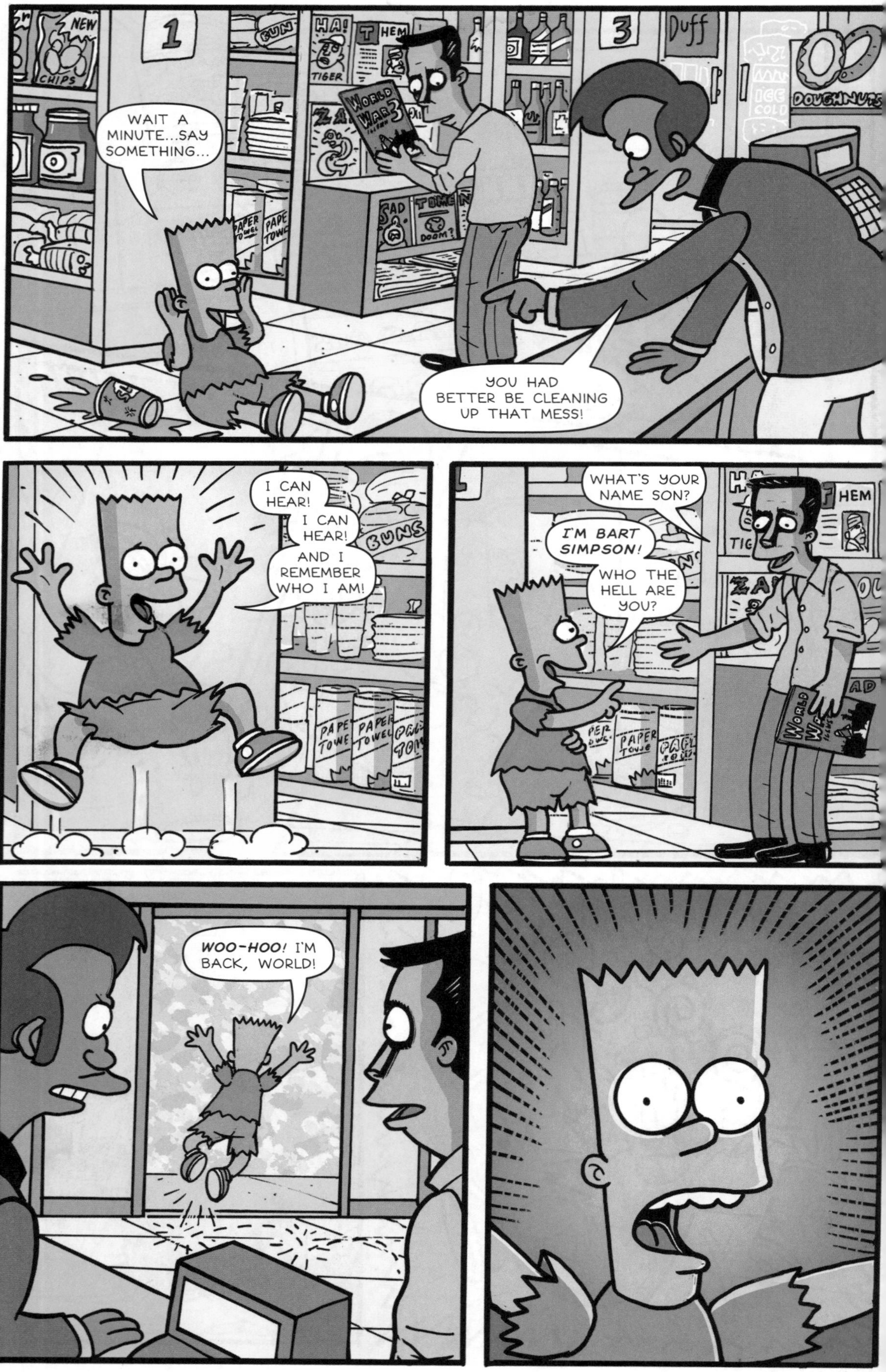

WAIT A MINUTE...SAY SOMETHING...
YOU HAD BETTER BE CLEANING UP THAT MESS!
I CAN HEAR!
I CAN HEAR!
AND I REMEMBER WHO I AM!
WHAT'S YOUR NAME SON?
I'M BART SIMPSON!
WHO THE HELL ARE YOU?
WOO-HOO! I'M BACK, WORLD!

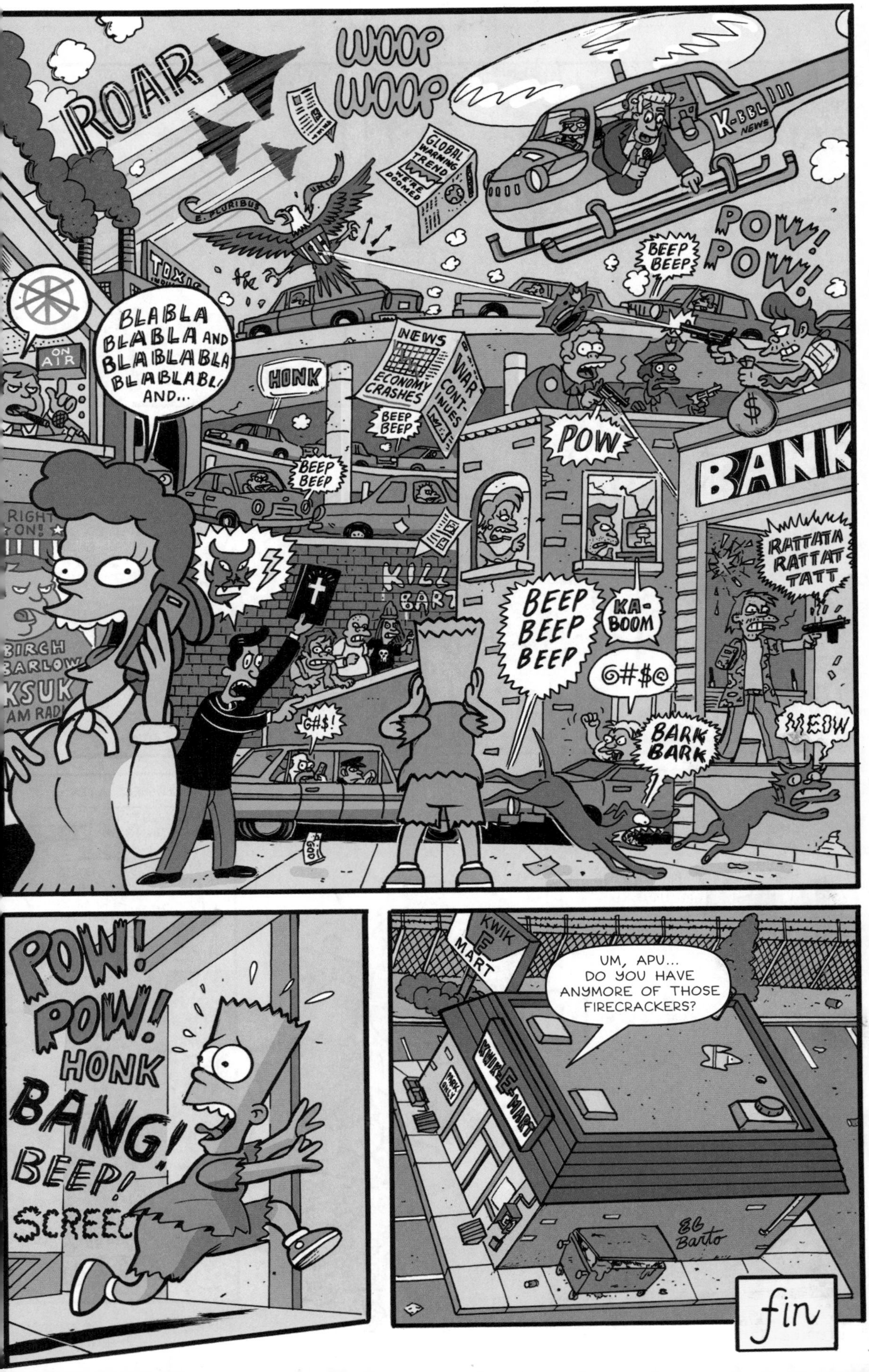

ROAR
WOOP WOOP
GLOBAL WARMING TREND
WE'RE DOOMED
E. PLURIBUS
UNUM
K-BBL NEWS
POW! POW!
BEEP BEEP
TOXIC
ON AIR
BLABLA BLABLA AND BLABLABLA BLABLABL! AND...
HONK
NEWS
ECONOMY CRASHES
WAR CONTINUES
BEEP BEEP
BEEP BEEP
POW
BANK
RIGHT ON!
BIRCH BARLOW
KSUK AM RADIO
KILL BART
RATTATA RATTAT TATT
BEEP BEEP BEEP
KA-BOOM
@#$@
@#$!
BARK BARK
MEOW
GOD
POW! POW! HONK BANG! BEEP! SCREEC
KWIK E MART
UM, APU... DO YOU HAVE ANYMORE OF THOSE FIRECRACKERS?
KWIK-E-MART
EG Barto

fin

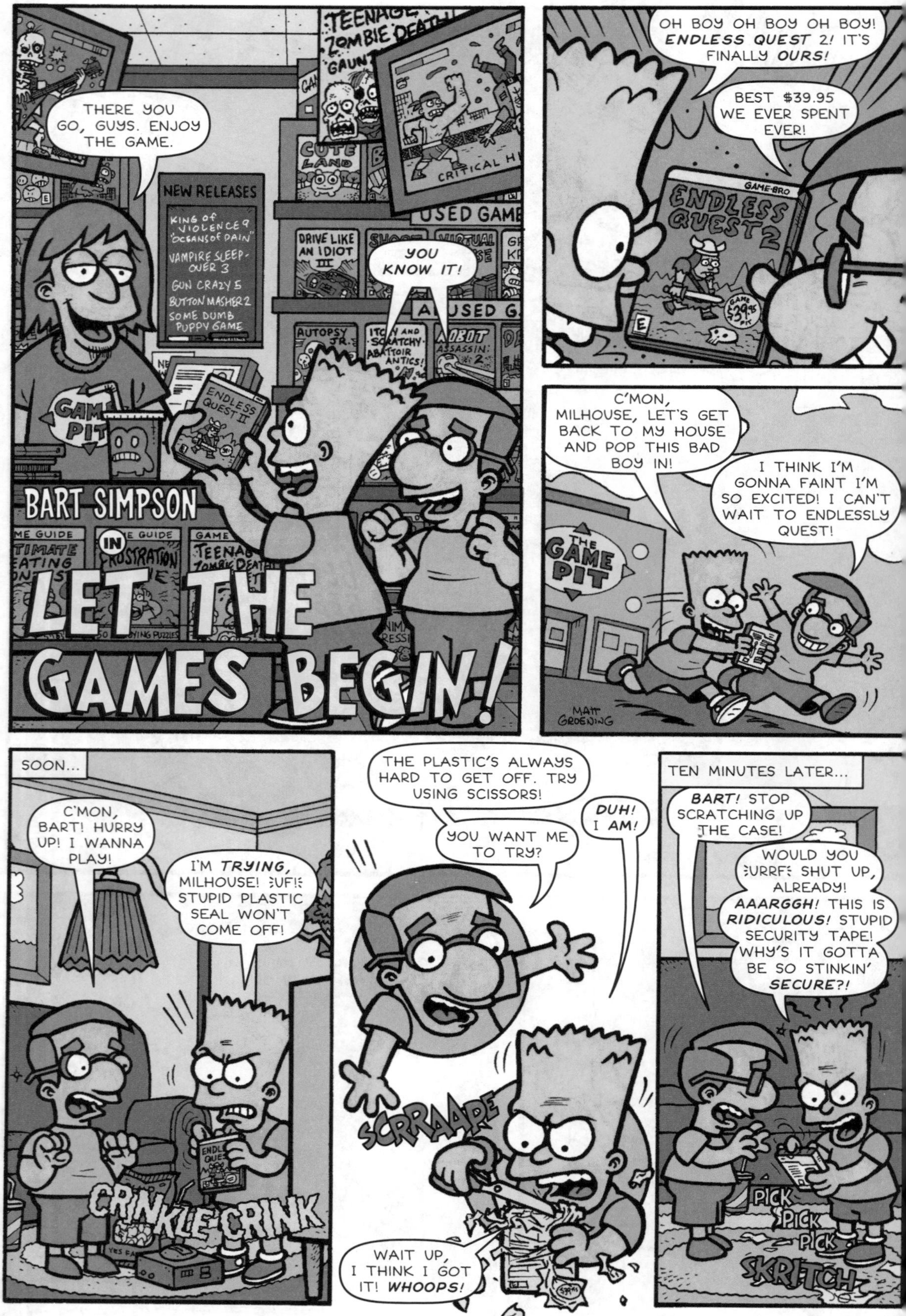
THERE YOU GO, GUYS. ENJOY THE GAME.
NEW RELEASES
KING OF VIOLENCE 9 "OCEANS OF PAIN"
VAMPIRE SLEEP-OVER 3
GUN CRAZY 5
BUTTON MASHER 2
SOME DUMB PUPPY GAME
USED GAMES
DRIVE LIKE AN IDIOT III
AUTOPSY JR.
ITCHY AND SCRATCHY ABATTOIR ANTICS!
ROBOT ASSASSIN 2
CUTE LAND
CRITICAL HIT
TEENAGE ZOMBIE DEATH GAUNT
ENDLESS QUEST II
GAME PIT
YOU KNOW IT!
BART SIMPSON IN
LET THE GAMES BEGIN!
OH BOY OH BOY OH BOY! ENDLESS QUEST 2! IT'S FINALLY OURS!
BEST $39.95 WE EVER SPENT EVER!
GAME-BRO
ENDLESS QUEST 2
C'MON, MILHOUSE, LET'S GET BACK TO MY HOUSE AND POP THIS BAD BOY IN!
I THINK I'M GONNA FAINT I'M SO EXCITED! I CAN'T WAIT TO ENDLESSLY QUEST!
THE GAME PIT
MATT GROENING
SOON...
C'MON, BART! HURRY UP! I WANNA PLAY!
I'M TRYING, MILHOUSE! UF! STUPID PLASTIC SEAL WON'T COME OFF!
CRINKLE CRINK
THE PLASTIC'S ALWAYS HARD TO GET OFF. TRY USING SCISSORS!
YOU WANT ME TO TRY?
DUH! I AM!
SCRRAAPE
WAIT UP, I THINK I GOT IT! WHOOPS!
TEN MINUTES LATER...
BART! STOP SCRATCHING UP THE CASE!
WOULD YOU URRF SHUT UP, ALREADY! AAARGGH! THIS IS RIDICULOUS! STUPID SECURITY TAPE! WHY'S IT GOTTA BE SO STINKIN' SECURE?!
PICK PICK PICK
SKRITCH

EVAN DORKIN STORY & ART

SARAH DYER COLORS

KAREN BATES LETTERS

BILL MORRISON EDITOR

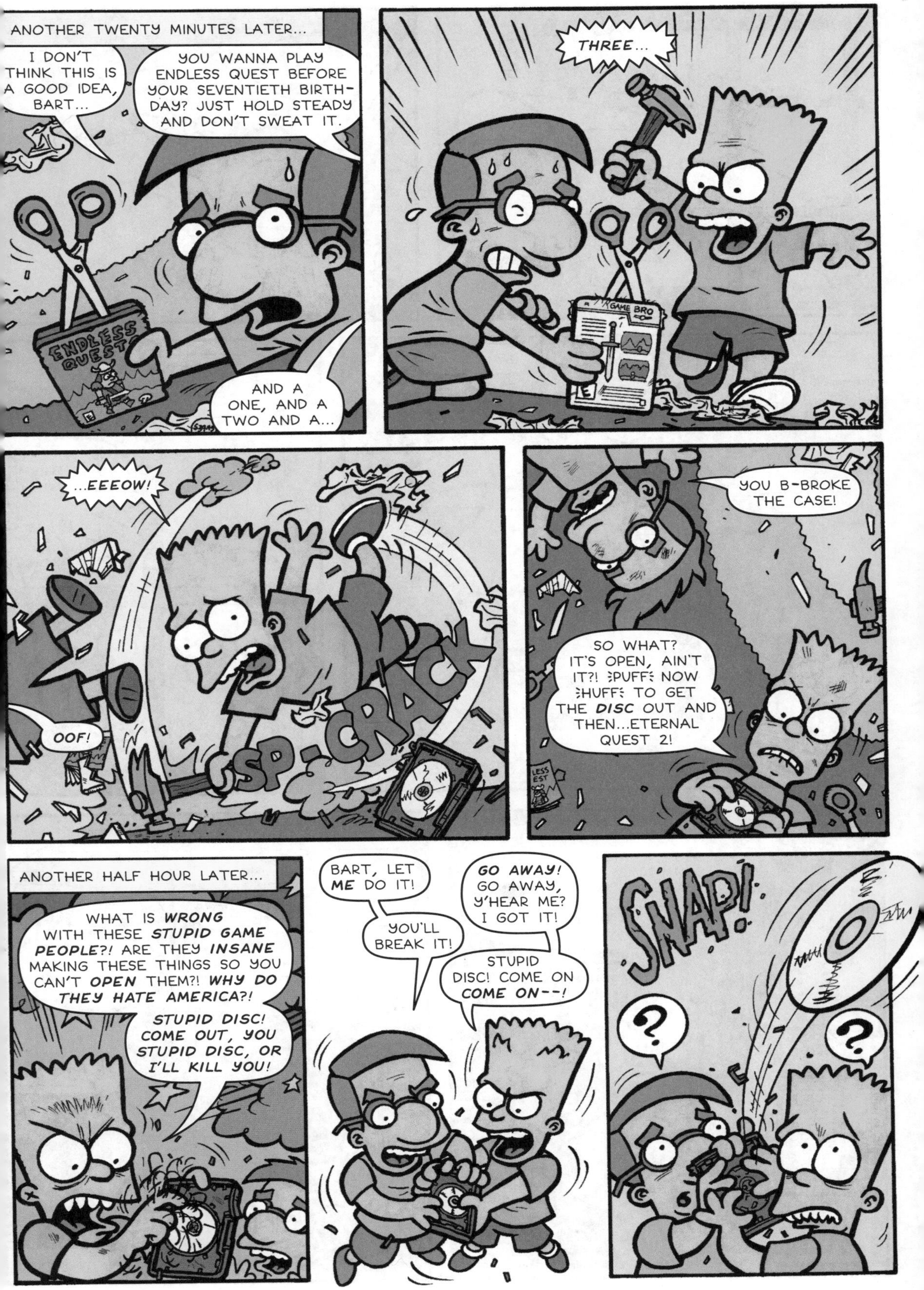
ANOTHER TWENTY MINUTES LATER...
I DON'T THINK THIS IS A GOOD IDEA, BART...
YOU WANNA PLAY ENDLESS QUEST BEFORE YOUR SEVENTIETH BIRTH-DAY? JUST HOLD STEADY AND DON'T SWEAT IT.
ENDLESS QUEST
AND A ONE, AND A TWO AND A...
THREE...
GAME BRO
...EEEOW!
OOF!
SP-CRACK
YOU B-BROKE THE CASE!
SO WHAT? IT'S OPEN, AIN'T IT?! PUFF NOW HUFF TO GET THE DISC OUT AND THEN...ETERNAL QUEST 2!
ANOTHER HALF HOUR LATER...
WHAT IS WRONG WITH THESE STUPID GAME PEOPLE?! ARE THEY INSANE MAKING THESE THINGS SO YOU CAN'T OPEN THEM?! WHY DO THEY HATE AMERICA?!
STUPID DISC! COME OUT, YOU STUPID DISC, OR I'LL KILL YOU!
BART, LET ME DO IT!
YOU'LL BREAK IT!
GO AWAY! GO AWAY, Y'HEAR ME? I GOT IT!
STUPID DISC! COME ON COME ON--!
SNAP!
?
?

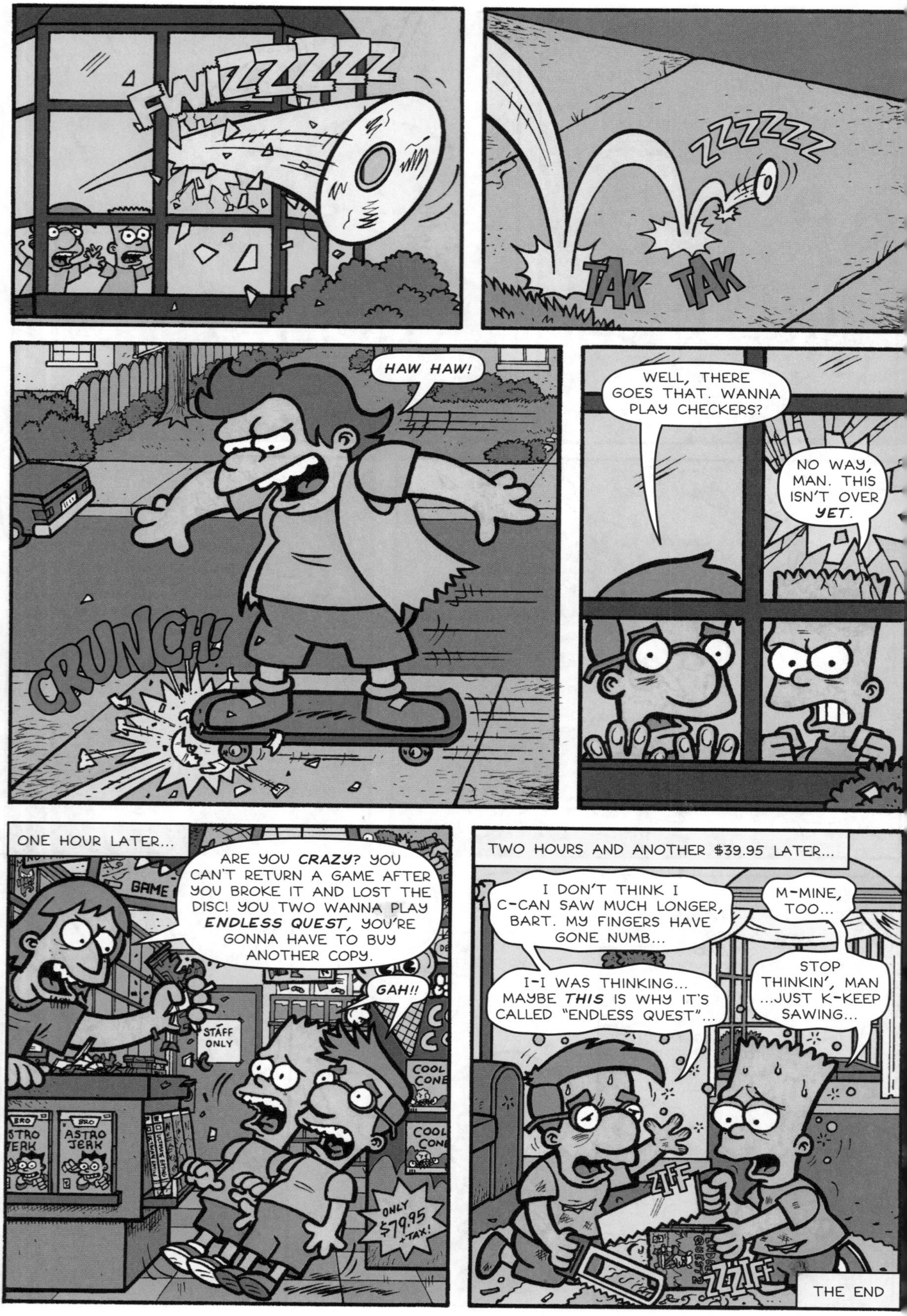
FWIZZZZZZ
ZZZZZZZ
TAK TAK
HAW HAW!
CRUNCH!
WELL, THERE GOES THAT. WANNA PLAY CHECKERS?
NO WAY, MAN. THIS ISN'T OVER YET.
ONE HOUR LATER...
ARE YOU CRAZY? YOU CAN'T RETURN A GAME AFTER YOU BROKE IT AND LOST THE DISC! YOU TWO WANNA PLAY ENDLESS QUEST, YOU'RE GONNA HAVE TO BUY ANOTHER COPY.
GAH!!
STAFF ONLY
GAME
COOL CONE
COOL CONE
ASTRO JERK
ASTRO JERK
ONLY $79.95 +TAX!
TWO HOURS AND ANOTHER $39.95 LATER...
I DON'T THINK I C-CAN SAW MUCH LONGER, BART. MY FINGERS HAVE GONE NUMB...
M-MINE, TOO...
I-I WAS THINKING... MAYBE THIS IS WHY IT'S CALLED "ENDLESS QUEST"...
STOP THINKIN', MAN ...JUST K-KEEP SAWING...
ZIFF
ZZIFF
THE END

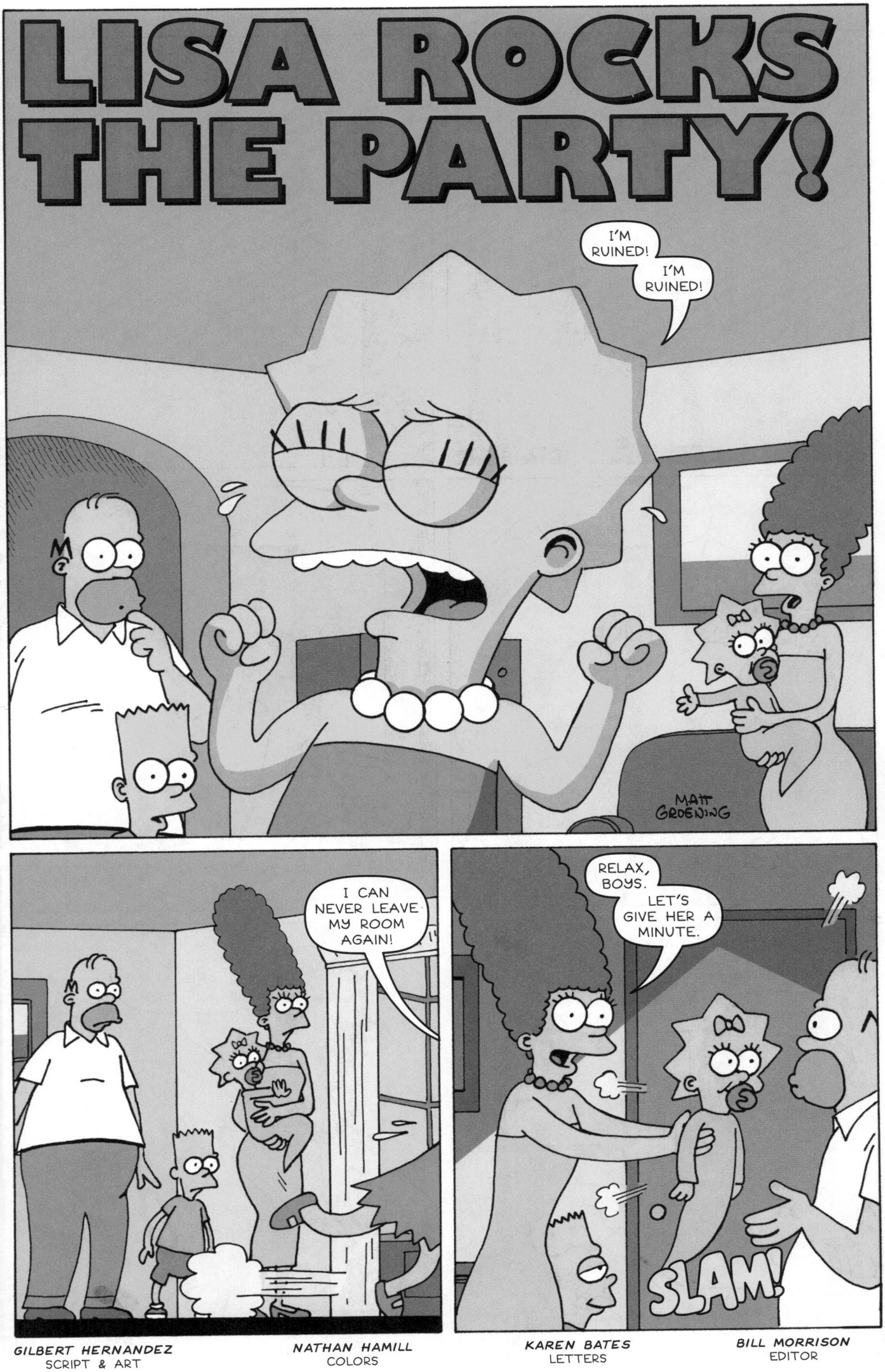
LISA ROCKS THE PARTY!
I'M RUINED! I'M RUINED!
MATT GROENING
I CAN NEVER LEAVE MY ROOM AGAIN!
RELAX, BOYS.
LET'S GIVE HER A MINUTE.
SLAM!

GILBERT HERNANDEZ
SCRIPT & ART

NATHAN HAMILL
COLORS

KAREN BATES
LETTERS

BILL MORRISON
EDITOR

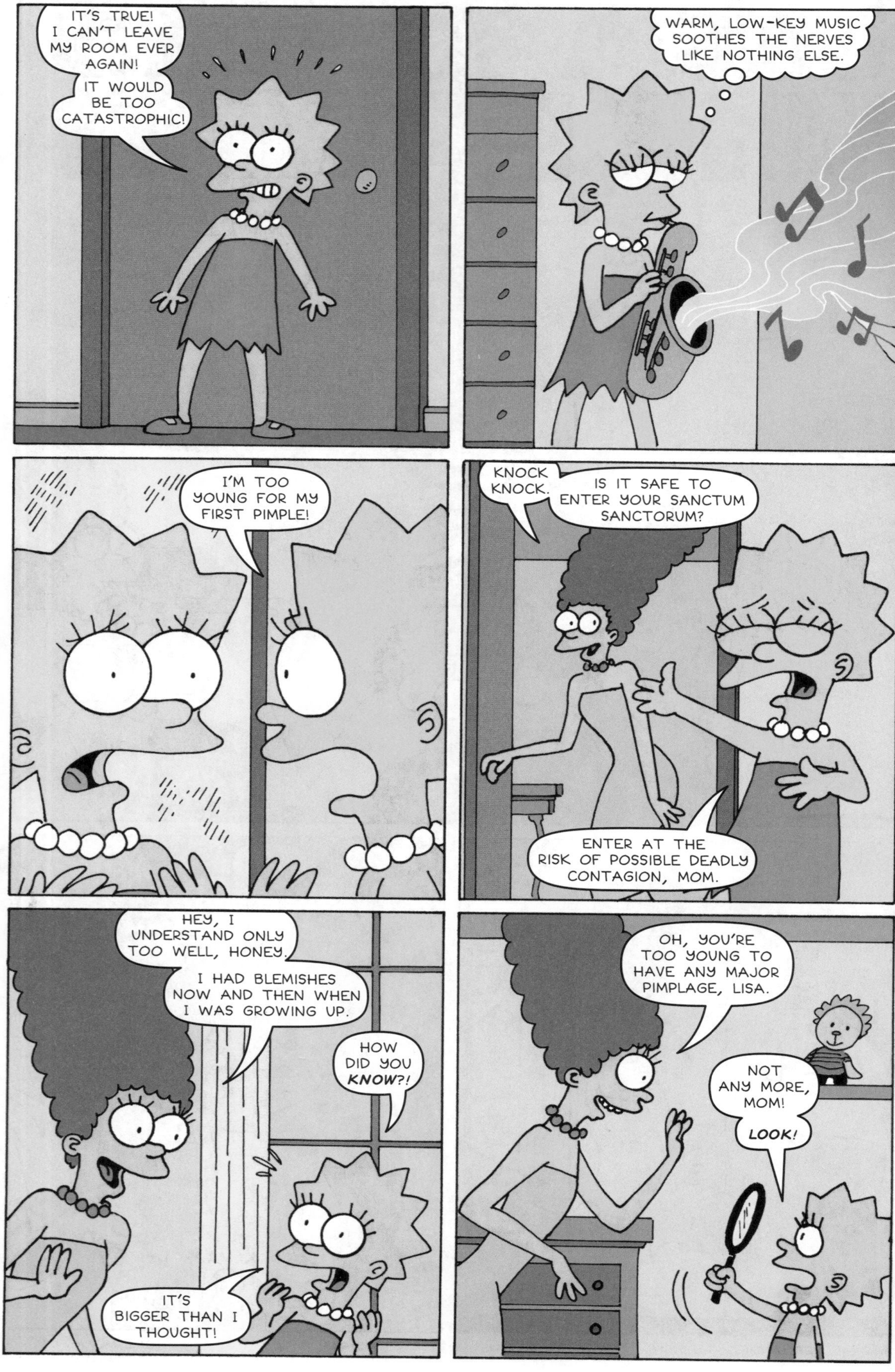
IT'S TRUE! I CAN'T LEAVE MY ROOM EVER AGAIN!
IT WOULD BE TOO CATASTROPHIC!
WARM, LOW-KEY MUSIC SOOTHES THE NERVES LIKE NOTHING ELSE.
I'M TOO YOUNG FOR MY FIRST PIMPLE!
KNOCK KNOCK.
IS IT SAFE TO ENTER YOUR SANCTUM SANCTORUM?
ENTER AT THE RISK OF POSSIBLE DEADLY CONTAGION, MOM.
HEY, I UNDERSTAND ONLY TOO WELL, HONEY.
I HAD BLEMISHES NOW AND THEN WHEN I WAS GROWING UP.
HOW DID YOU *KNOW*?!
IT'S BIGGER THAN I THOUGHT!
OH, YOU'RE TOO YOUNG TO HAVE ANY MAJOR PIMPLAGE, LISA.
NOT ANY MORE, MOM!
LOOK!

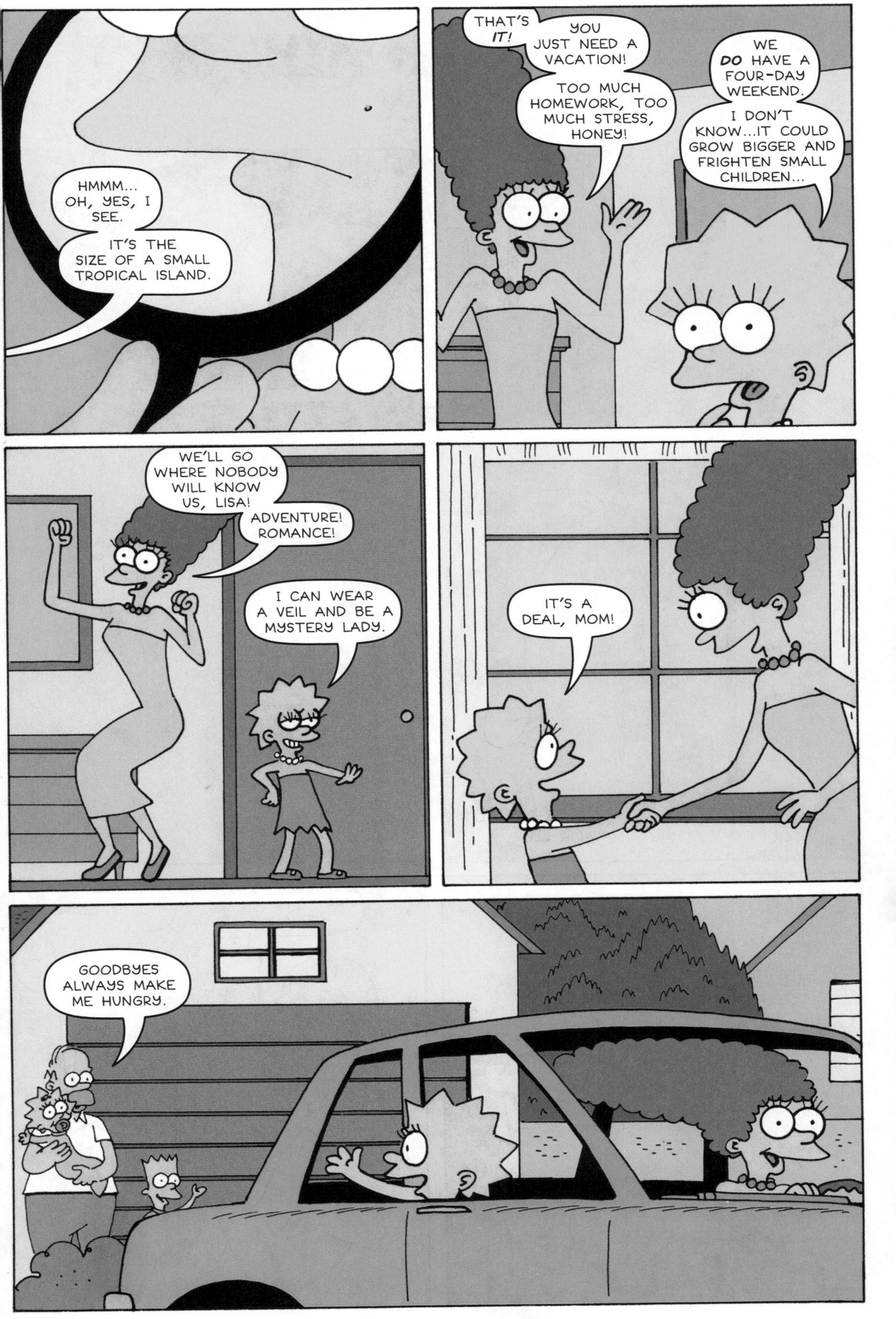
HMMM... OH, YES, I SEE.
IT'S THE SIZE OF A SMALL TROPICAL ISLAND.
THAT'S IT!
YOU JUST NEED A VACATION!
TOO MUCH HOMEWORK, TOO MUCH STRESS, HONEY!
WE DO HAVE A FOUR-DAY WEEKEND.
I DON'T KNOW...IT COULD GROW BIGGER AND FRIGHTEN SMALL CHILDREN...
WE'LL GO WHERE NOBODY WILL KNOW US, LISA!
ADVENTURE! ROMANCE!
I CAN WEAR A VEIL AND BE A MYSTERY LADY.
IT'S A DEAL, MOM!
GOODBYES ALWAYS MAKE ME HUNGRY.

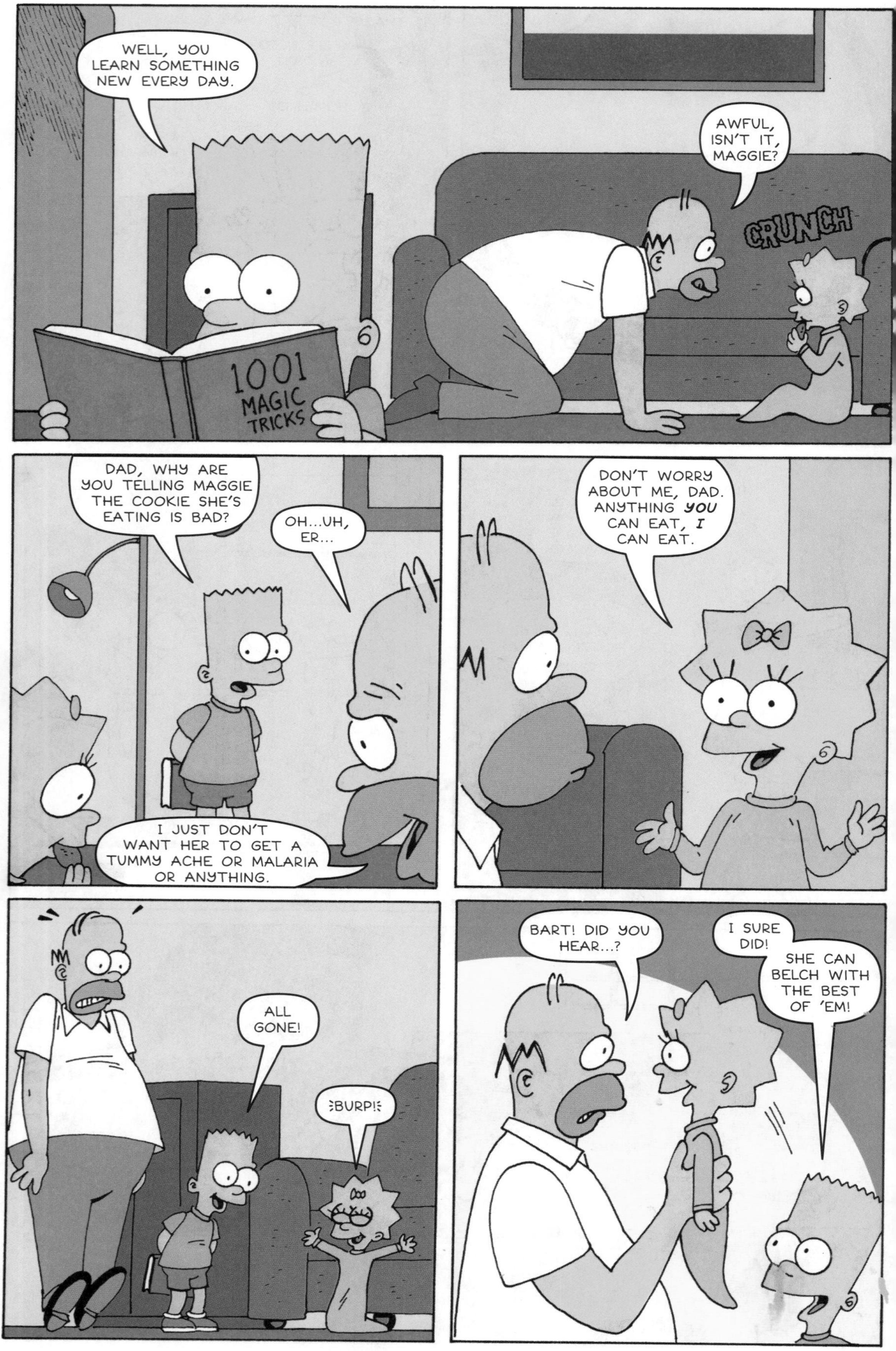

WELL, YOU LEARN SOMETHING NEW EVERY DAY.
1001 MAGIC TRICKS
AWFUL, ISN'T IT, MAGGIE?
CRUNCH
DAD, WHY ARE YOU TELLING MAGGIE THE COOKIE SHE'S EATING IS BAD?
OH...UH, ER...
I JUST DON'T WANT HER TO GET A TUMMY ACHE OR MALARIA OR ANYTHING.
DON'T WORRY ABOUT ME, DAD. ANYTHING *YOU* CAN EAT, *I* CAN EAT.
ALL GONE!
BURP!
BART! DID YOU HEAR...?
I SURE DID!
SHE CAN BELCH WITH THE BEST OF 'EM!

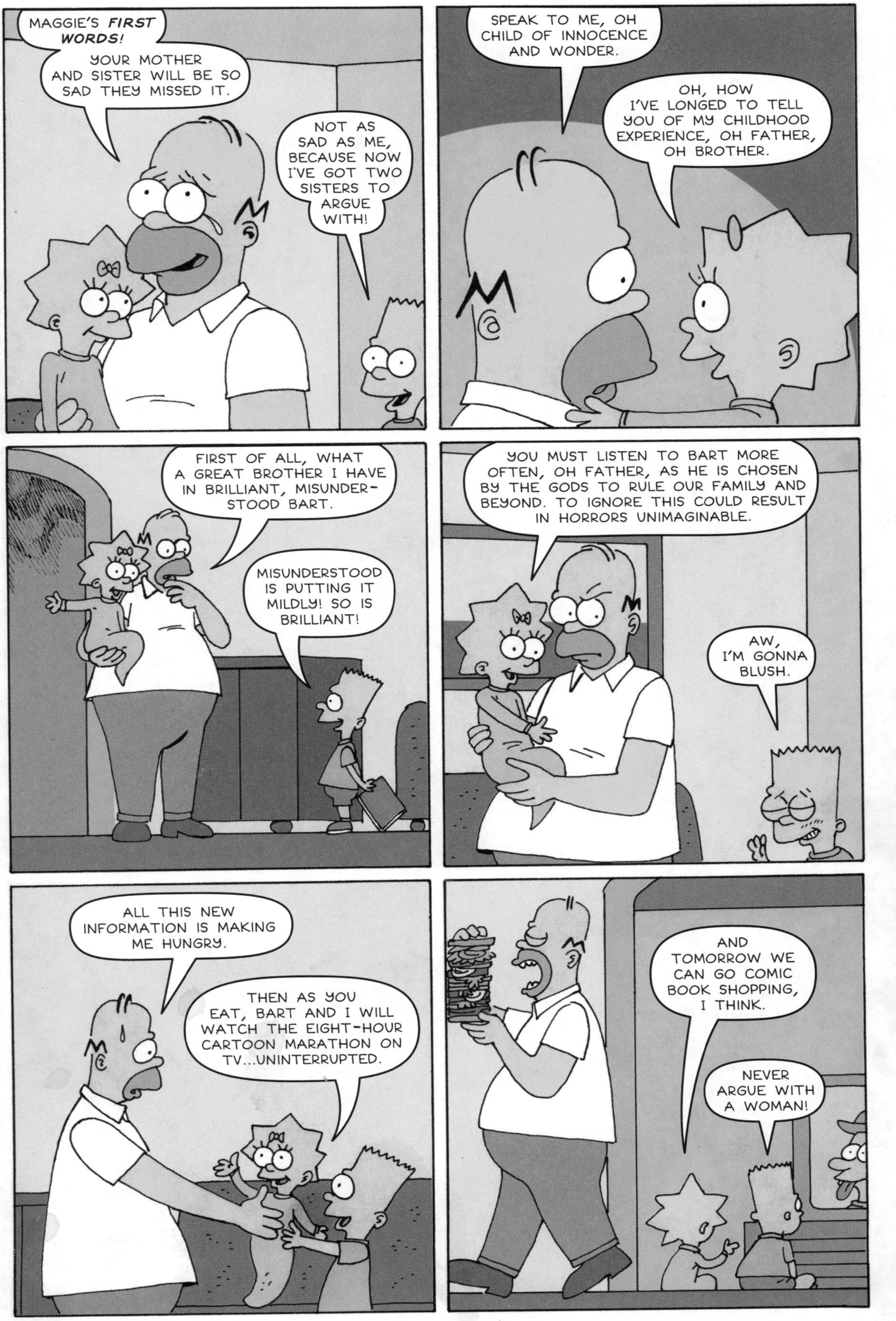
MAGGIE'S **FIRST WORDS!**
YOUR MOTHER AND SISTER WILL BE SO SAD THEY MISSED IT.
NOT AS SAD AS ME, BECAUSE NOW I'VE GOT TWO SISTERS TO ARGUE WITH!
SPEAK TO ME, OH CHILD OF INNOCENCE AND WONDER.
OH, HOW I'VE LONGED TO TELL YOU OF MY CHILDHOOD EXPERIENCE, OH FATHER, OH BROTHER.
FIRST OF ALL, WHAT A GREAT BROTHER I HAVE IN BRILLIANT, MISUNDERSTOOD BART.
MISUNDERSTOOD IS PUTTING IT MILDLY! SO IS BRILLIANT!
YOU MUST LISTEN TO BART MORE OFTEN, OH FATHER, AS HE IS CHOSEN BY THE GODS TO RULE OUR FAMILY AND BEYOND. TO IGNORE THIS COULD RESULT IN HORRORS UNIMAGINABLE.
AW, I'M GONNA BLUSH.
ALL THIS NEW INFORMATION IS MAKING ME HUNGRY.
THEN AS YOU EAT, BART AND I WILL WATCH THE EIGHT-HOUR CARTOON MARATHON ON TV...UNINTERRUPTED.
AND TOMORROW WE CAN GO COMIC BOOK SHOPPING, I THINK.
NEVER ARGUE WITH A WOMAN!

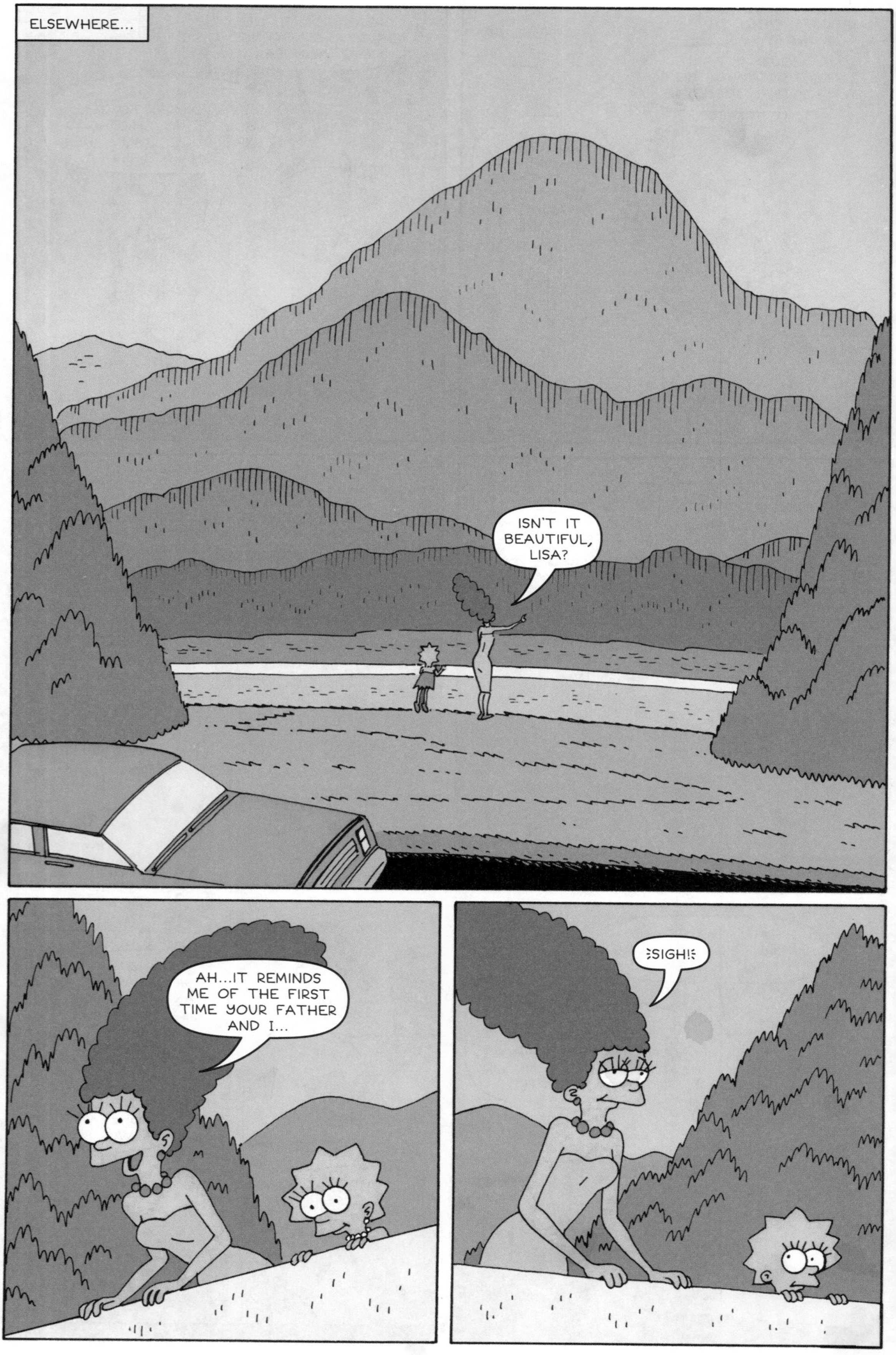
ELSEWHERE...
ISN'T IT BEAUTIFUL, LISA?
AH...IT REMINDS ME OF THE FIRST TIME YOUR FATHER AND I...
SIGH!

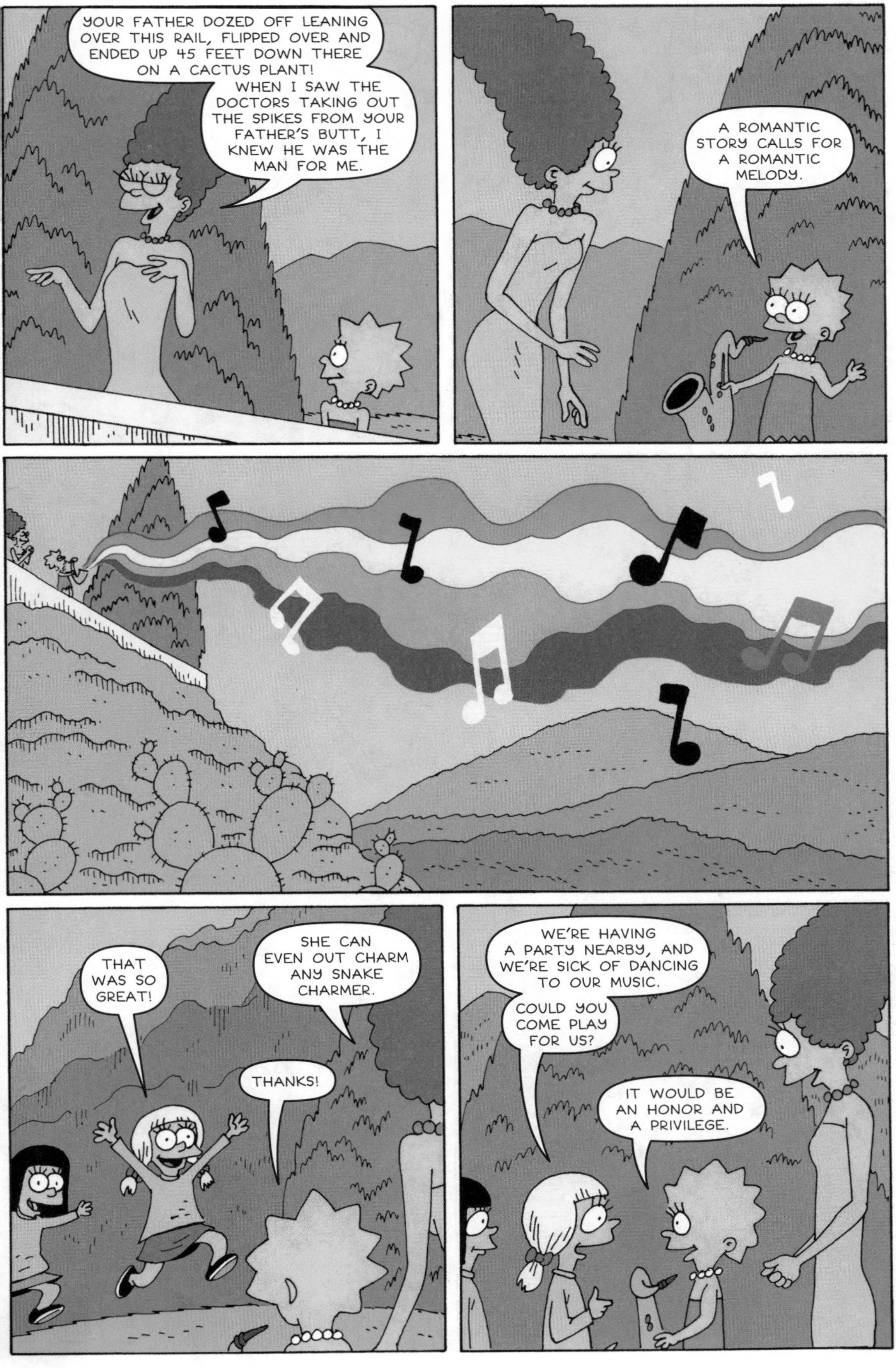
YOUR FATHER DOZED OFF LEANING OVER THIS RAIL, FLIPPED OVER AND ENDED UP 45 FEET DOWN THERE ON A CACTUS PLANT!
WHEN I SAW THE DOCTORS TAKING OUT THE SPIKES FROM YOUR FATHER'S BUTT, I KNEW HE WAS THE MAN FOR ME.
A ROMANTIC STORY CALLS FOR A ROMANTIC MELODY.
THAT WAS SO GREAT!
SHE CAN EVEN OUT CHARM ANY SNAKE CHARMER.
THANKS!
WE'RE HAVING A PARTY NEARBY, AND WE'RE SICK OF DANCING TO OUR MUSIC.
COULD YOU COME PLAY FOR US?
IT WOULD BE AN HONOR AND A PRIVILEGE.

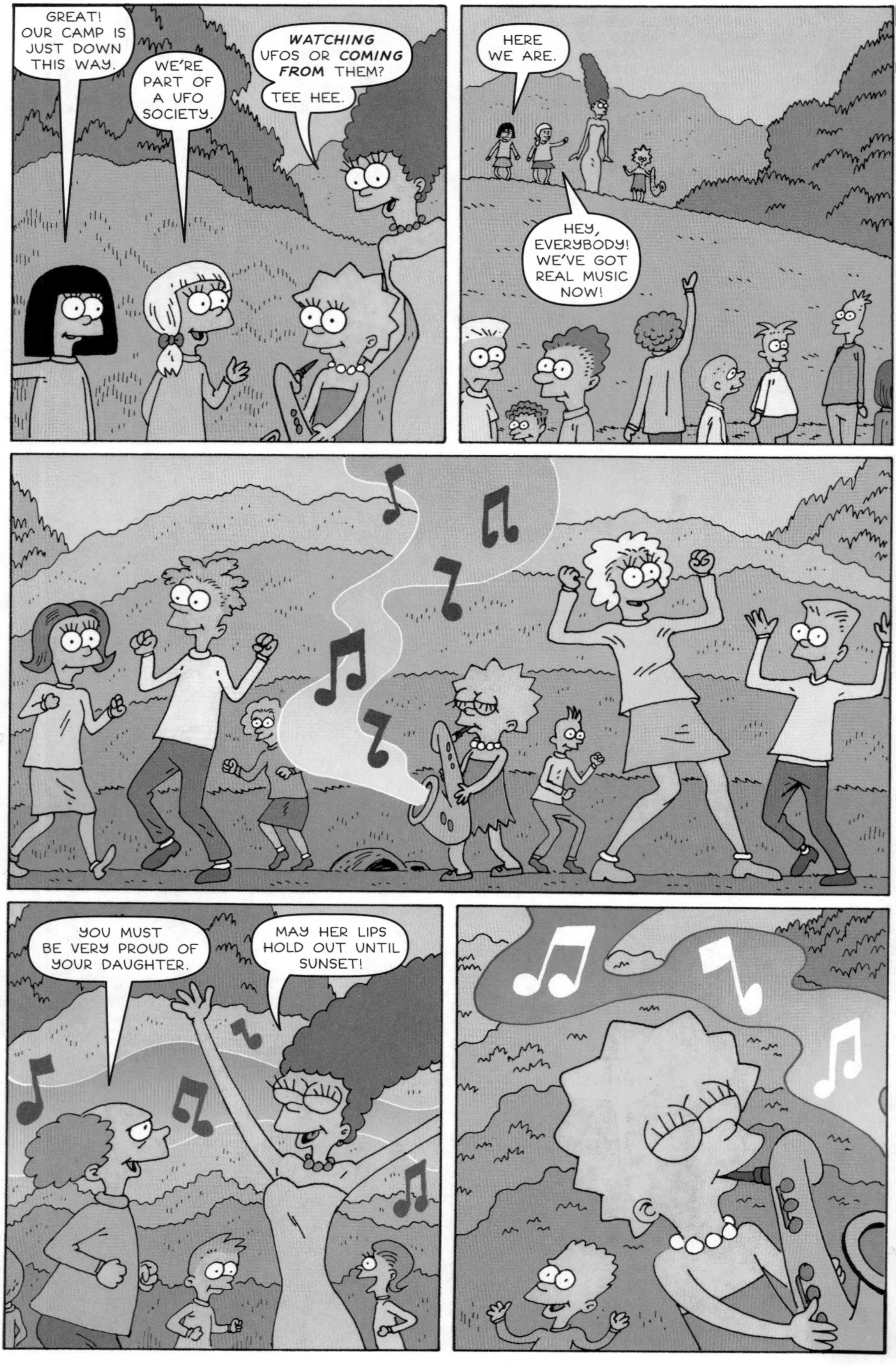
GREAT! OUR CAMP IS JUST DOWN THIS WAY.
WE'RE PART OF A UFO SOCIETY.
WATCHING UFOS OR COMING FROM THEM?
TEE HEE.
HERE WE ARE.
HEY, EVERYBODY! WE'VE GOT REAL MUSIC NOW!
YOU MUST BE VERY PROUD OF YOUR DAUGHTER.
MAY HER LIPS HOLD OUT UNTIL SUNSET!

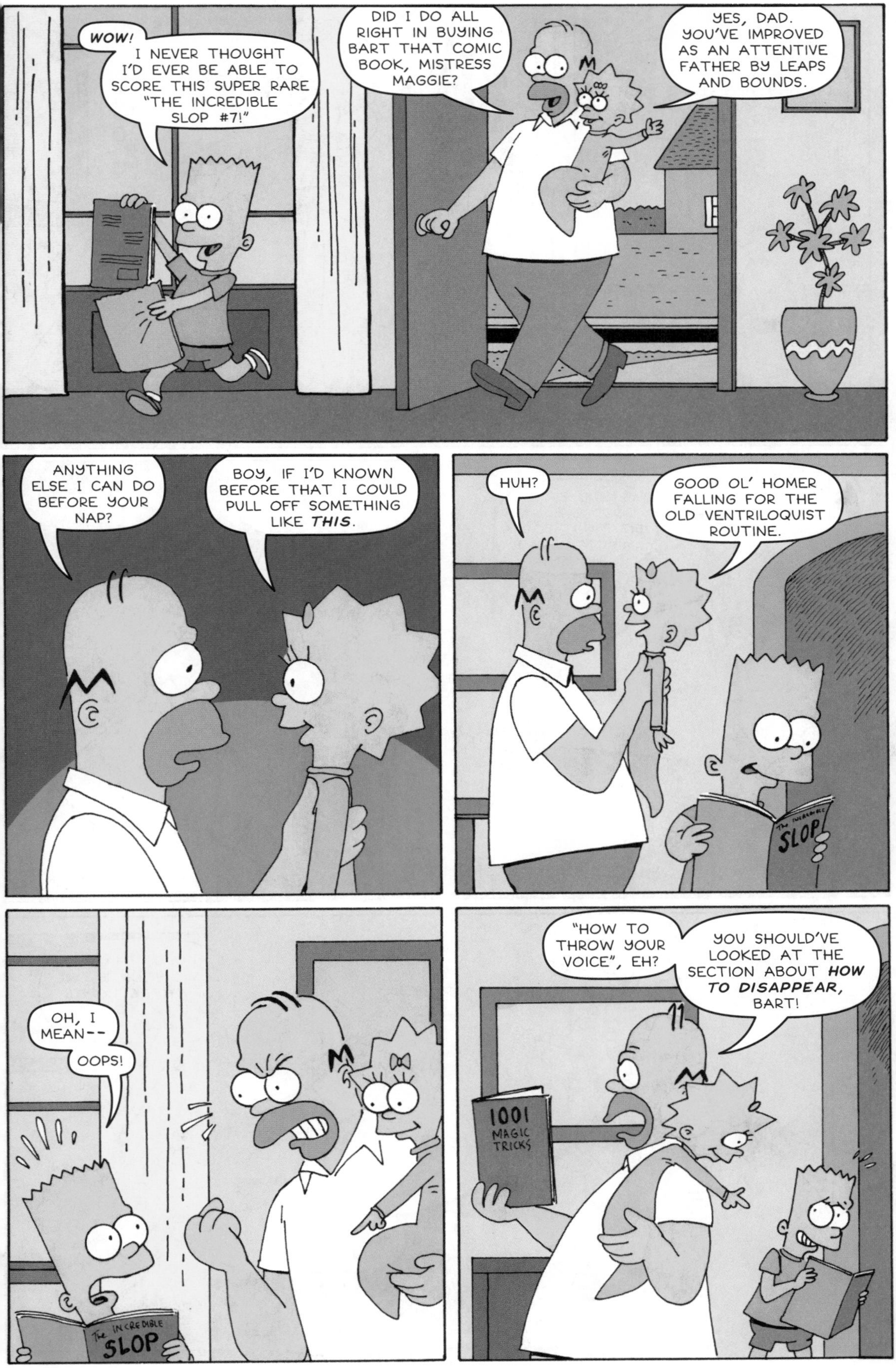
WOW! I NEVER THOUGHT I'D EVER BE ABLE TO SCORE THIS SUPER RARE "THE INCREDIBLE SLOP #7!"
DID I DO ALL RIGHT IN BUYING BART THAT COMIC BOOK, MISTRESS MAGGIE?
YES, DAD. YOU'VE IMPROVED AS AN ATTENTIVE FATHER BY LEAPS AND BOUNDS.
ANYTHING ELSE I CAN DO BEFORE YOUR NAP?
BOY, IF I'D KNOWN BEFORE THAT I COULD PULL OFF SOMETHING LIKE *THIS*.
HUH?
GOOD OL' HOMER FALLING FOR THE OLD VENTRILOQUIST ROUTINE.
The INCREDIBLE SLOP
OH, I MEAN--
OOPS!
The INCREDIBLE SLOP
"HOW TO THROW YOUR VOICE", EH?
YOU SHOULD'VE LOOKED AT THE SECTION ABOUT ***HOW TO DISAPPEAR,*** BART!
1001 MAGIC TRICKS

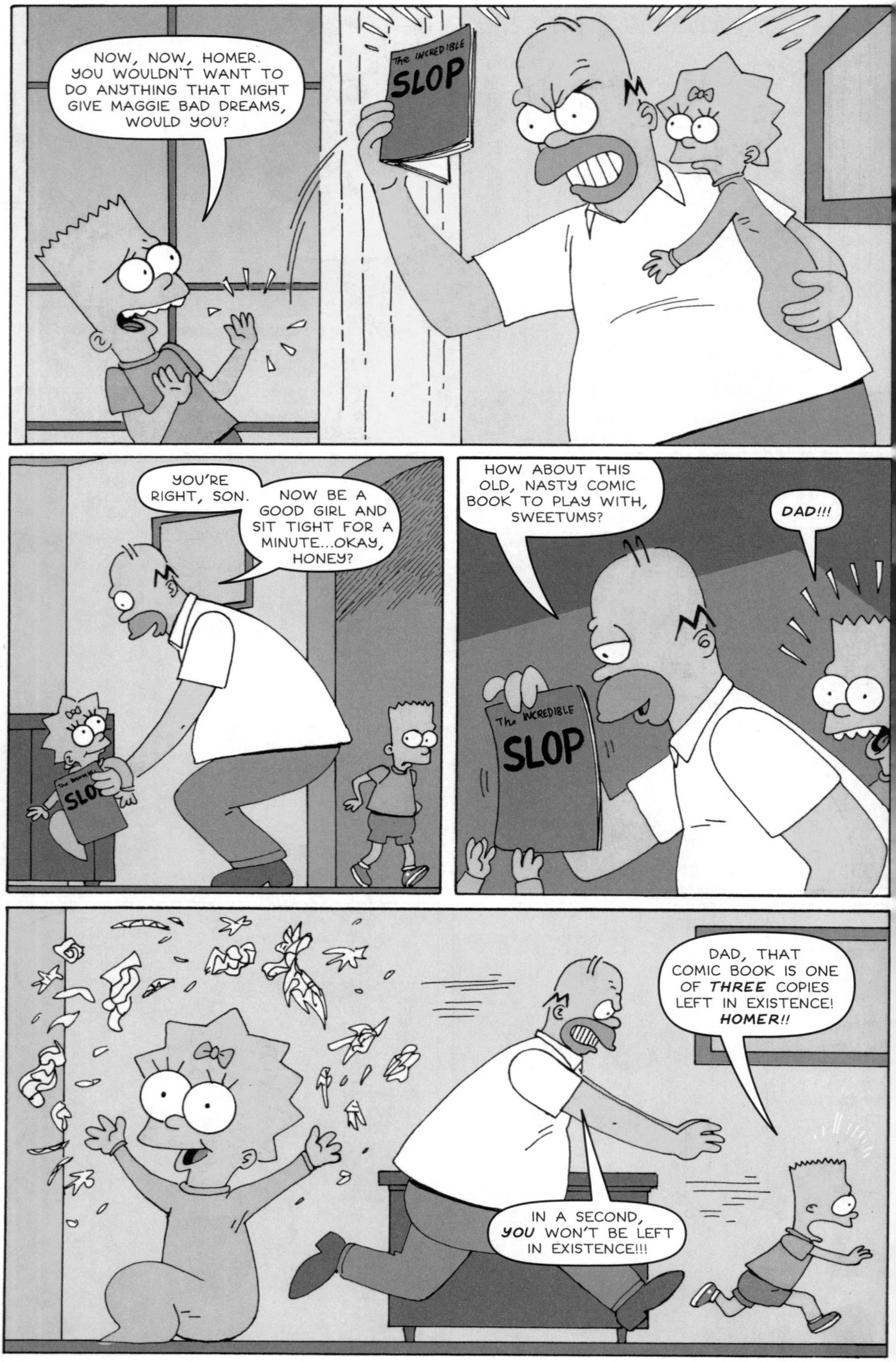
NOW, NOW, HOMER. YOU WOULDN'T WANT TO DO ANYTHING THAT MIGHT GIVE MAGGIE BAD DREAMS, WOULD YOU?
The INCREDIBLE SLOP
YOU'RE RIGHT, SON.
NOW BE A GOOD GIRL AND SIT TIGHT FOR A MINUTE...OKAY, HONEY?
SLOP
HOW ABOUT THIS OLD, NASTY COMIC BOOK TO PLAY WITH, SWEETUMS?
DAD!!!
The INCREDIBLE SLOP
DAD, THAT COMIC BOOK IS ONE OF THREE COPIES LEFT IN EXISTENCE! HOMER!!
IN A SECOND, YOU WON'T BE LEFT IN EXISTENCE!!!

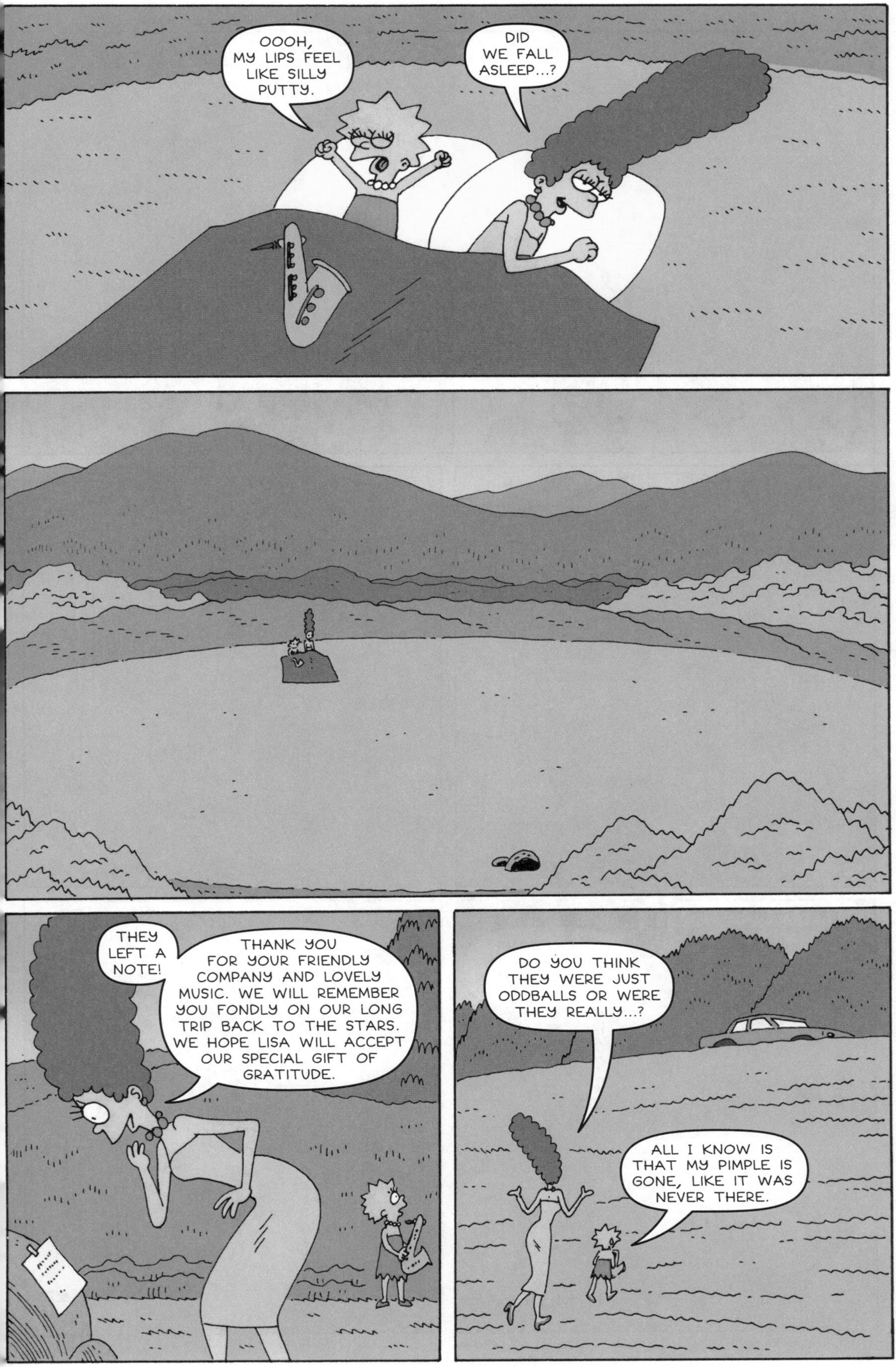
OOOH, MY LIPS FEEL LIKE SILLY PUTTY.
DID WE FALL ASLEEP...?
THEY LEFT A NOTE!
THANK YOU FOR YOUR FRIENDLY COMPANY AND LOVELY MUSIC. WE WILL REMEMBER YOU FONDLY ON OUR LONG TRIP BACK TO THE STARS. WE HOPE LISA WILL ACCEPT OUR SPECIAL GIFT OF GRATITUDE.
DO YOU THINK THEY WERE JUST ODDBALLS OR WERE THEY REALLY...?
ALL I KNOW IS THAT MY PIMPLE IS GONE, LIKE IT WAS NEVER THERE.

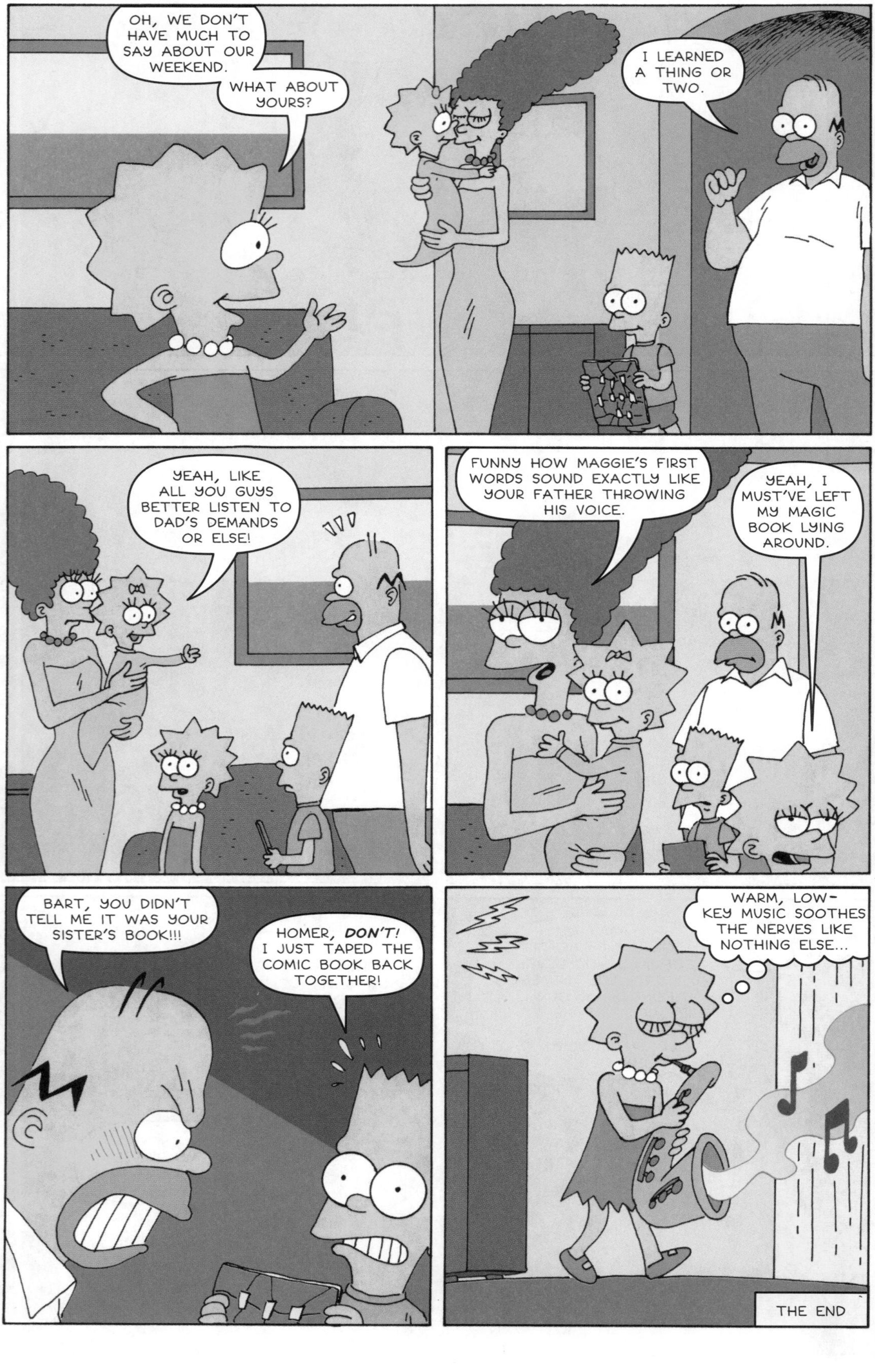
OH, WE DON'T HAVE MUCH TO SAY ABOUT OUR WEEKEND.
WHAT ABOUT YOURS?
I LEARNED A THING OR TWO.
YEAH, LIKE ALL YOU GUYS BETTER LISTEN TO DAD'S DEMANDS OR ELSE!
FUNNY HOW MAGGIE'S FIRST WORDS SOUND EXACTLY LIKE YOUR FATHER THROWING HIS VOICE.
YEAH, I MUST'VE LEFT MY MAGIC BOOK LYING AROUND.
BART, YOU DIDN'T TELL ME IT WAS YOUR SISTER'S BOOK!!!
HOMER, DON'T! I JUST TAPED THE COMIC BOOK BACK TOGETHER!
WARM, LOW-KEY MUSIC SOOTHES THE NERVES LIKE NOTHING ELSE...
THE END

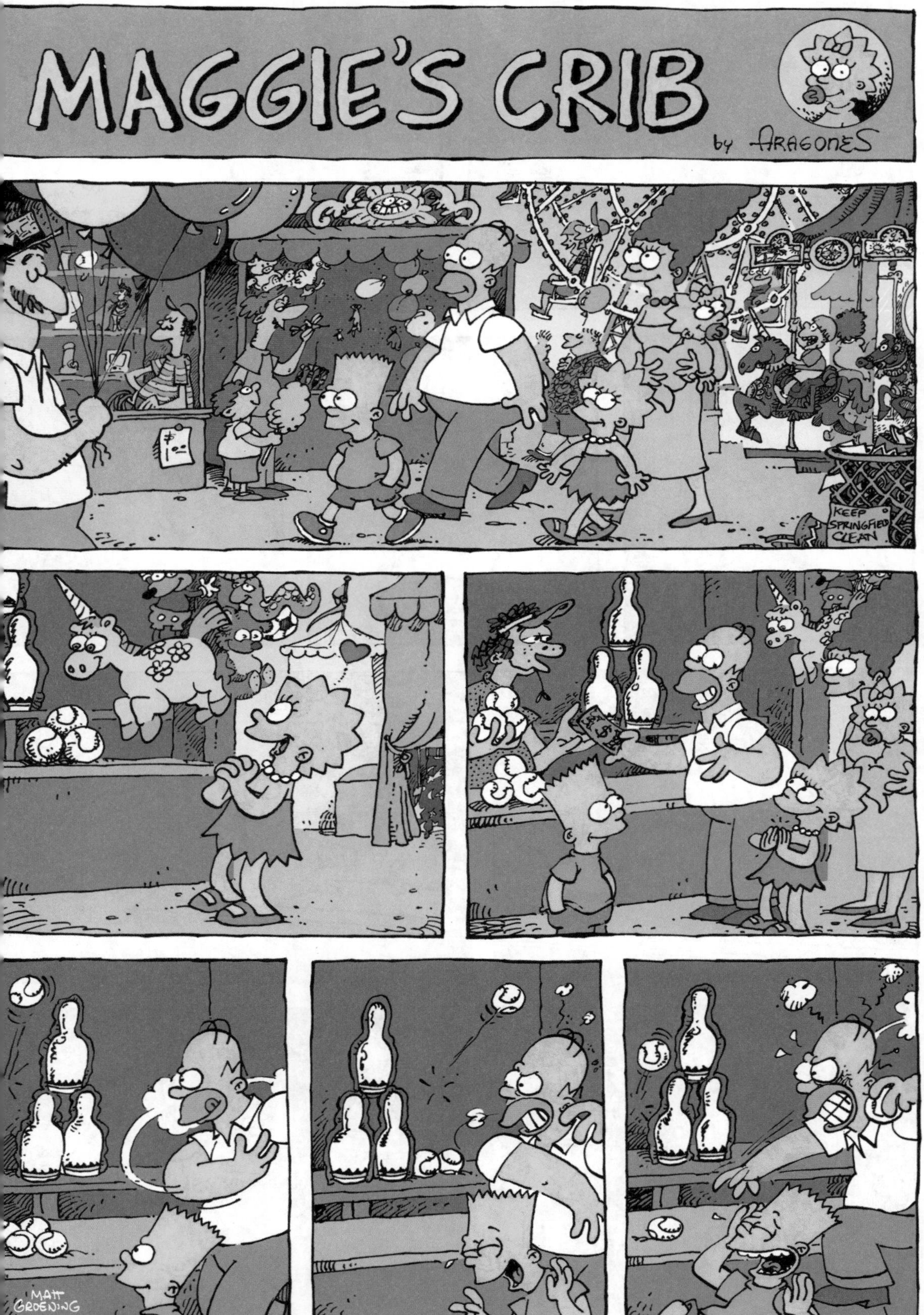
MAGGIE'S CRIB
by ARAGONES
KEEP SPRINGFIELD CLEAN
MATT GROENING

SERGIO ARAGONÉS
STORY & ART

ART VILLANUEVA
COLORS

BILL MORRISON
EDITOR

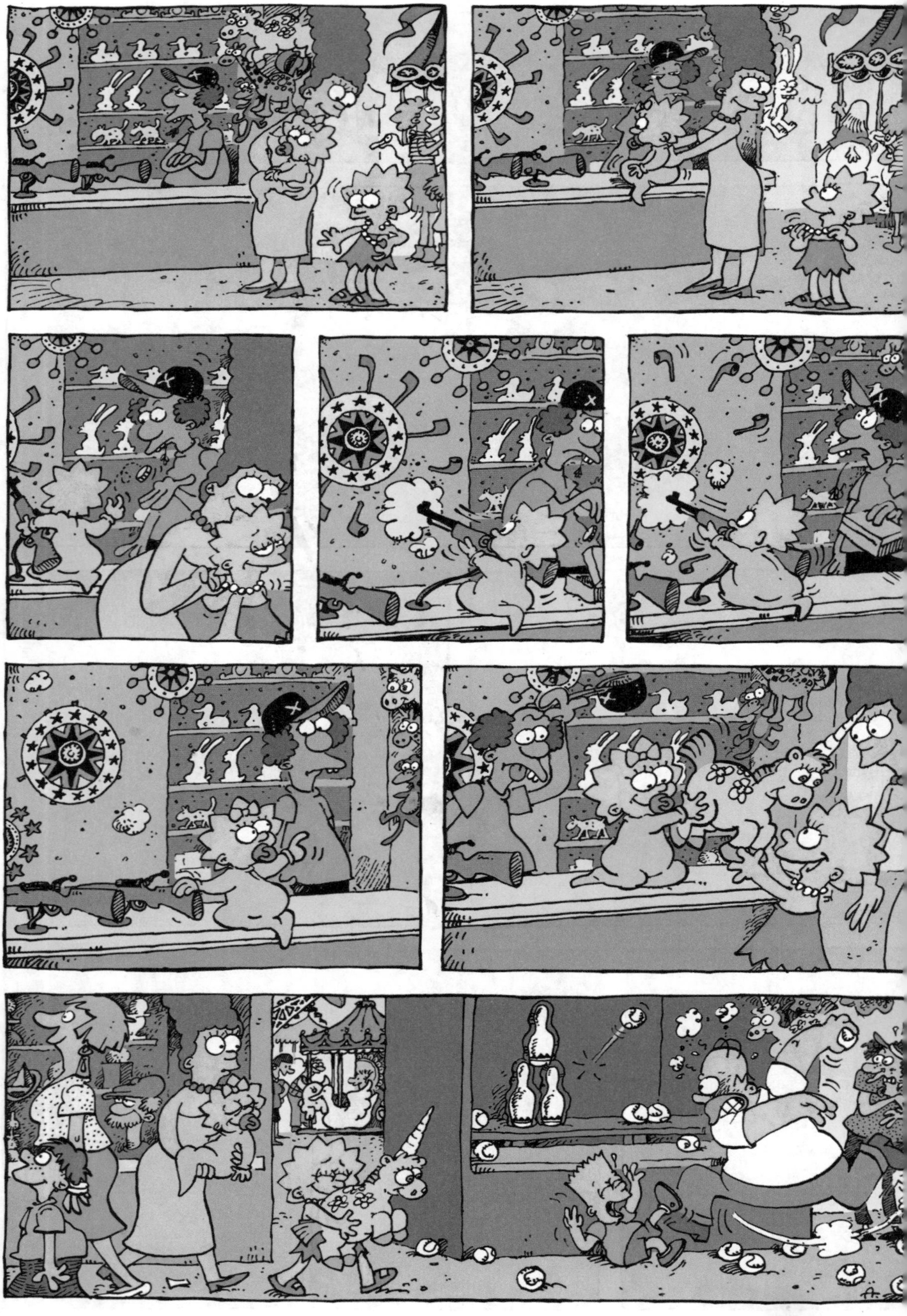

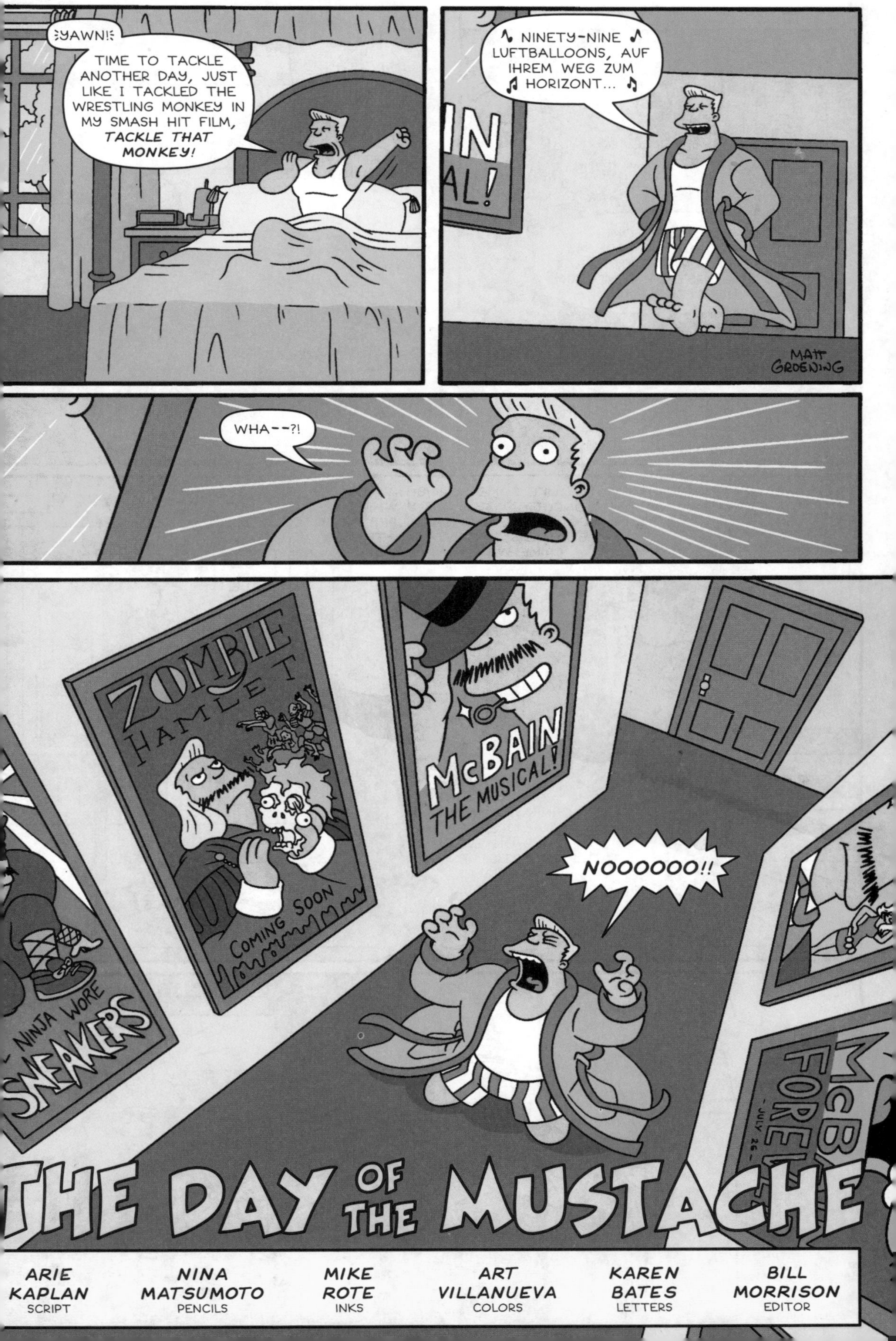

YAWN!
TIME TO TACKLE ANOTHER DAY, JUST LIKE I TACKLED THE WRESTLING MONKEY IN MY SMASH HIT FILM, *TACKLE THAT MONKEY!*
NINETY-NINE LUFTBALLOONS, AUF IHREM WEG ZUM HORIZONT...
MATT GROENING
WHA--?!
ZOMBIE HAMLET
COMING SOON
McBAIN THE MUSICAL!
NINJA WORE SNEAKERS
NOOOOOO!!
JULY 26
THE DAY OF THE MUSTACHE
ARIE KAPLAN
SCRIPT
NINA MATSUMOTO
PENCILS
MIKE ROTE
INKS
ART VILLANUEVA
COLORS
KAREN BATES
LETTERS
BILL MORRISON
EDITOR

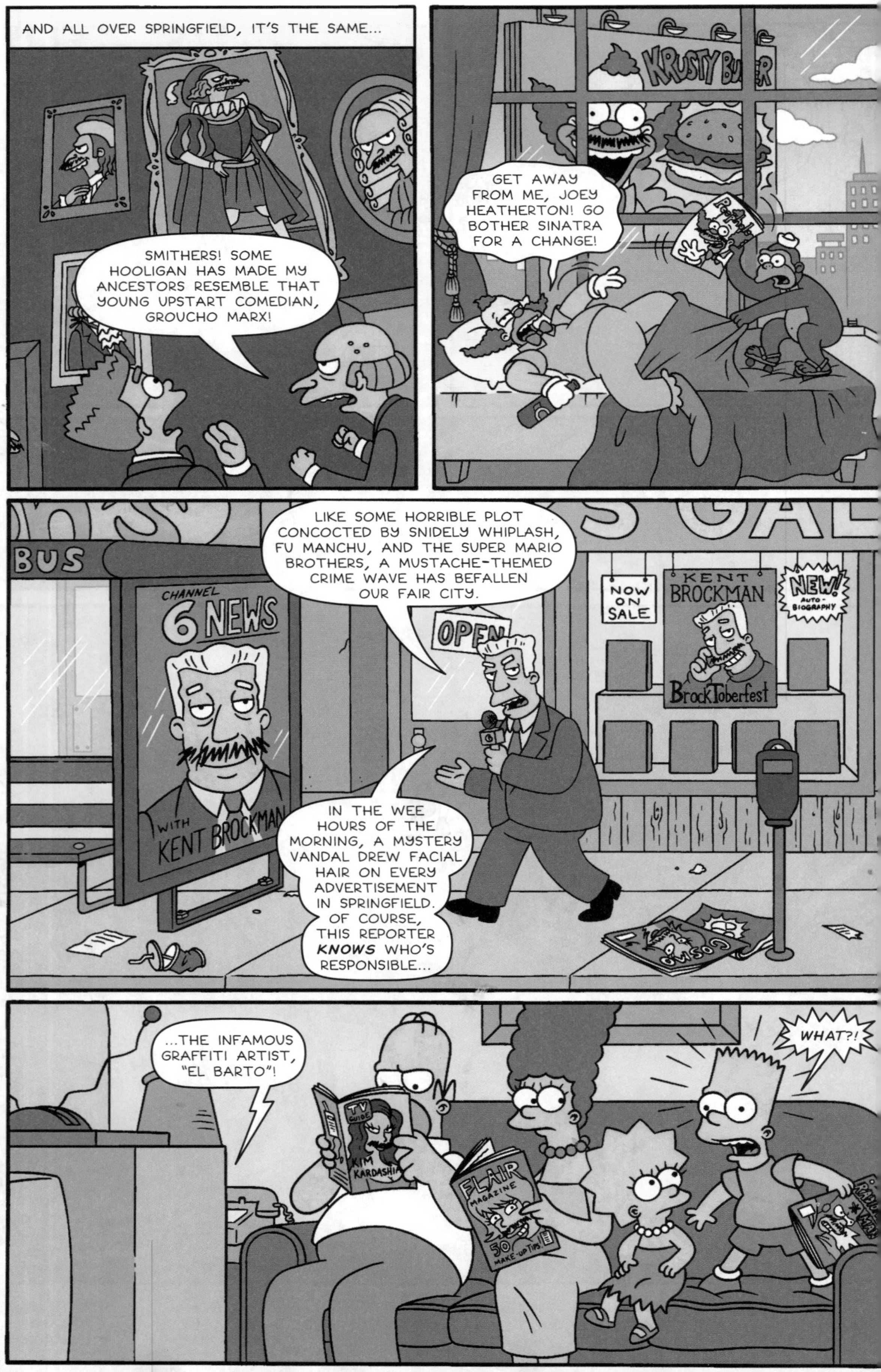
AND ALL OVER SPRINGFIELD, IT'S THE SAME...
SMITHERS! SOME HOOLIGAN HAS MADE MY ANCESTORS RESEMBLE THAT YOUNG UPSTART COMEDIAN, GROUCHO MARX!
KRUSTY BURGER
GET AWAY FROM ME, JOEY HEATHERTON! GO BOTHER SINATRA FOR A CHANGE!
BUS
CHANNEL 6 NEWS
WITH KENT BROCKMAN
LIKE SOME HORRIBLE PLOT CONCOCTED BY SNIDELY WHIPLASH, FU MANCHU, AND THE SUPER MARIO BROTHERS, A MUSTACHE-THEMED CRIME WAVE HAS BEFALLEN OUR FAIR CITY.
OPEN
NOW ON SALE
KENT BROCKMAN
BrockToberfest
NEW! AUTO-BIOGRAPHY
IN THE WEE HOURS OF THE MORNING, A MYSTERY VANDAL DREW FACIAL HAIR ON EVERY ADVERTISEMENT IN SPRINGFIELD. OF COURSE, THIS REPORTER ***KNOWS*** WHO'S RESPONSIBLE...
COSMO
...THE INFAMOUS GRAFFITI ARTIST, "EL BARTO"!
TV GUIDE
KIM KARDASHIA
FLAIR MAGAZINE
50 MAKE-UP TIPS
WHAT?!

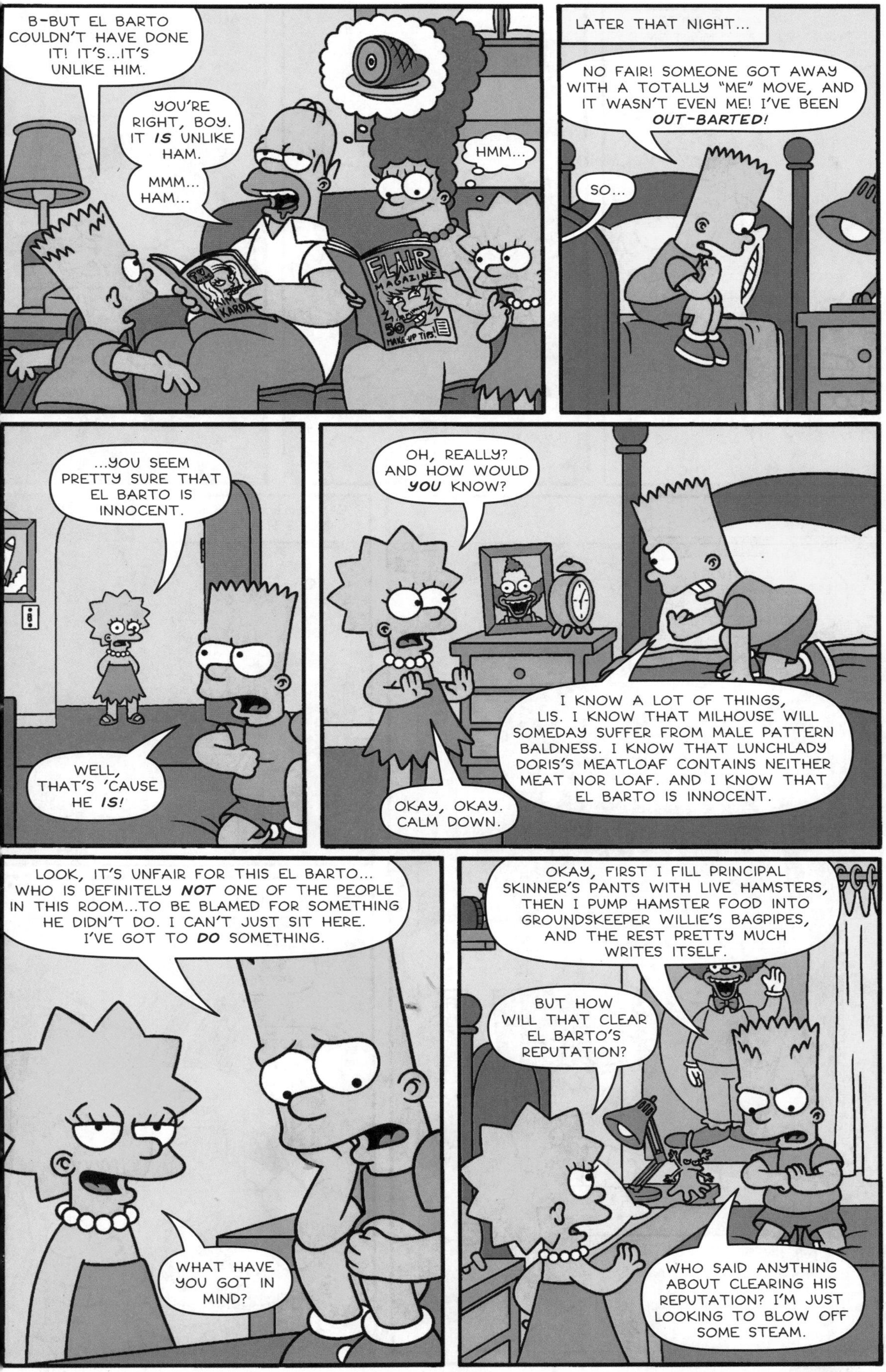
B-BUT EL BARTO COULDN'T HAVE DONE IT! IT'S...IT'S UNLIKE HIM.
YOU'RE RIGHT, BOY. IT ***IS*** UNLIKE HAM.
MMM... HAM...
HMM...
FLAIR MAGAZINE
50 MAKE-UP TIPS!
LATER THAT NIGHT...
NO FAIR! SOMEONE GOT AWAY WITH A TOTALLY "ME" MOVE, AND IT WASN'T EVEN ME! I'VE BEEN ***OUT-BARTED!***
SO...
...YOU SEEM PRETTY SURE THAT EL BARTO IS INNOCENT.
WELL, THAT'S 'CAUSE HE ***IS!***
OH, REALLY? AND HOW WOULD ***YOU*** KNOW?
I KNOW A LOT OF THINGS, LIS. I KNOW THAT MILHOUSE WILL SOMEDAY SUFFER FROM MALE PATTERN BALDNESS. I KNOW THAT LUNCHLADY DORIS'S MEATLOAF CONTAINS NEITHER MEAT NOR LOAF. AND I KNOW THAT EL BARTO IS INNOCENT.
OKAY, OKAY. CALM DOWN.
LOOK, IT'S UNFAIR FOR THIS EL BARTO... WHO IS DEFINITELY ***NOT*** ONE OF THE PEOPLE IN THIS ROOM...TO BE BLAMED FOR SOMETHING HE DIDN'T DO. I CAN'T JUST SIT HERE. I'VE GOT TO ***DO*** SOMETHING.
WHAT HAVE YOU GOT IN MIND?
OKAY, FIRST I FILL PRINCIPAL SKINNER'S PANTS WITH LIVE HAMSTERS, THEN I PUMP HAMSTER FOOD INTO GROUNDSKEEPER WILLIE'S BAGPIPES, AND THE REST PRETTY MUCH WRITES ITSELF.
BUT HOW WILL THAT CLEAR EL BARTO'S REPUTATION?
WHO SAID ANYTHING ABOUT CLEARING HIS REPUTATION? I'M JUST LOOKING TO BLOW OFF SOME STEAM.

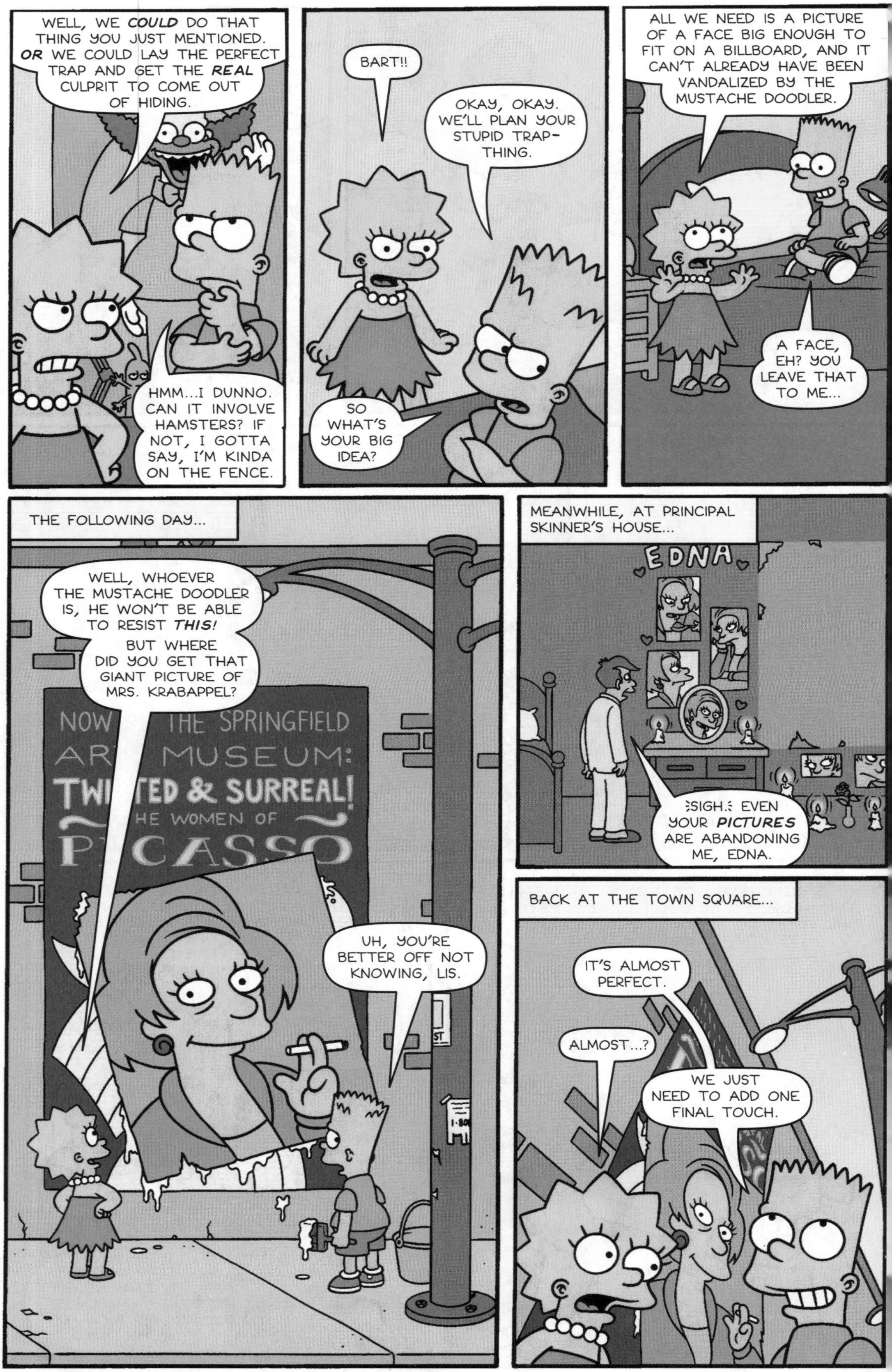
WELL, WE *COULD* DO THAT THING YOU JUST MENTIONED. *OR* WE COULD LAY THE PERFECT TRAP AND GET THE *REAL* CULPRIT TO COME OUT OF HIDING.
HMM...I DUNNO. CAN IT INVOLVE HAMSTERS? IF NOT, I GOTTA SAY, I'M KINDA ON THE FENCE.
BART!!
OKAY, OKAY. WE'LL PLAN YOUR STUPID TRAP-THING.
SO WHAT'S YOUR BIG IDEA?
ALL WE NEED IS A PICTURE OF A FACE BIG ENOUGH TO FIT ON A BILLBOARD, AND IT CAN'T ALREADY HAVE BEEN VANDALIZED BY THE MUSTACHE DOODLER.
A FACE, EH? YOU LEAVE THAT TO ME...
THE FOLLOWING DAY...
WELL, WHOEVER THE MUSTACHE DOODLER IS, HE WON'T BE ABLE TO RESIST *THIS!*
BUT WHERE DID YOU GET THAT GIANT PICTURE OF MRS. KRABAPPEL?
UH, YOU'RE BETTER OFF NOT KNOWING, LIS.
MEANWHILE, AT PRINCIPAL SKINNER'S HOUSE...
EDNA
SIGH. EVEN YOUR *PICTURES* ARE ABANDONING ME, EDNA.
BACK AT THE TOWN SQUARE...
IT'S ALMOST PERFECT.
ALMOST...?
WE JUST NEED TO ADD ONE FINAL TOUCH.

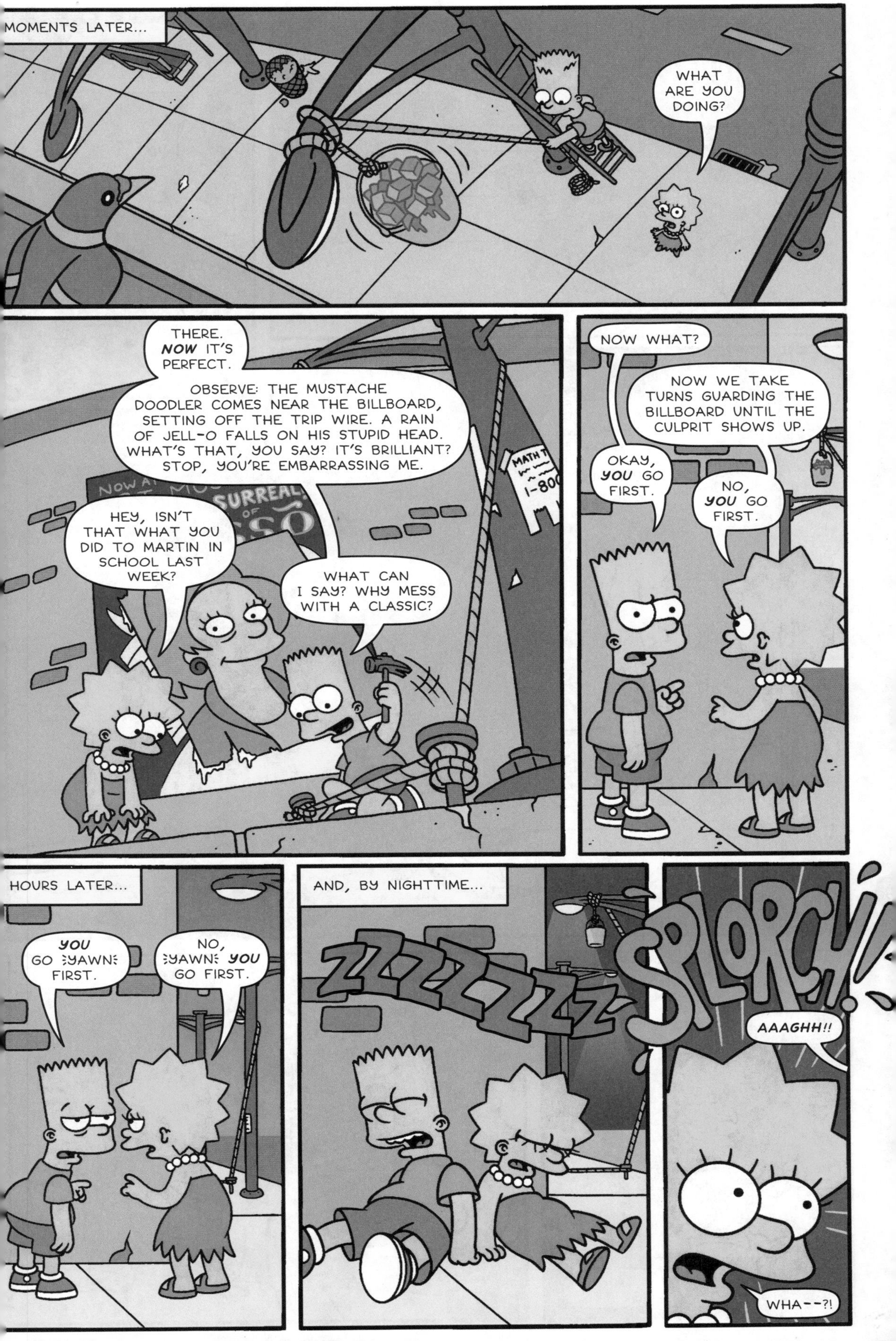
MOMENTS LATER...
WHAT ARE YOU DOING?
THERE. NOW IT'S PERFECT.
OBSERVE: THE MUSTACHE DOODLER COMES NEAR THE BILLBOARD, SETTING OFF THE TRIP WIRE. A RAIN OF JELL-O FALLS ON HIS STUPID HEAD. WHAT'S THAT, YOU SAY? IT'S BRILLIANT? STOP, YOU'RE EMBARRASSING ME.
HEY, ISN'T THAT WHAT YOU DID TO MARTIN IN SCHOOL LAST WEEK?
WHAT CAN I SAY? WHY MESS WITH A CLASSIC?
NOW WHAT?
NOW WE TAKE TURNS GUARDING THE BILLBOARD UNTIL THE CULPRIT SHOWS UP.
OKAY, YOU GO FIRST.
NO, YOU GO FIRST.
HOURS LATER...
YOU GO :YAWN: FIRST.
NO, :YAWN: YOU GO FIRST.
AND, BY NIGHTTIME...
ZZZZZZZZ
SPLORCH!!
AAAGHH!!
WHA--?!

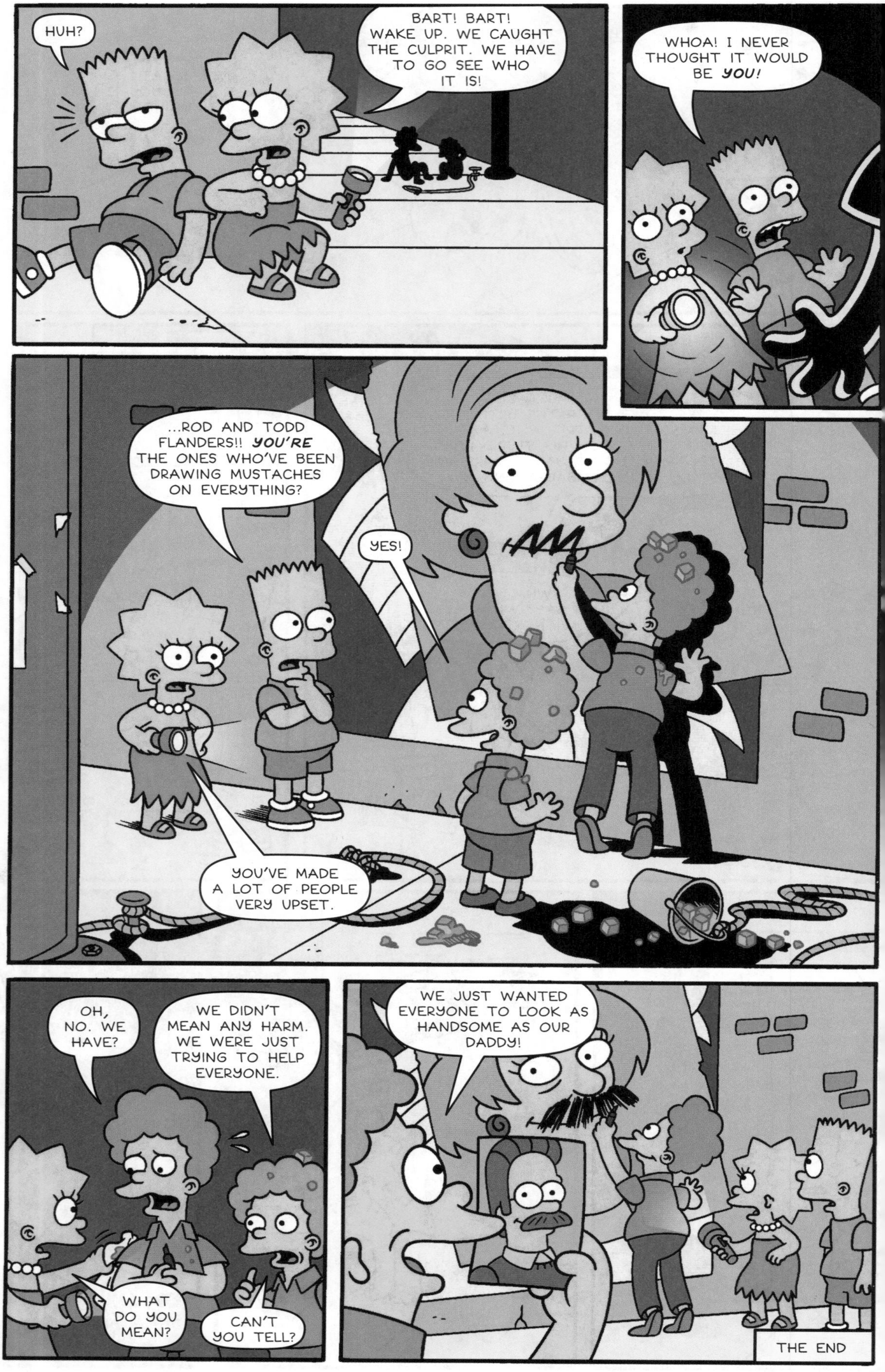
HUH?
BART! BART! WAKE UP. WE CAUGHT THE CULPRIT. WE HAVE TO GO SEE WHO IT IS!
WHOA! I NEVER THOUGHT IT WOULD BE *YOU!*
...ROD AND TODD FLANDERS!! *YOU'RE* THE ONES WHO'VE BEEN DRAWING MUSTACHES ON EVERYTHING?
YES!
YOU'VE MADE A LOT OF PEOPLE VERY UPSET.
OH, NO. WE HAVE?
WE DIDN'T MEAN ANY HARM. WE WERE JUST TRYING TO HELP EVERYONE.
WHAT DO YOU MEAN?
CAN'T YOU TELL?
WE JUST WANTED EVERYONE TO LOOK AS HANDSOME AS OUR DADDY!
THE END

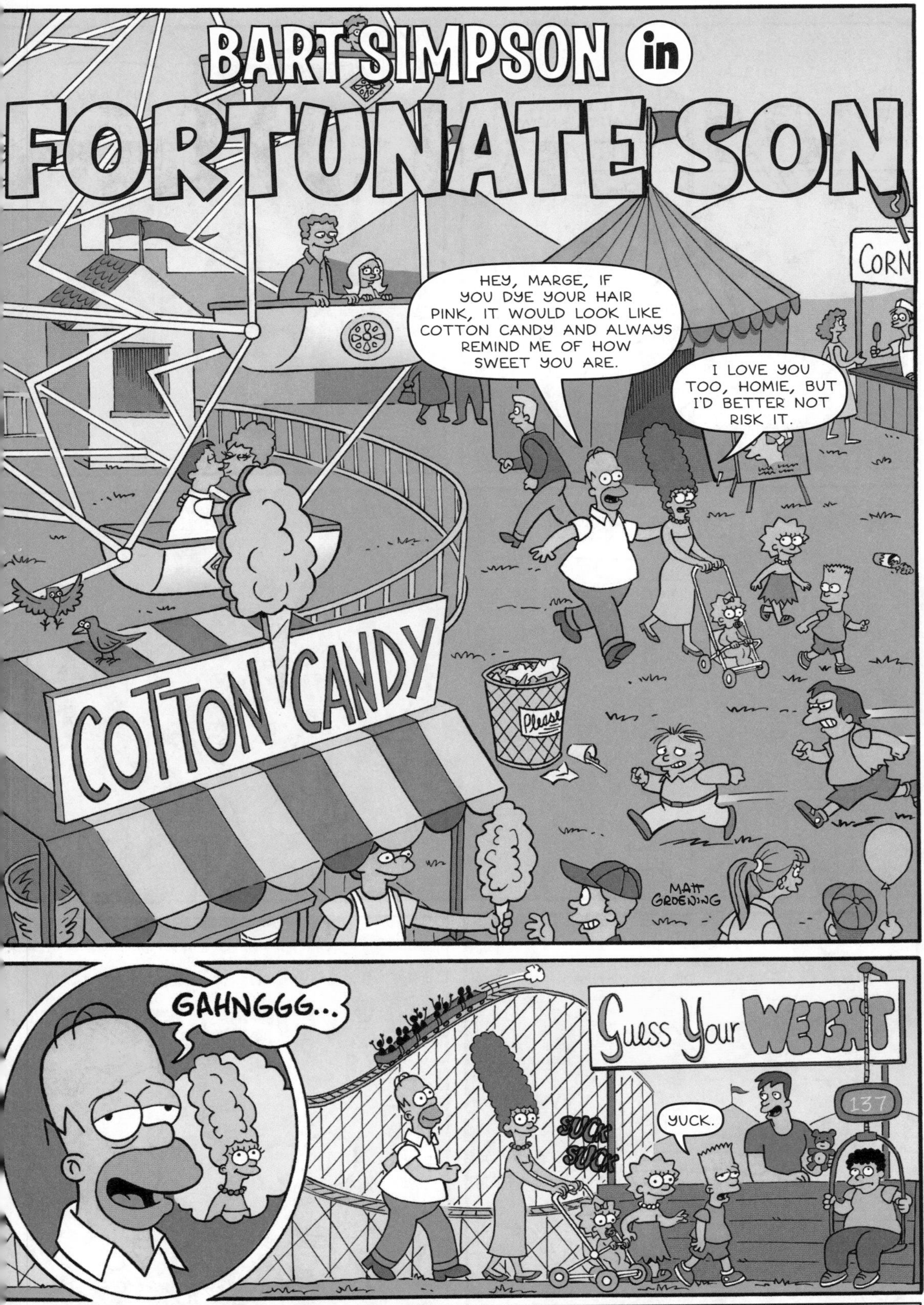
BART SIMPSON in
FORTUNATE SON
CORN
HEY, MARGE, IF YOU DYE YOUR HAIR PINK, IT WOULD LOOK LIKE COTTON CANDY AND ALWAYS REMIND ME OF HOW SWEET YOU ARE.
I LOVE YOU TOO, HOMIE, BUT I'D BETTER NOT RISK IT.
COTTON CANDY
Please
MATT GROENING
GAHNGGG...
Guess Your WEIGHT
137
SUCK SUCK
YUCK.

CAROL LAY
STORY & ART

ART VILLANUEVA
COLORS

KAREN BATES
LETTERS

BILL MORRISON
EDITOR

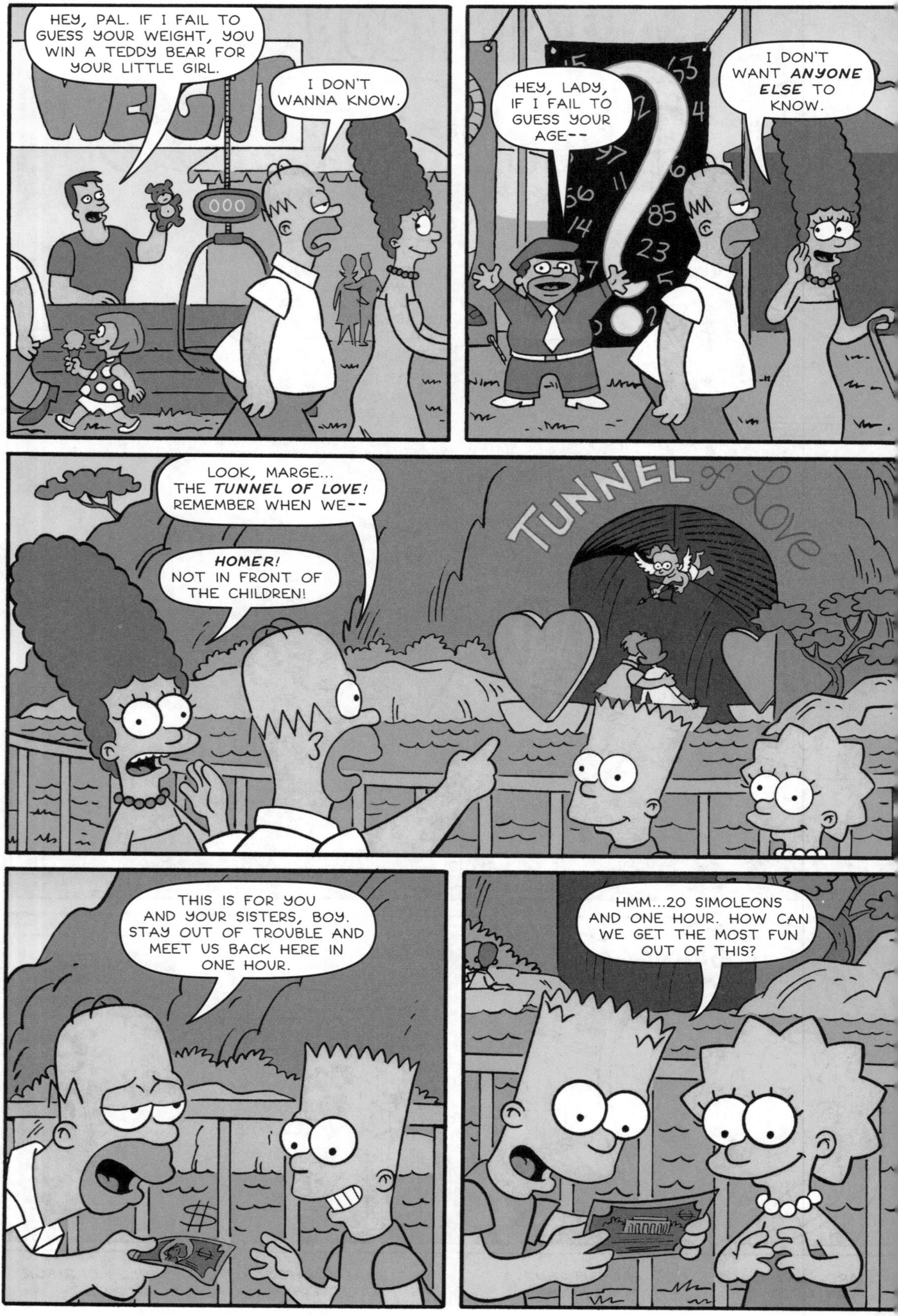
HEY, PAL. IF I FAIL TO GUESS YOUR WEIGHT, YOU WIN A TEDDY BEAR FOR YOUR LITTLE GIRL.
I DON'T WANNA KNOW.
HEY, LADY, IF I FAIL TO GUESS YOUR AGE--
I DON'T WANT **ANYONE ELSE** TO KNOW.
LOOK, MARGE... THE ***TUNNEL OF LOVE!*** REMEMBER WHEN WE--
HOMER! NOT IN FRONT OF THE CHILDREN!
TUNNEL of LOVE
THIS IS FOR YOU AND YOUR SISTERS, BOY. STAY OUT OF TROUBLE AND MEET US BACK HERE IN ONE HOUR.
HMM...20 SIMOLEONS AND ONE HOUR. HOW CAN WE GET THE MOST FUN OUT OF THIS?

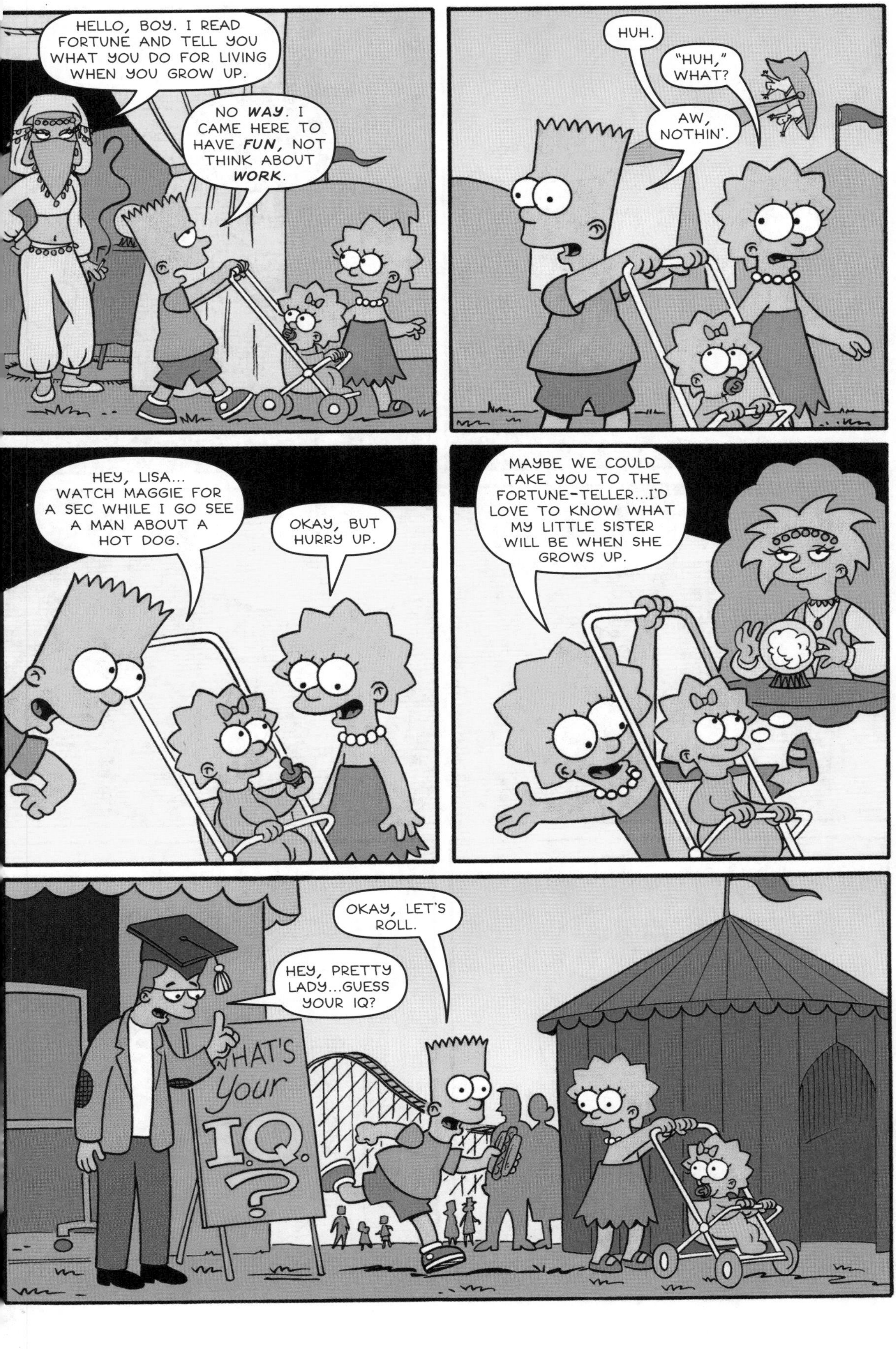
HELLO, BOY. I READ FORTUNE AND TELL YOU WHAT YOU DO FOR LIVING WHEN YOU GROW UP.
NO **WAY**. I CAME HERE TO HAVE **FUN**, NOT THINK ABOUT **WORK**.
HUH.
"HUH," WHAT?
AW, NOTHIN'.
HEY, LISA... WATCH MAGGIE FOR A SEC WHILE I GO SEE A MAN ABOUT A HOT DOG.
OKAY, BUT HURRY UP.
MAYBE WE COULD TAKE YOU TO THE FORTUNE-TELLER...I'D LOVE TO KNOW WHAT MY LITTLE SISTER WILL BE WHEN SHE GROWS UP.
HEY, PRETTY LADY...GUESS YOUR IQ?
OKAY, LET'S ROLL.
WHAT'S Your I.Q. ?

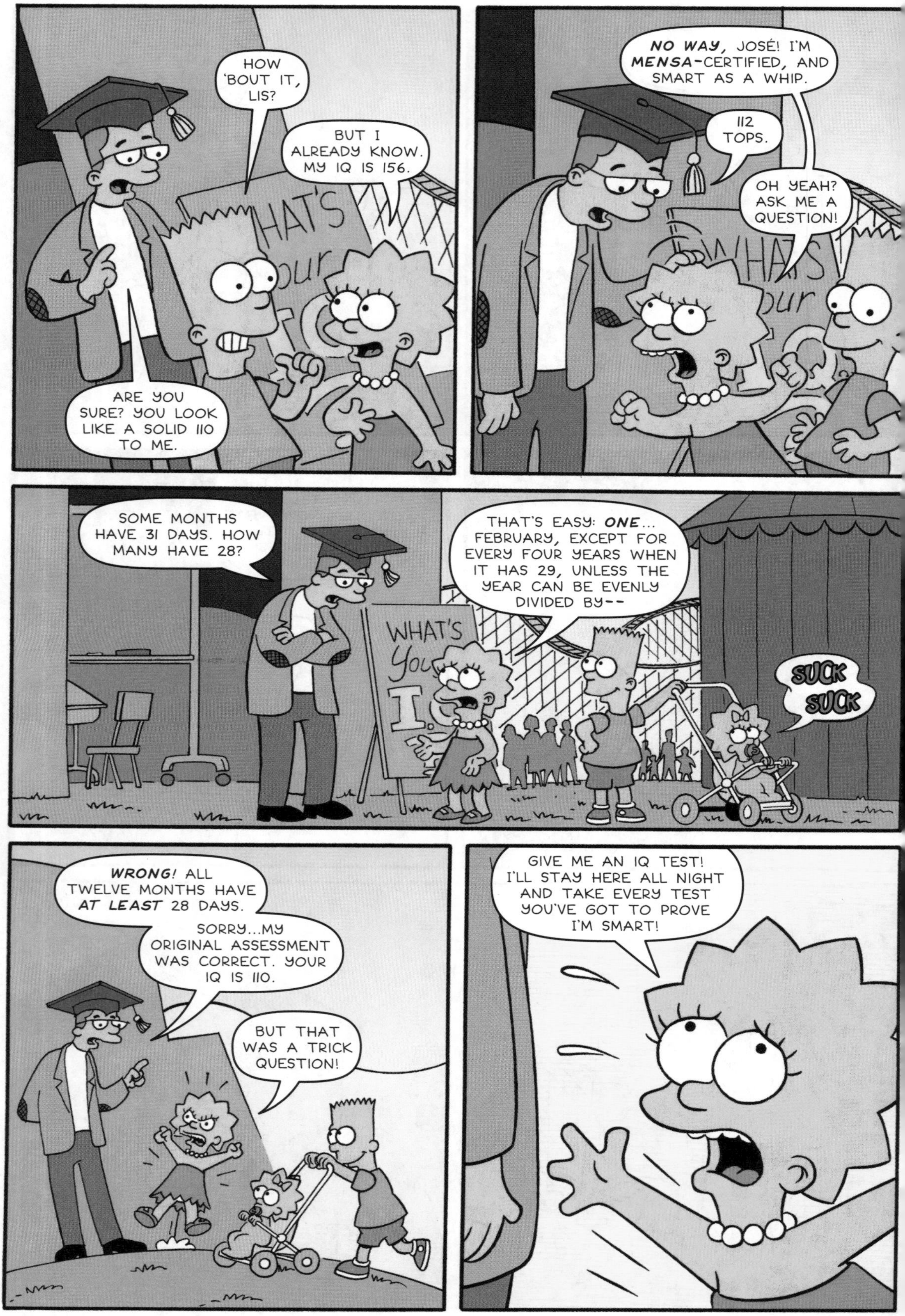
HOW 'BOUT IT, LIS?
BUT I ALREADY KNOW. MY IQ IS 156.
ARE YOU SURE? YOU LOOK LIKE A SOLID 110 TO ME.
NO WAY, JOSÉ! I'M MENSA-CERTIFIED, AND SMART AS A WHIP.
112 TOPS.
OH YEAH? ASK ME A QUESTION!
SOME MONTHS HAVE 31 DAYS. HOW MANY HAVE 28?
THAT'S EASY: ONE... FEBRUARY, EXCEPT FOR EVERY FOUR YEARS WHEN IT HAS 29, UNLESS THE YEAR CAN BE EVENLY DIVIDED BY--
SUCK SUCK
WRONG! ALL TWELVE MONTHS HAVE AT LEAST 28 DAYS.
SORRY...MY ORIGINAL ASSESSMENT WAS CORRECT. YOUR IQ IS 110.
BUT THAT WAS A TRICK QUESTION!
GIVE ME AN IQ TEST! I'LL STAY HERE ALL NIGHT AND TAKE EVERY TEST YOU'VE GOT TO PROVE I'M SMART!

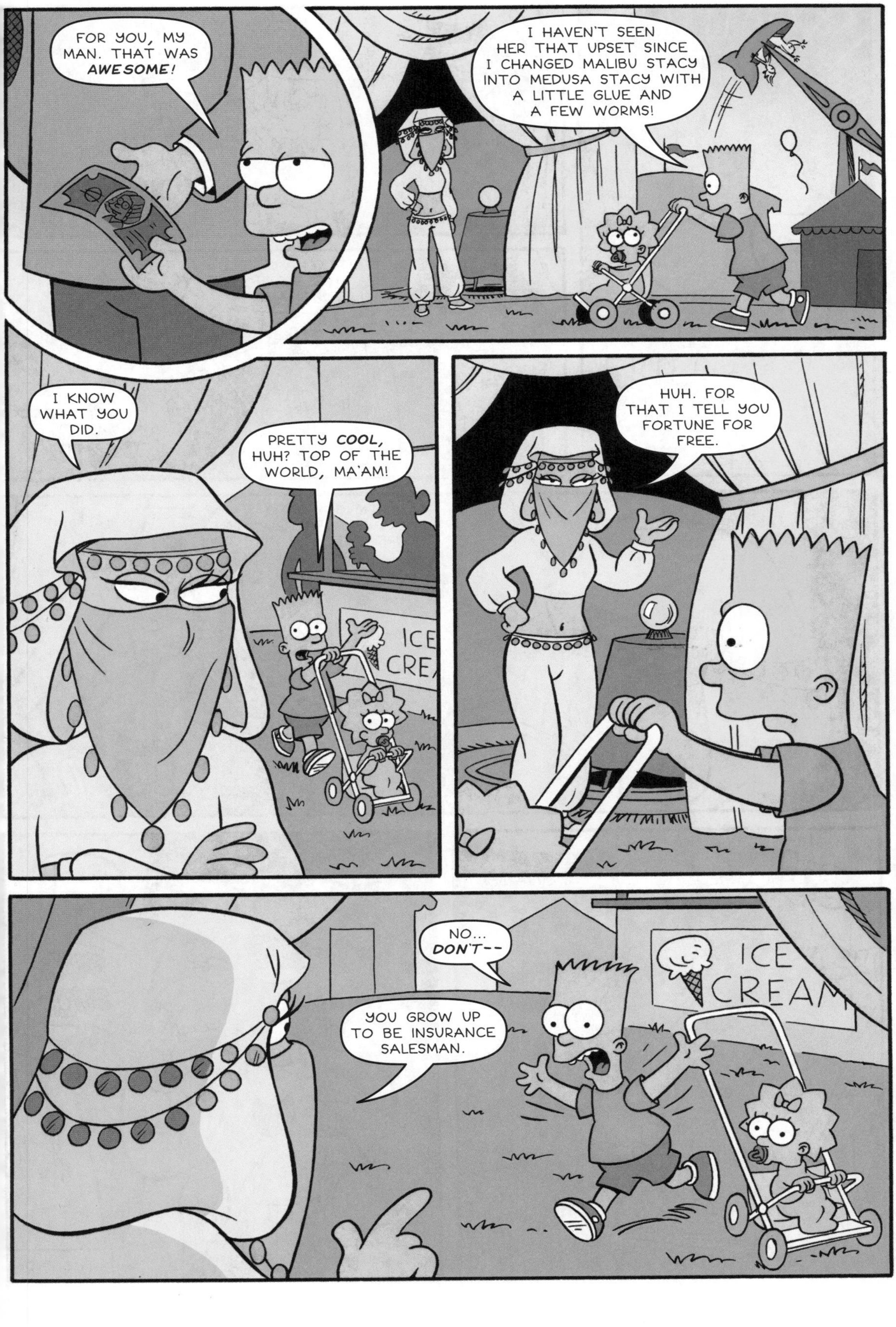
FOR YOU, MY MAN. THAT WAS **AWESOME**!
I HAVEN'T SEEN HER THAT UPSET SINCE I CHANGED MALIBU STACY INTO MEDUSA STACY WITH A LITTLE GLUE AND A FEW WORMS!
I KNOW WHAT YOU DID.
PRETTY **COOL,** HUH? TOP OF THE WORLD, MA'AM!
ICE CREA
HUH. FOR THAT I TELL YOU FORTUNE FOR FREE.
NO... **DON'T--**
YOU GROW UP TO BE INSURANCE SALESMAN.
ICE CREAM

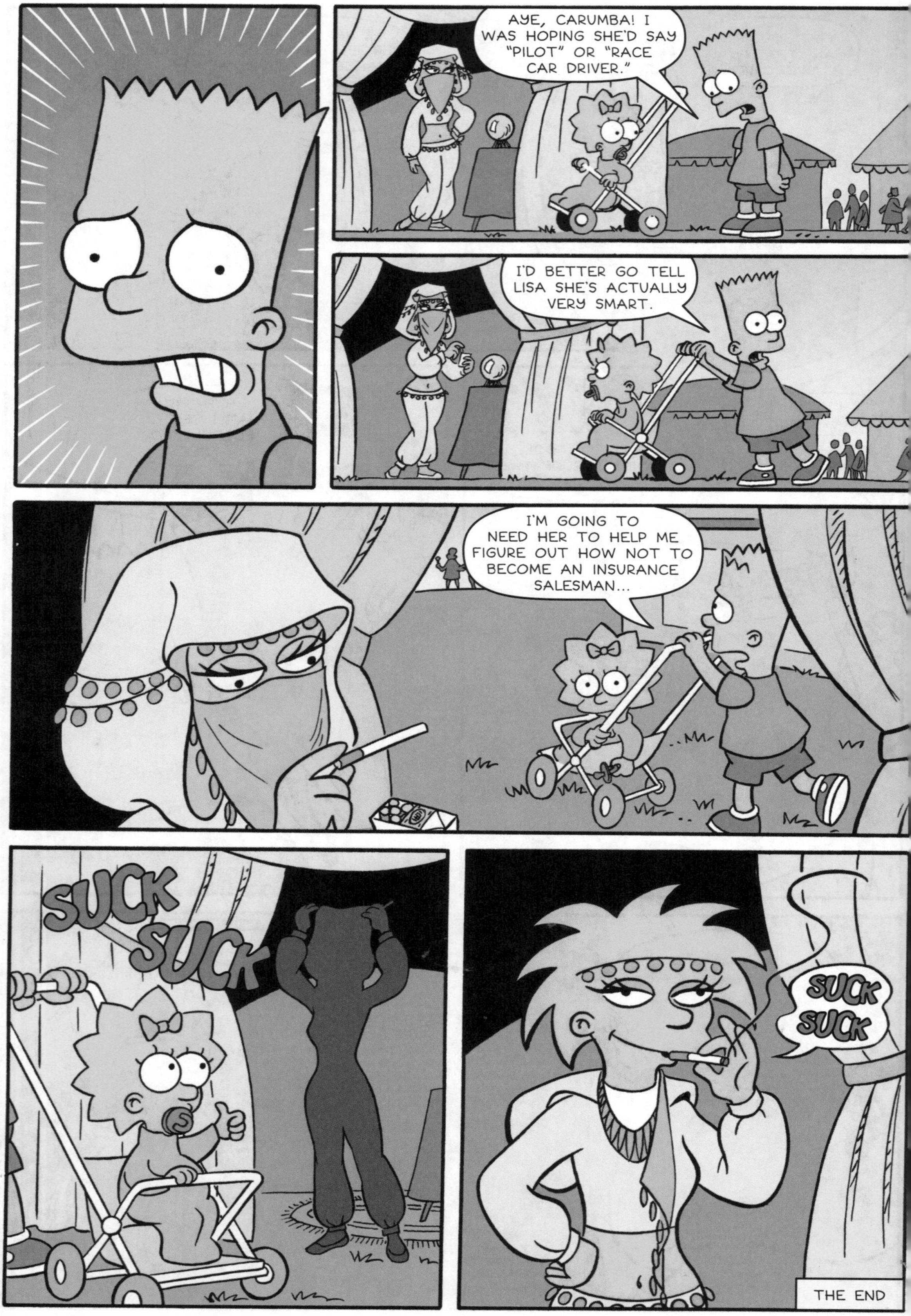
AYE, CARUMBA! I WAS HOPING SHE'D SAY "PILOT" OR "RACE CAR DRIVER."
I'D BETTER GO TELL LISA SHE'S ACTUALLY VERY SMART.
I'M GOING TO NEED HER TO HELP ME FIGURE OUT HOW NOT TO BECOME AN INSURANCE SALESMAN...
SUCK
SUCK
SUCK
SUCK
THE END

BART vs. BART

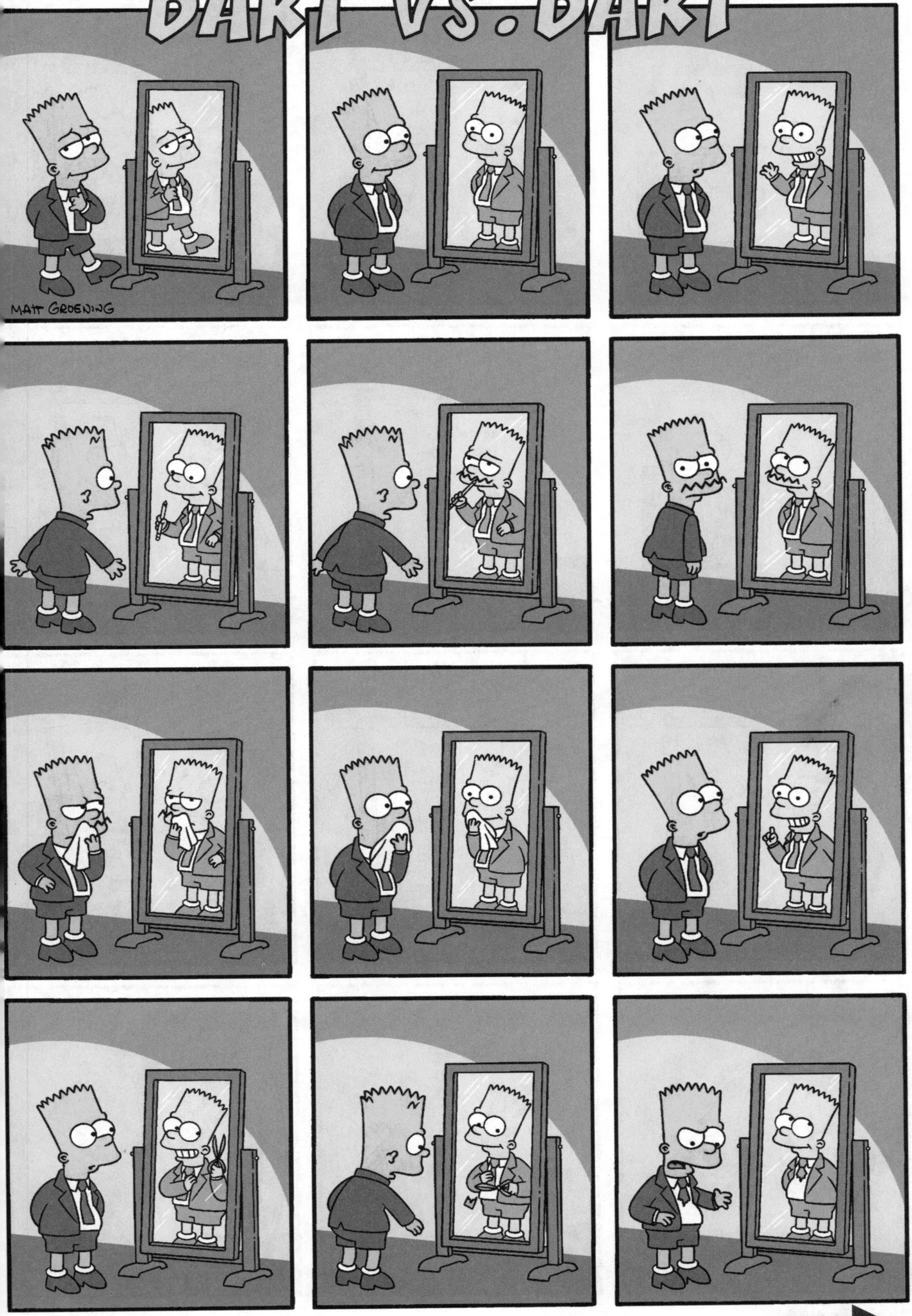
MATT GROENING

CONTINUED

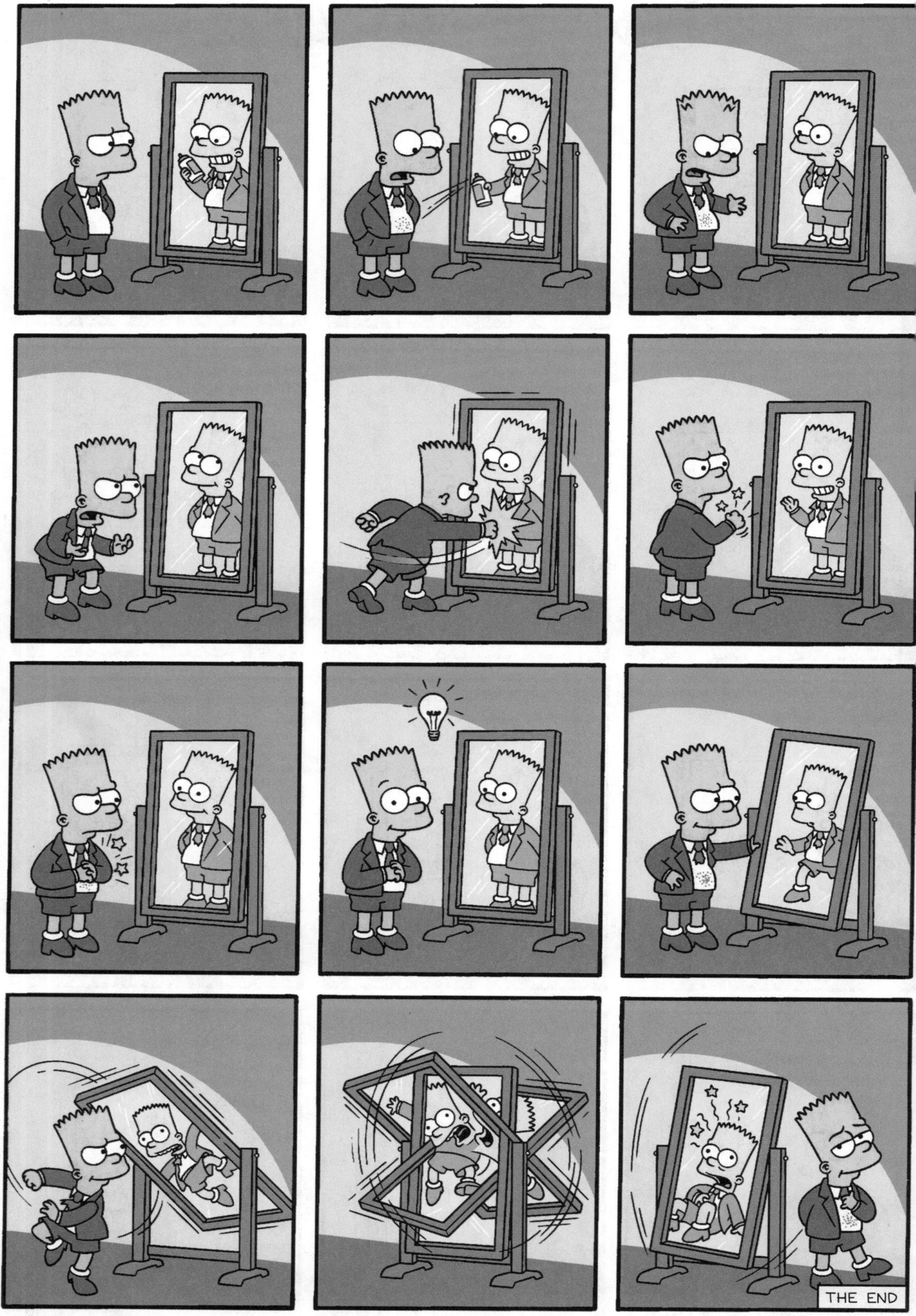
THE END

MARY TRAINOR
STORY & LAYOUTS

MIKE ROTE
PENCILS & INKS

ART VILLANUEVA
COLORS

BILL MORRISON
EDITOR

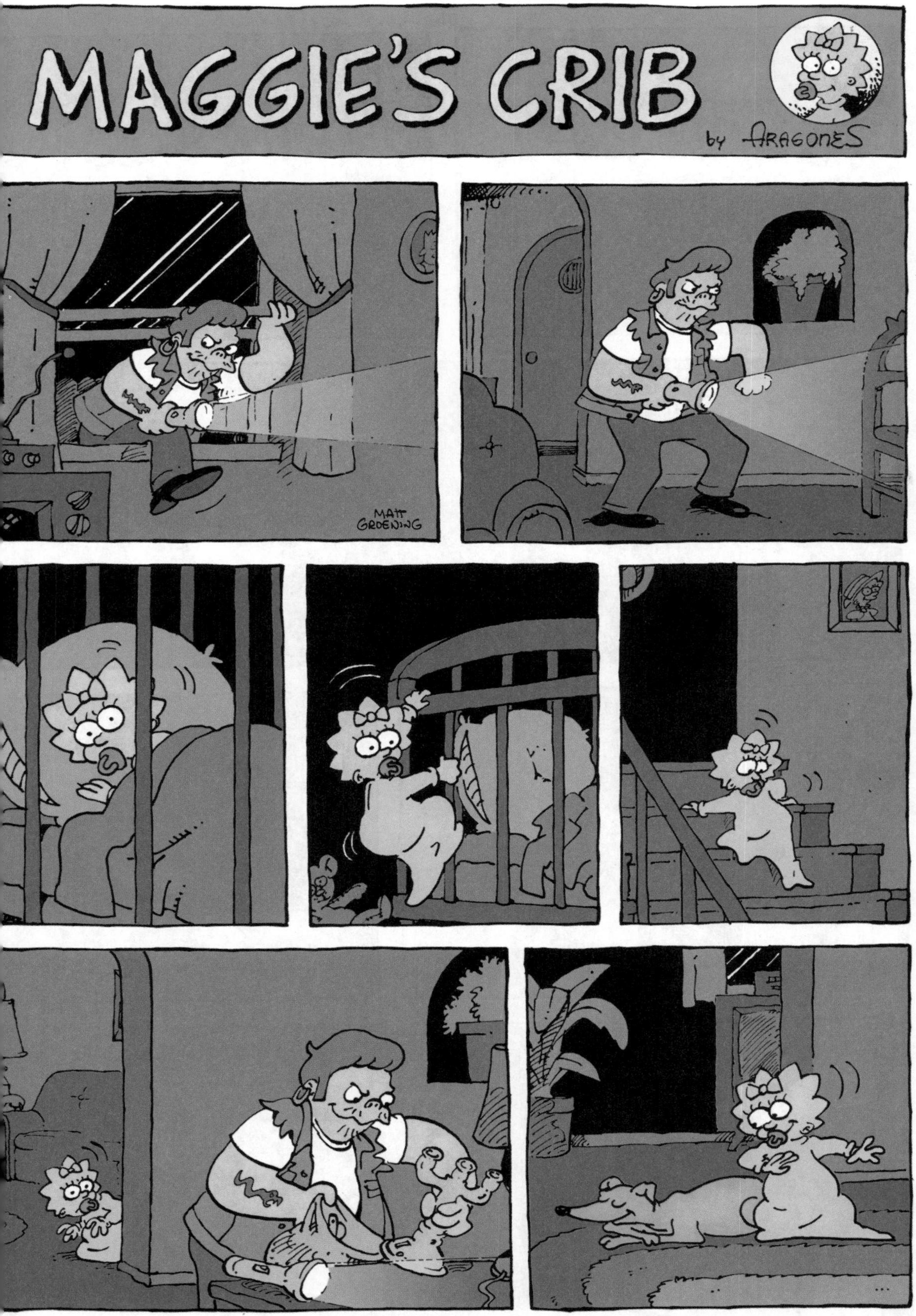
MAGGIE'S CRIB
by ARAGONES
MATT GROENING

SERGIO ARAGONÉS
STORY & ART

ART VILLANUEVA
COLORS

BILL MORRISON
EDITOR

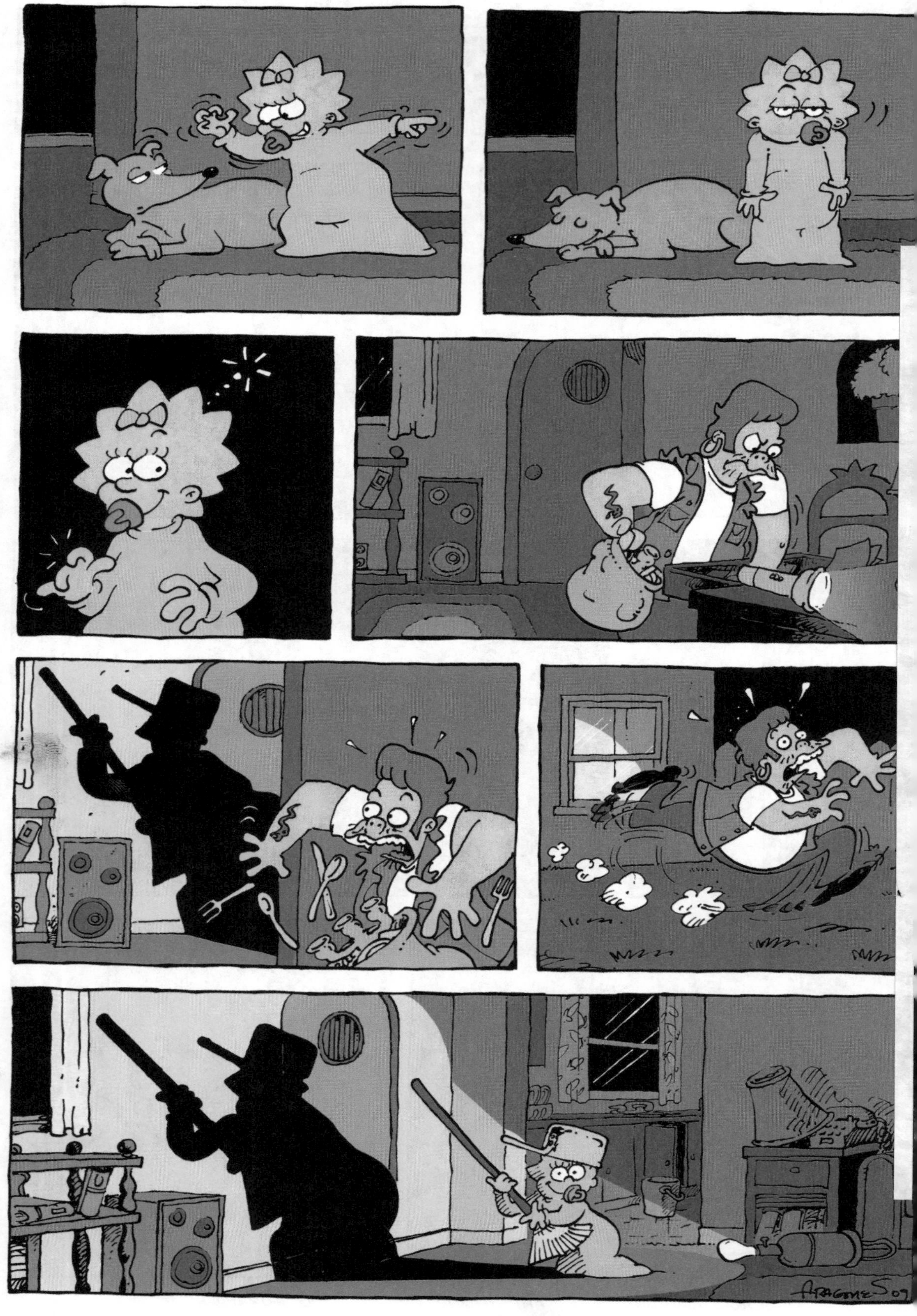

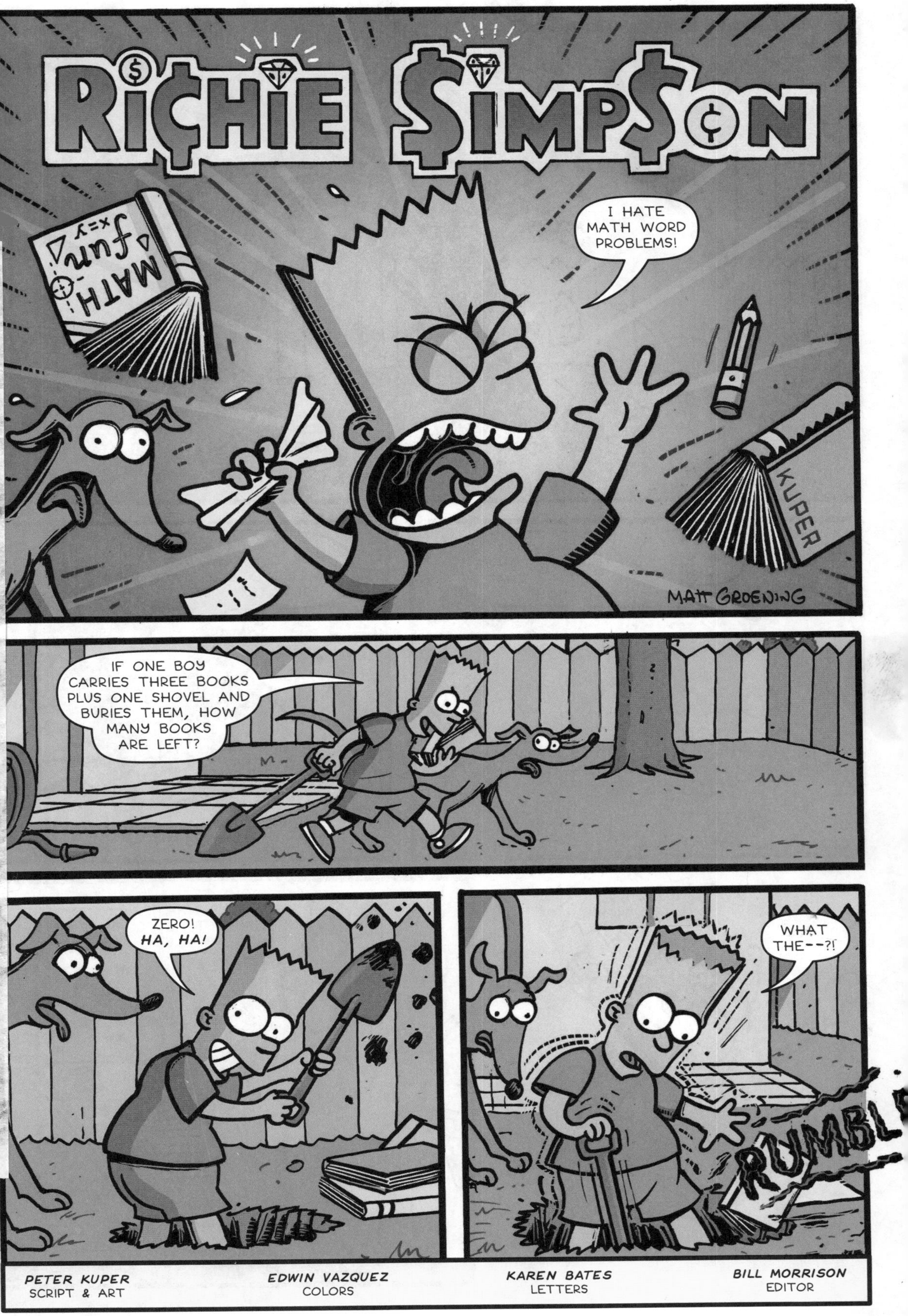
RI¢HIE IMPON
MATH fun x=y
I HATE MATH WORD PROBLEMS!
KUPER
MATT GROENING
IF ONE BOY CARRIES THREE BOOKS PLUS ONE SHOVEL AND BURIES THEM, HOW MANY BOOKS ARE LEFT?
ZERO! *HA, HA!*
WHAT THE--?!
RUMBL

PETER KUPER SCRIPT & ART

EDWIN VAZQUEZ COLORS

KAREN BATES LETTERS

BILL MORRISON EDITOR

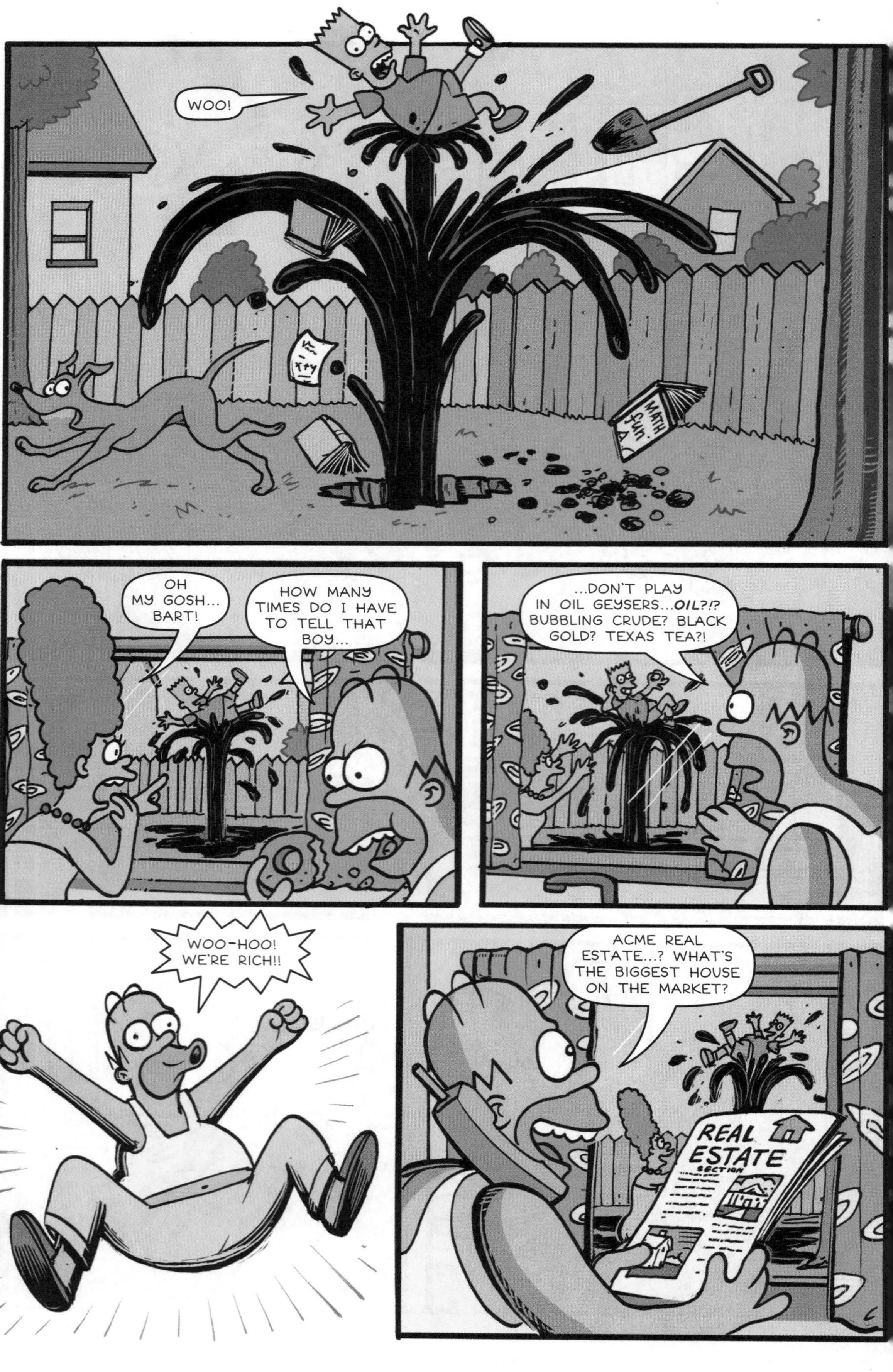
WOO!
MATH fun
OH MY GOSH... BART!
HOW MANY TIMES DO I HAVE TO TELL THAT BOY...
...DON'T PLAY IN OIL GEYSERS...OIL?!? BUBBLING CRUDE? BLACK GOLD? TEXAS TEA?!
WOO-HOO! WE'RE RICH!!
ACME REAL ESTATE...? WHAT'S THE BIGGEST HOUSE ON THE MARKET?
REAL ESTATE SECTION

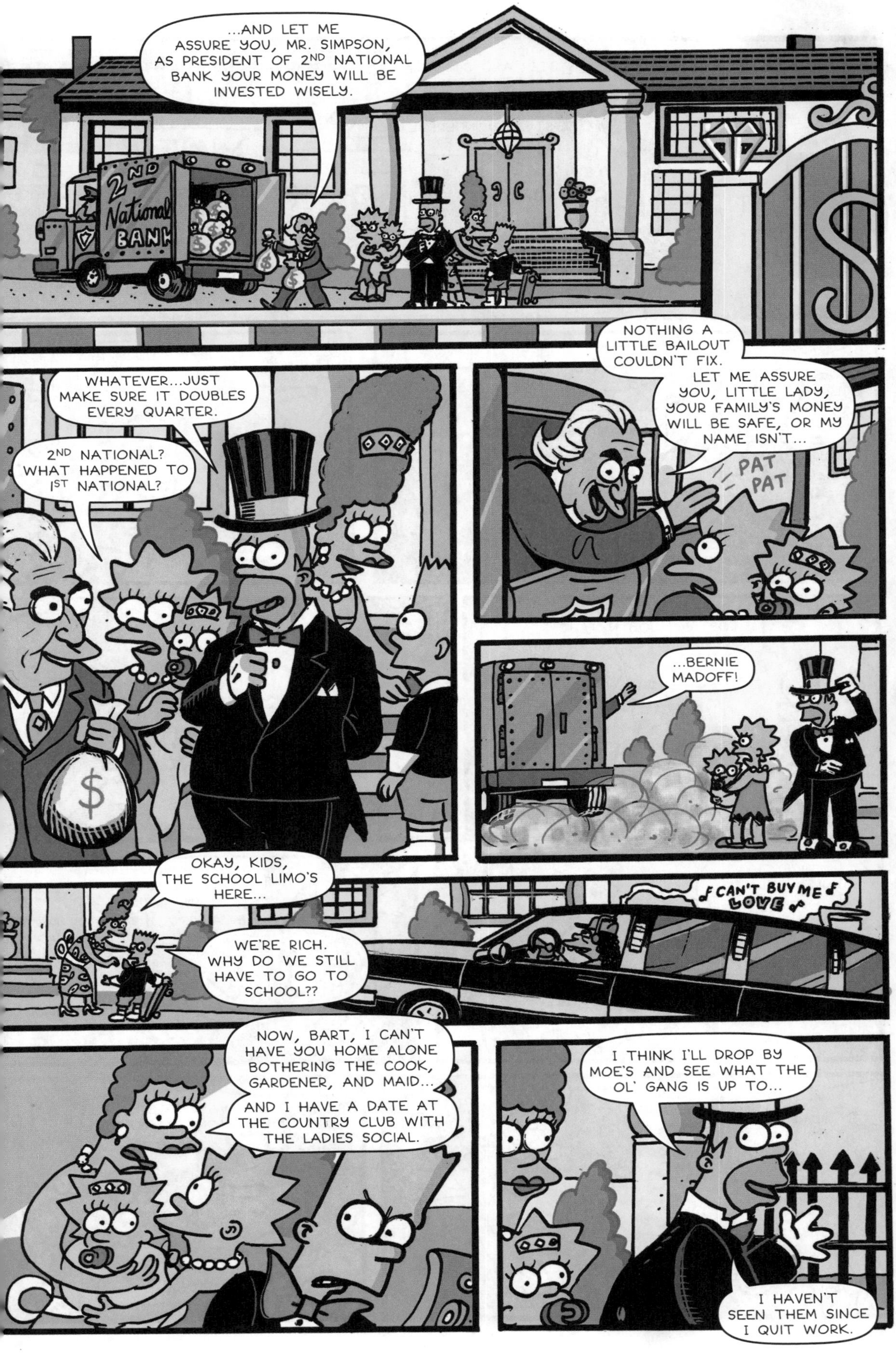
...AND LET ME ASSURE YOU, MR. SIMPSON, AS PRESIDENT OF 2ND NATIONAL BANK YOUR MONEY WILL BE INVESTED WISELY.
2ND National BANK
WHATEVER...JUST MAKE SURE IT DOUBLES EVERY QUARTER.
2ND NATIONAL? WHAT HAPPENED TO 1ST NATIONAL?
$
NOTHING A LITTLE BAILOUT COULDN'T FIX.
LET ME ASSURE YOU, LITTLE LADY, YOUR FAMILY'S MONEY WILL BE SAFE, OR MY NAME ISN'T...
PAT PAT
...BERNIE MADOFF!
OKAY, KIDS, THE SCHOOL LIMO'S HERE...
WE'RE RICH. WHY DO WE STILL HAVE TO GO TO SCHOOL??
CAN'T BUY ME LOVE
NOW, BART, I CAN'T HAVE YOU HOME ALONE BOTHERING THE COOK, GARDENER, AND MAID...
AND I HAVE A DATE AT THE COUNTRY CLUB WITH THE LADIES SOCIAL.
I THINK I'LL DROP BY MOE'S AND SEE WHAT THE OL' GANG IS UP TO...
I HAVEN'T SEEN THEM SINCE I QUIT WORK.

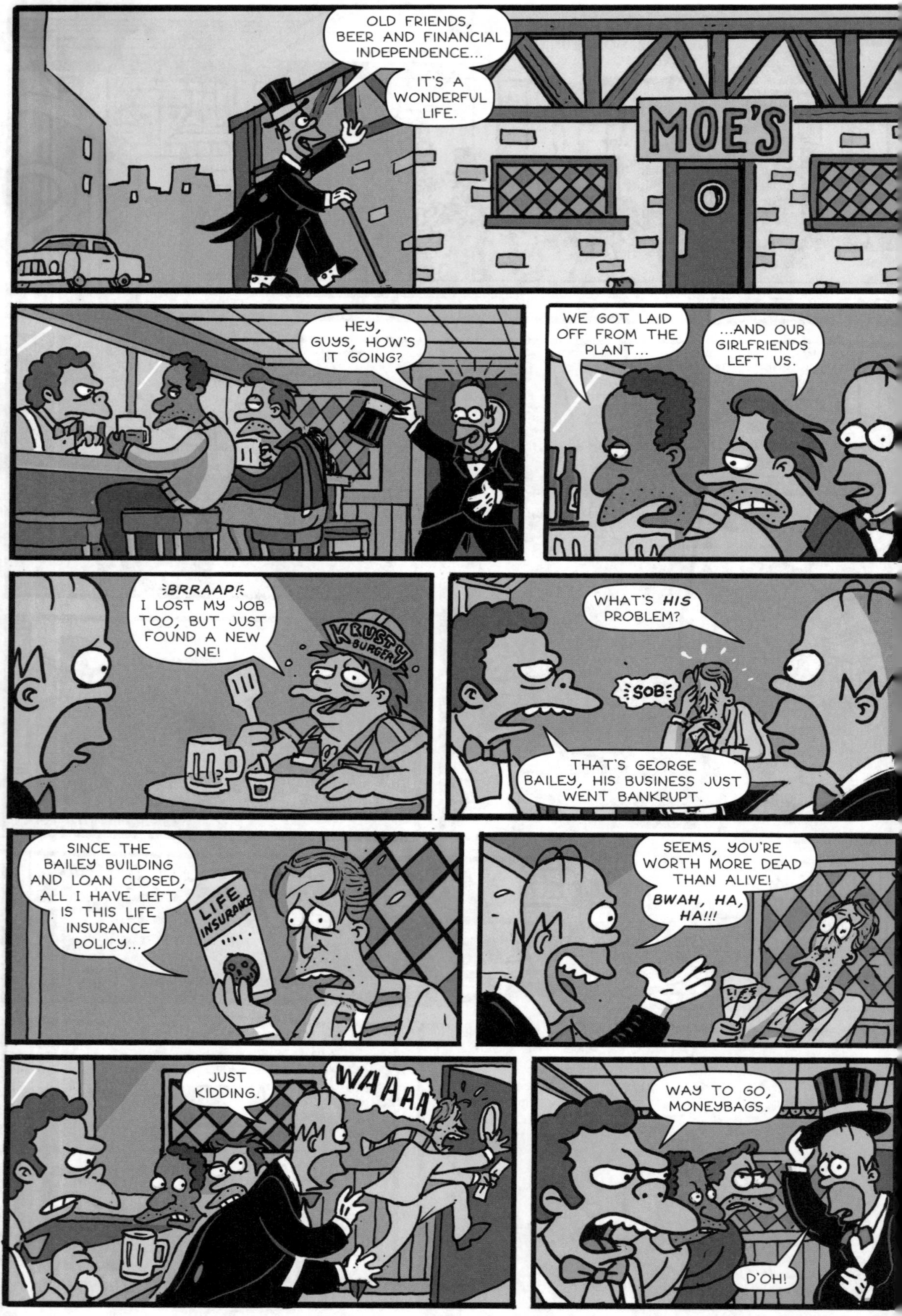

OLD FRIENDS, BEER AND FINANCIAL INDEPENDENCE...
IT'S A WONDERFUL LIFE.
MOE'S
HEY, GUYS, HOW'S IT GOING?
WE GOT LAID OFF FROM THE PLANT...
...AND OUR GIRLFRIENDS LEFT US.
BRRAAP!
I LOST MY JOB TOO, BUT JUST FOUND A NEW ONE!
KRUSTY BURGER
WHAT'S HIS PROBLEM?
SOB
THAT'S GEORGE BAILEY, HIS BUSINESS JUST WENT BANKRUPT.
SINCE THE BAILEY BUILDING AND LOAN CLOSED, ALL I HAVE LEFT IS THIS LIFE INSURANCE POLICY...
LIFE INSURANCE
SEEMS, YOU'RE WORTH MORE DEAD THAN ALIVE!
BWAH, HA, HA!!!
JUST KIDDING.
WAAAAA
WAY TO GO, MONEYBAGS.
D'OH!

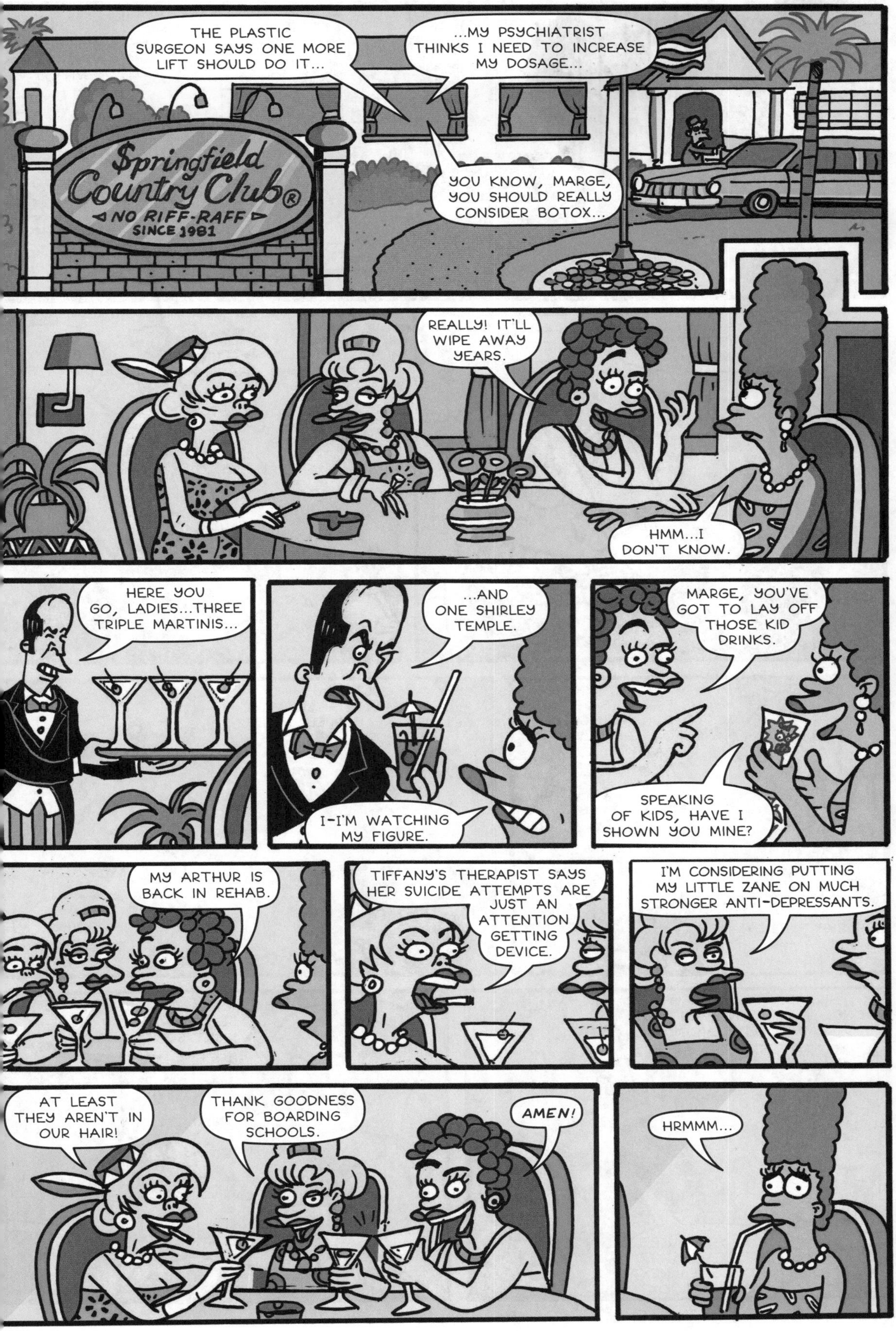
THE PLASTIC SURGEON SAYS ONE MORE LIFT SHOULD DO IT...
...MY PSYCHIATRIST THINKS I NEED TO INCREASE MY DOSAGE...
$pringfield Country Club®
NO RIFF-RAFF
SINCE 1981
YOU KNOW, MARGE, YOU SHOULD REALLY CONSIDER BOTOX...
REALLY! IT'LL WIPE AWAY YEARS.
HMM...I DON'T KNOW.
HERE YOU GO, LADIES...THREE TRIPLE MARTINIS...
...AND ONE SHIRLEY TEMPLE.
I-I'M WATCHING MY FIGURE.
MARGE, YOU'VE GOT TO LAY OFF THOSE KID DRINKS.
SPEAKING OF KIDS, HAVE I SHOWN YOU MINE?
MY ARTHUR IS BACK IN REHAB.
TIFFANY'S THERAPIST SAYS HER SUICIDE ATTEMPTS ARE JUST AN ATTENTION GETTING DEVICE.
I'M CONSIDERING PUTTING MY LITTLE ZANE ON MUCH STRONGER ANTI-DEPRESSANTS.
AT LEAST THEY AREN'T IN OUR HAIR!
THANK GOODNESS FOR BOARDING SCHOOLS.
AMEN!
HRMMM...

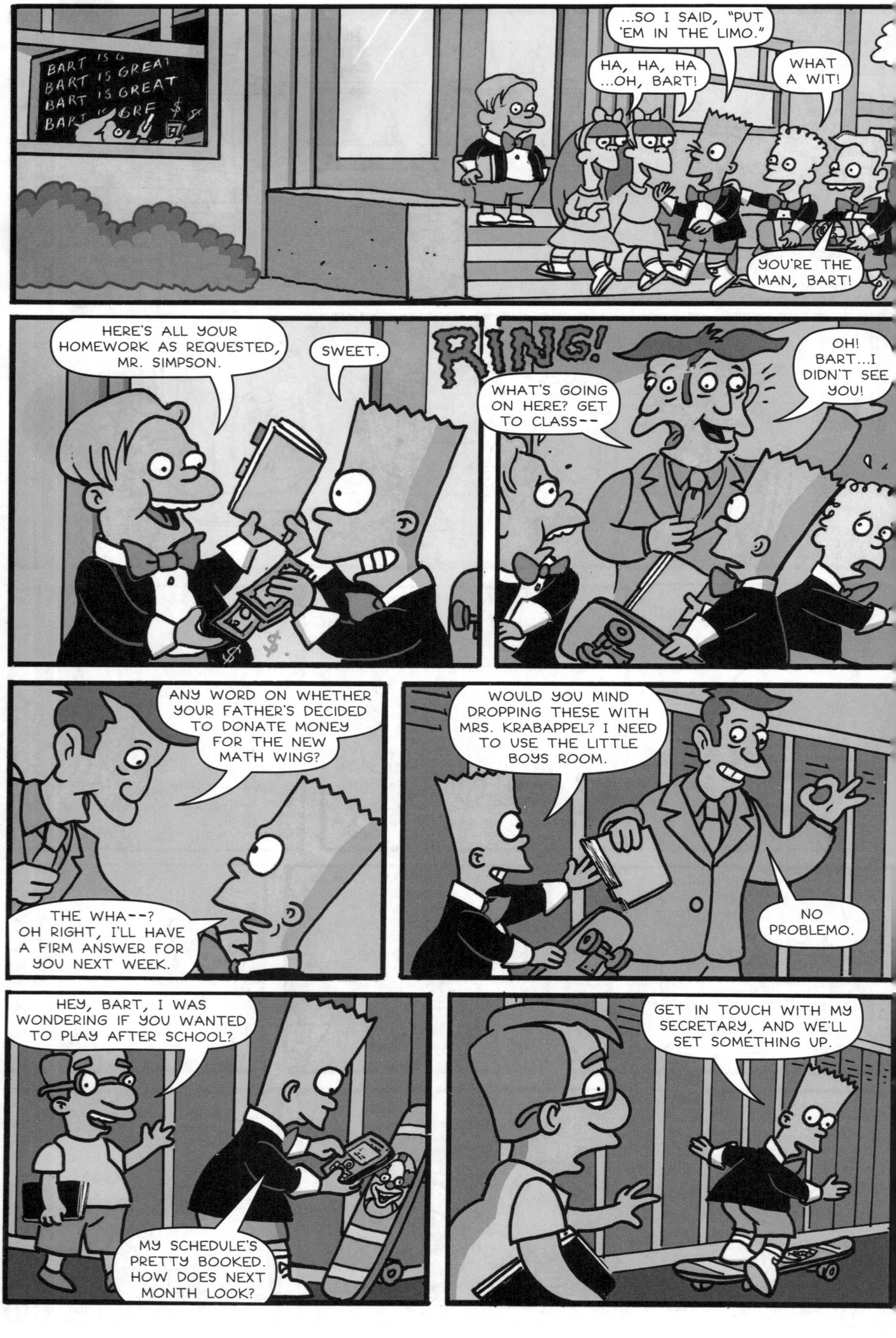
BART IS G
BART IS GREAT
BART IS GREAT
BART IS GRE
...SO I SAID, "PUT 'EM IN THE LIMO."
HA, HA, HA ...OH, BART!
WHAT A WIT!
YOU'RE THE MAN, BART!
HERE'S ALL YOUR HOMEWORK AS REQUESTED, MR. SIMPSON.
SWEET.
RING!
WHAT'S GOING ON HERE? GET TO CLASS--
OH! BART...I DIDN'T SEE YOU!
ANY WORD ON WHETHER YOUR FATHER'S DECIDED TO DONATE MONEY FOR THE NEW MATH WING?
THE WHA--? OH RIGHT, I'LL HAVE A FIRM ANSWER FOR YOU NEXT WEEK.
WOULD YOU MIND DROPPING THESE WITH MRS. KRABAPPEL? I NEED TO USE THE LITTLE BOYS ROOM.
NO PROBLEMO.
HEY, BART, I WAS WONDERING IF YOU WANTED TO PLAY AFTER SCHOOL?
MY SCHEDULE'S PRETTY BOOKED. HOW DOES NEXT MONTH LOOK?
GET IN TOUCH WITH MY SECRETARY, AND WE'LL SET SOMETHING UP.

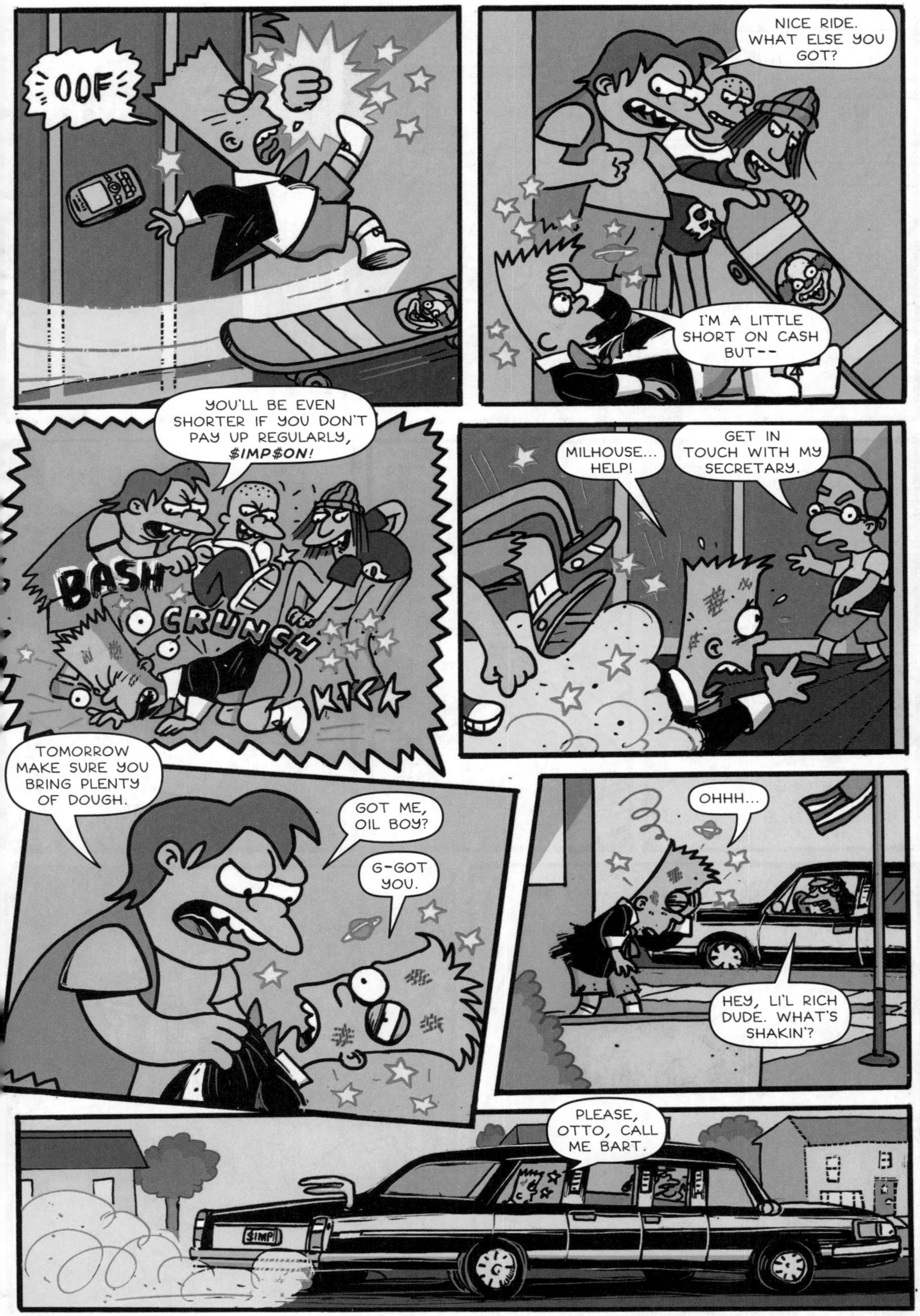
OOF
NICE RIDE. WHAT ELSE YOU GOT?
I'M A LITTLE SHORT ON CASH BUT--
YOU'LL BE EVEN SHORTER IF YOU DON'T PAY UP REGULARLY, IMPON!
BASH
CRUNCH
KICK
MILHOUSE... HELP!
GET IN TOUCH WITH MY SECRETARY.
TOMORROW MAKE SURE YOU BRING PLENTY OF DOUGH.
GOT ME, OIL BOY?
G-GOT YOU.
OHHH...
HEY, LI'L RICH DUDE. WHAT'S SHAKIN'?
PLEASE, OTTO, CALL ME BART.
$IMP

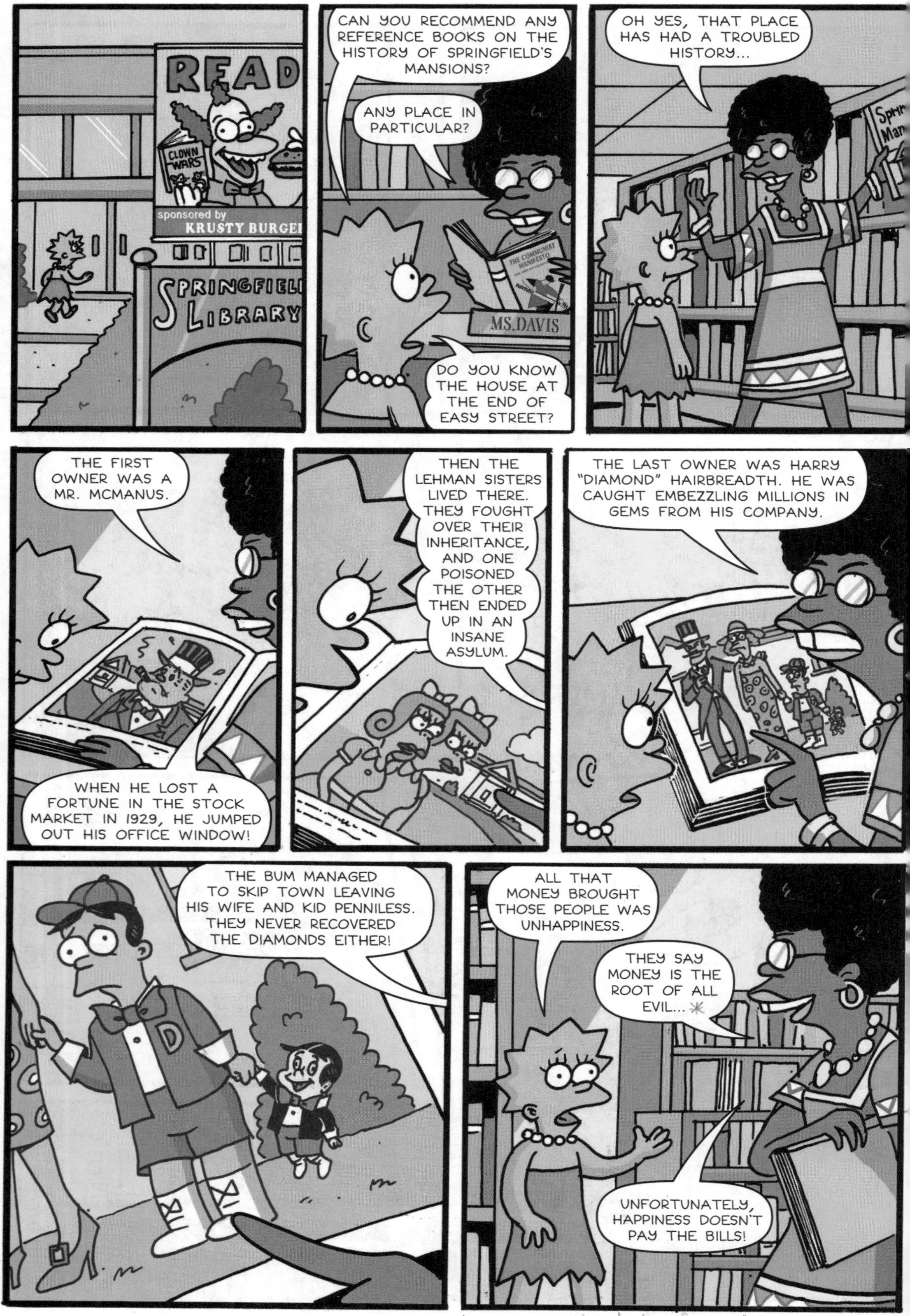
READ
CLOWN WARS
sponsored by
KRUSTY BURGER
SPRINGFIELD LIBRARY
CAN YOU RECOMMEND ANY REFERENCE BOOKS ON THE HISTORY OF SPRINGFIELD'S MANSIONS?
ANY PLACE IN PARTICULAR?
THE COMMUNIST MANIFESTO
MS. DAVIS
DO YOU KNOW THE HOUSE AT THE END OF EASY STREET?
OH YES, THAT PLACE HAS HAD A TROUBLED HISTORY...
THE FIRST OWNER WAS A MR. MCMANUS.
WHEN HE LOST A FORTUNE IN THE STOCK MARKET IN 1929, HE JUMPED OUT HIS OFFICE WINDOW!
THEN THE LEHMAN SISTERS LIVED THERE. THEY FOUGHT OVER THEIR INHERITANCE, AND ONE POISONED THE OTHER THEN ENDED UP IN AN INSANE ASYLUM.
THE LAST OWNER WAS HARRY "DIAMOND" HAIRBREADTH. HE WAS CAUGHT EMBEZZLING MILLIONS IN GEMS FROM HIS COMPANY.
THE BUM MANAGED TO SKIP TOWN LEAVING HIS WIFE AND KID PENNILESS. THEY NEVER RECOVERED THE DIAMONDS EITHER!
D
ALL THAT MONEY BROUGHT THOSE PEOPLE WAS UNHAPPINESS.
THEY SAY MONEY IS THE ROOT OF ALL EVIL... *
UNFORTUNATELY, HAPPINESS DOESN'T PAY THE BILLS!

* wrong — the love of money...

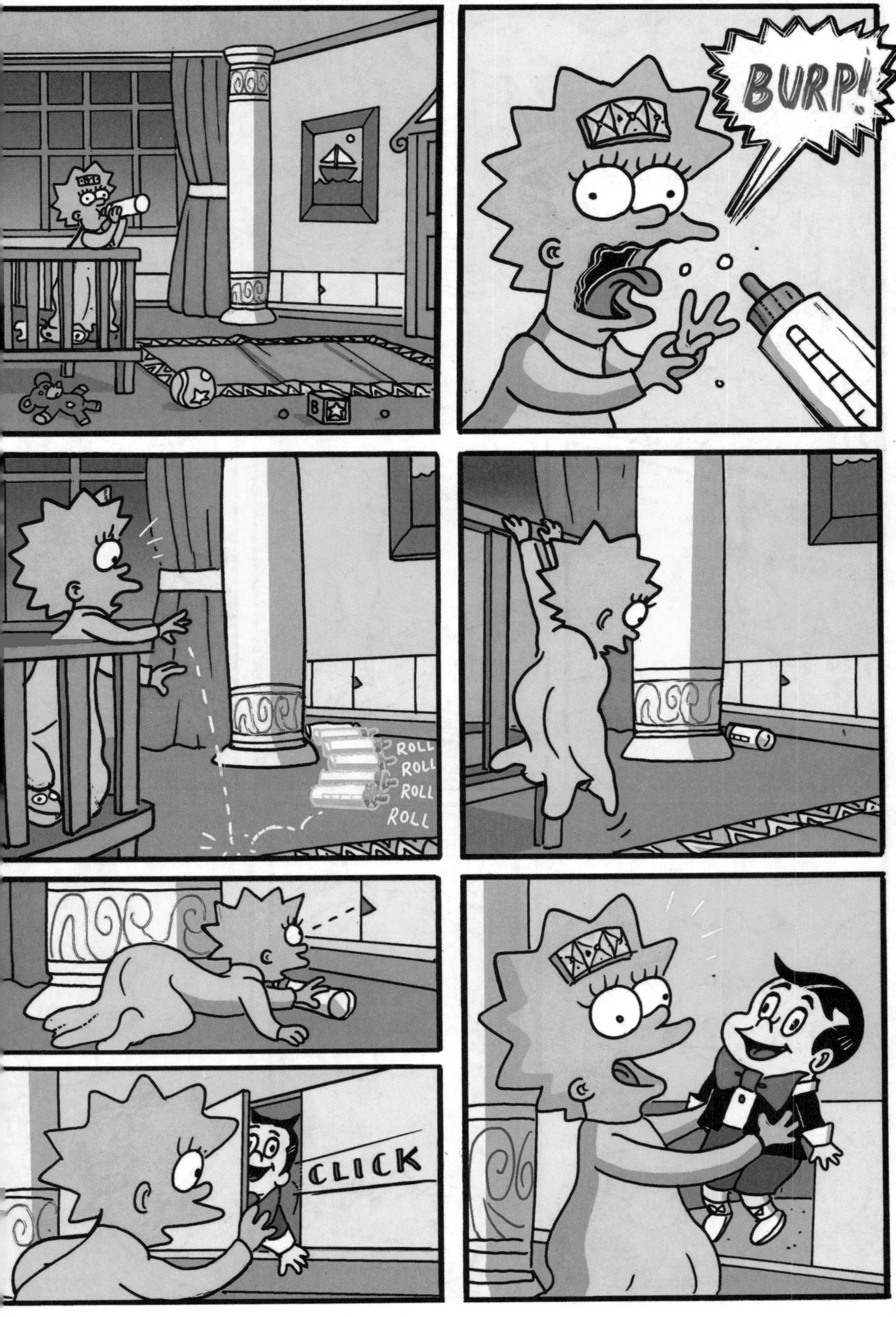

BURP!
ROLL
ROLL
ROLL
ROLL
CLICK

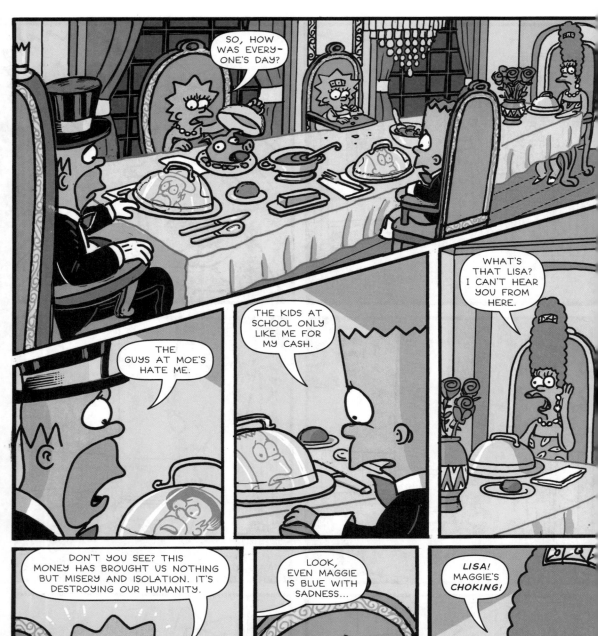

SO, HOW WAS EVERY-ONE'S DAY?

THE GUYS AT MOE'S HATE ME.

THE KIDS AT SCHOOL ONLY LIKE ME FOR MY CASH.

WHAT'S THAT LISA? I CAN'T HEAR YOU FROM HERE.

DON'T YOU SEE? THIS MONEY HAS BROUGHT US NOTHING BUT MISERY AND ISOLATION. IT'S DESTROYING OUR HUMANITY.

LOOK, EVEN MAGGIE IS BLUE WITH SADNESS...

LISA! MAGGIE'S CHOKING!

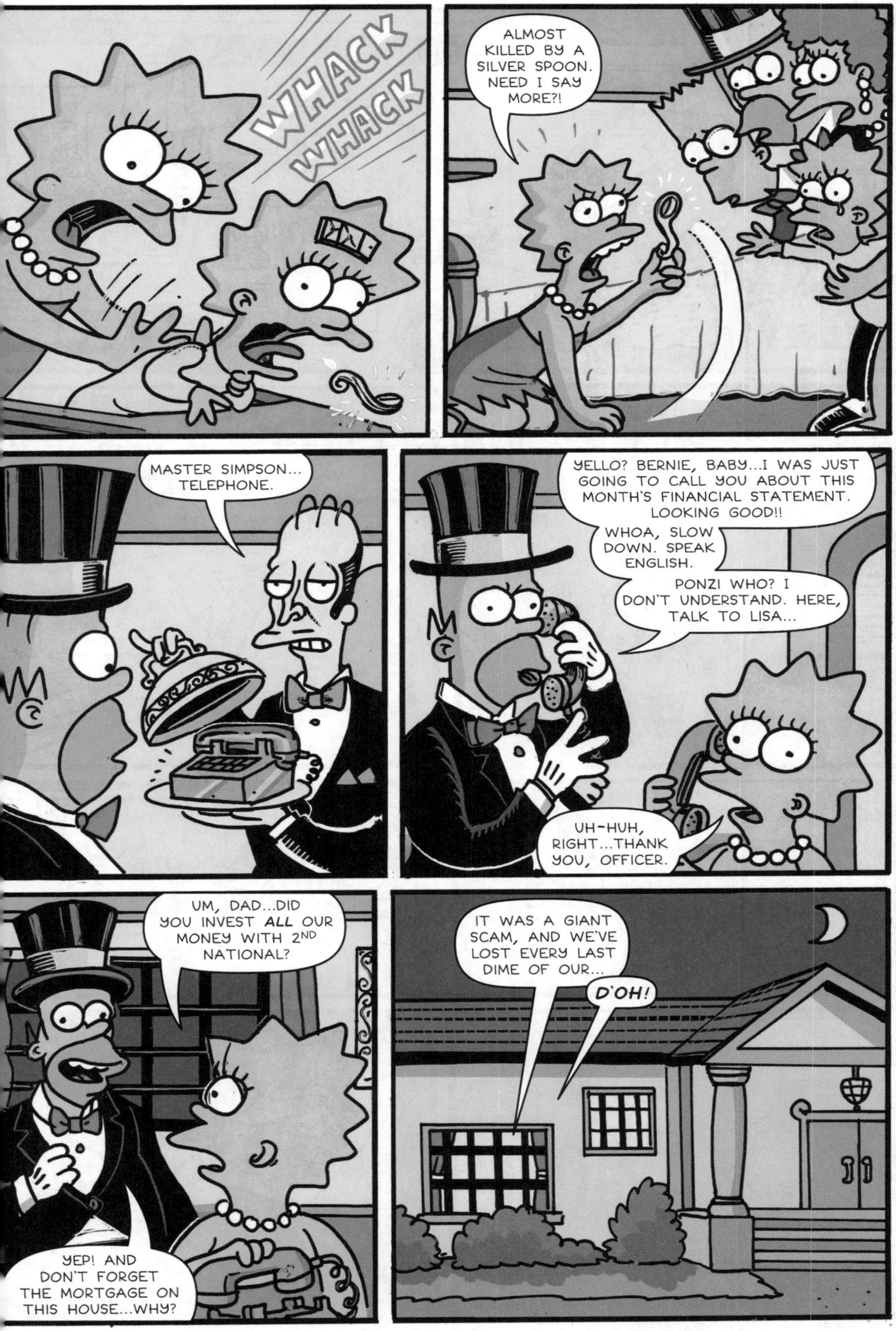
WHACK
WHACK
ALMOST KILLED BY A SILVER SPOON. NEED I SAY MORE?!
MASTER SIMPSON... TELEPHONE.
YELLO? BERNIE, BABY...I WAS JUST GOING TO CALL YOU ABOUT THIS MONTH'S FINANCIAL STATEMENT. LOOKING GOOD!!
WHOA, SLOW DOWN. SPEAK ENGLISH.
PONZI WHO? I DON'T UNDERSTAND. HERE, TALK TO LISA...
UH-HUH, RIGHT...THANK YOU, OFFICER.
UM, DAD...DID YOU INVEST ALL OUR MONEY WITH 2ND NATIONAL?
YEP! AND DON'T FORGET THE MORTGAGE ON THIS HOUSE...WHY?
IT WAS A GIANT SCAM, AND WE'VE LOST EVERY LAST DIME OF OUR...
D'OH!

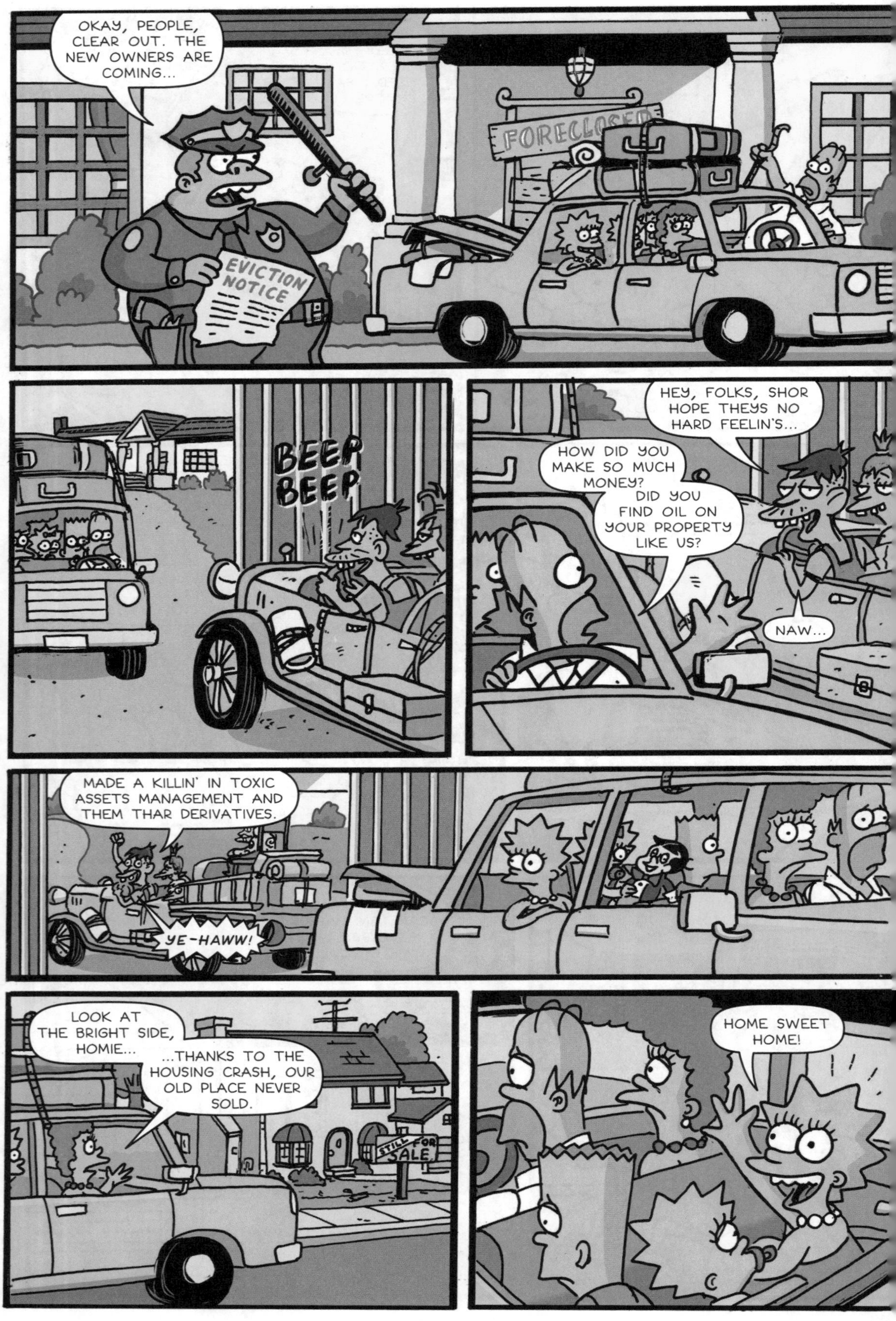

OKAY, PEOPLE, CLEAR OUT. THE NEW OWNERS ARE COMING...
FORECLOSED
EVICTION NOTICE
BEEP BEEP
HEY, FOLKS, SHOR HOPE THEYS NO HARD FEELIN'S...
HOW DID YOU MAKE SO MUCH MONEY?
DID YOU FIND OIL ON YOUR PROPERTY LIKE US?
NAW...
MADE A KILLIN' IN TOXIC ASSETS MANAGEMENT AND THEM THAR DERIVATIVES.
YE-HAWW!
LOOK AT THE BRIGHT SIDE, HOMIE...
...THANKS TO THE HOUSING CRASH, OUR OLD PLACE NEVER SOLD.
STILL FOR SALE
HOME SWEET HOME!

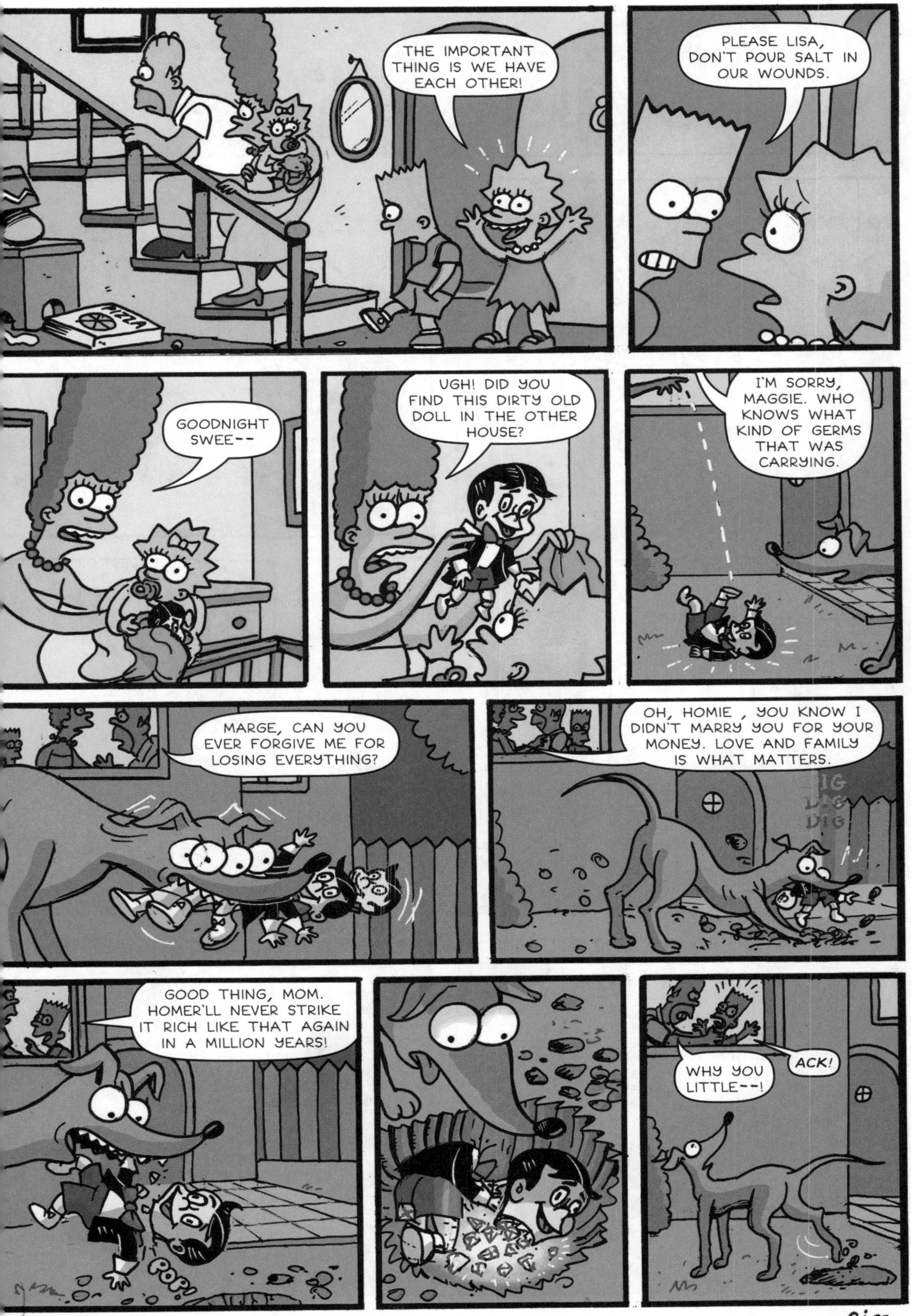
THE IMPORTANT THING IS WE HAVE EACH OTHER!
PLEASE LISA, DON'T POUR SALT IN OUR WOUNDS.
GOODNIGHT SWEE--
UGH! DID YOU FIND THIS DIRTY OLD DOLL IN THE OTHER HOUSE?
I'M SORRY, MAGGIE. WHO KNOWS WHAT KIND OF GERMS THAT WAS CARRYING.
MARGE, CAN YOU EVER FORGIVE ME FOR LOSING EVERYTHING?
OH, HOMIE, YOU KNOW I DIDN'T MARRY YOU FOR YOUR MONEY. LOVE AND FAMILY IS WHAT MATTERS.
GOOD THING, MOM. HOMER'LL NEVER STRIKE IT RICH LIKE THAT AGAIN IN A MILLION YEARS!
POP!
WHY YOU LITTLE--!
ACK!

fin

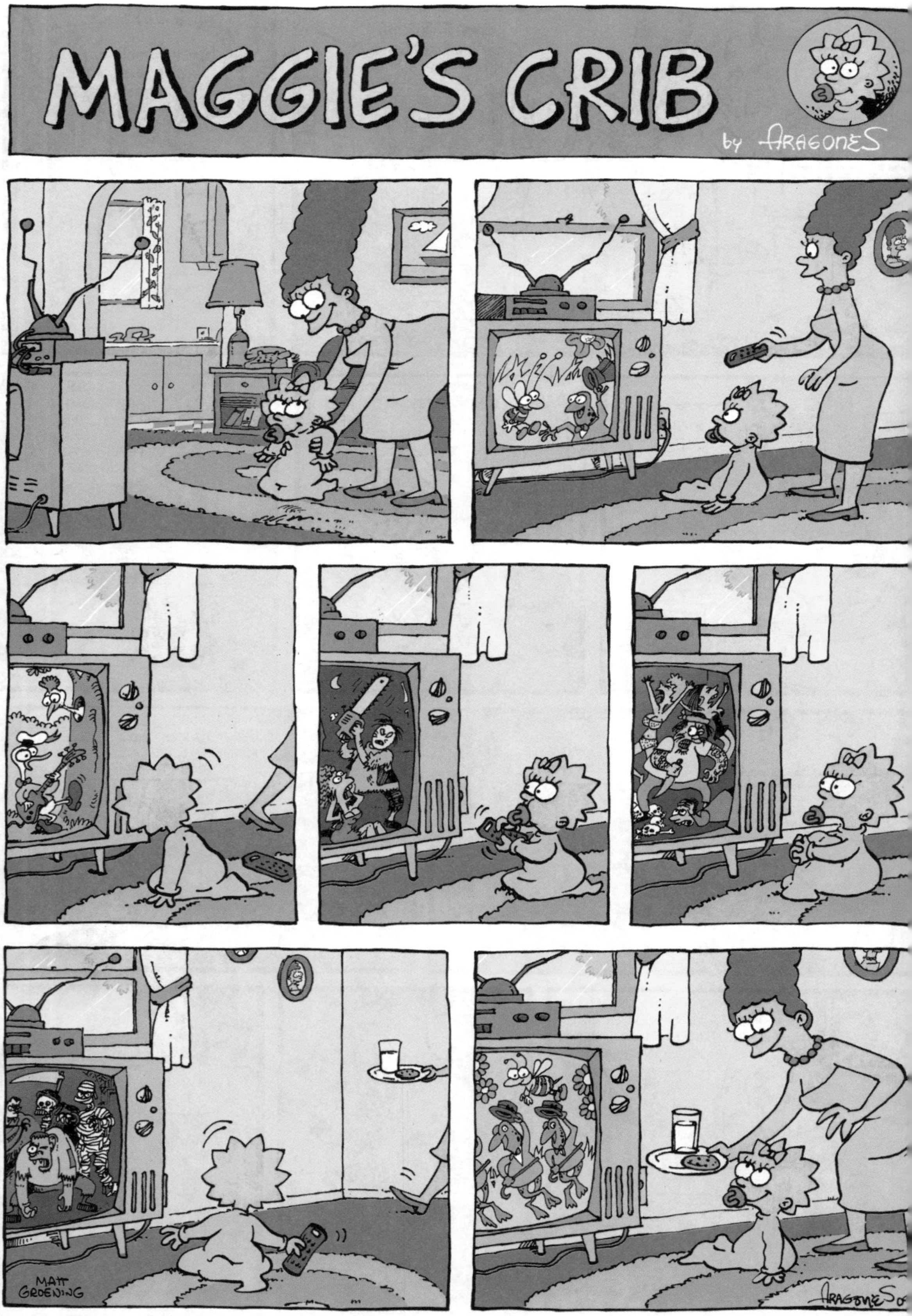
MAGGIE'S CRIB
by ARAGONES
MATT GROENING
ARAGONÉS

SERGIO ARAGONÉS
STORY & ART

ART VILLANUEVA
COLORS

BILL MORRISON
EDITOR

LISA & BART SIMPSON

in

A TOMB WITH A VIEW

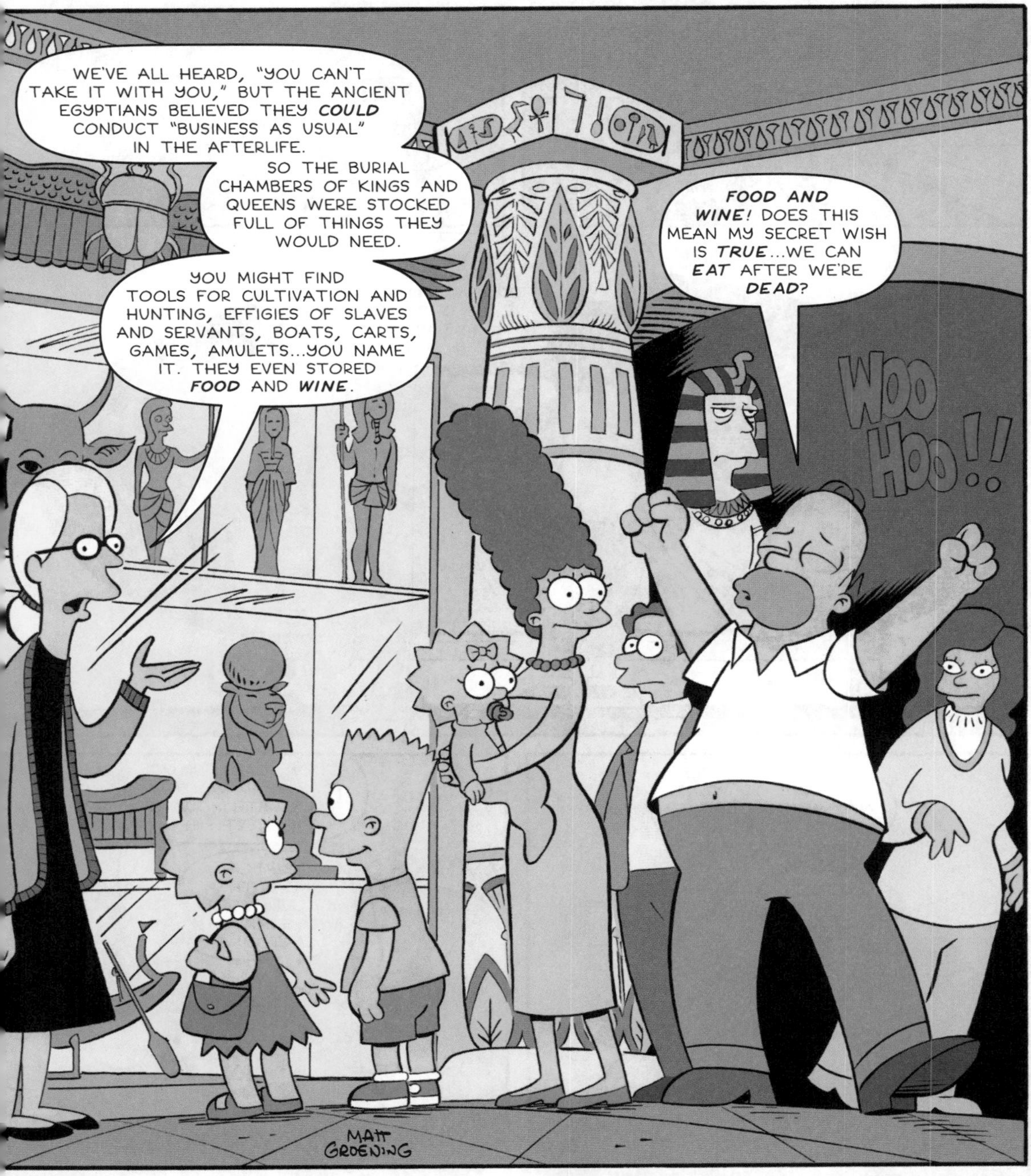
WE'VE ALL HEARD, "YOU CAN'T TAKE IT WITH YOU," BUT THE ANCIENT EGYPTIANS BELIEVED THEY *COULD* CONDUCT "BUSINESS AS USUAL" IN THE AFTERLIFE.
SO THE BURIAL CHAMBERS OF KINGS AND QUEENS WERE STOCKED FULL OF THINGS THEY WOULD NEED.
YOU MIGHT FIND TOOLS FOR CULTIVATION AND HUNTING, EFFIGIES OF SLAVES AND SERVANTS, BOATS, CARTS, GAMES, AMULETS...YOU NAME IT. THEY EVEN STORED *FOOD* AND *WINE*.
FOOD AND WINE! DOES THIS MEAN MY SECRET WISH IS *TRUE*...WE CAN *EAT* AFTER WE'RE *DEAD*?
WOO HOO!!
MATT GROENING

CAROL LAY SCRIPT & ART

NATHAN HAMILL COLORS

KAREN BATES LETTERS

BILL MORRISON EDITOR

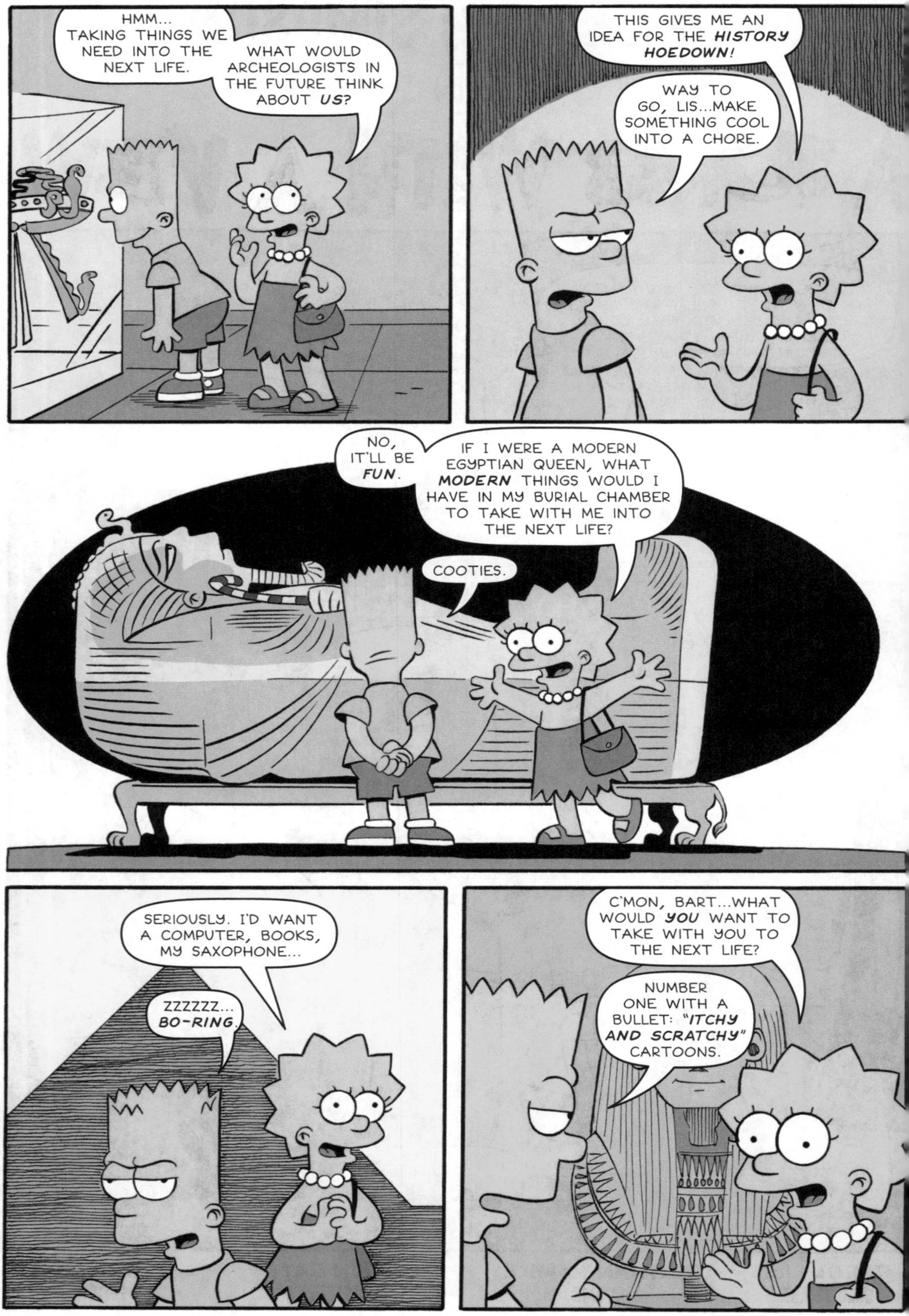
HMM... TAKING THINGS WE NEED INTO THE NEXT LIFE.
WHAT WOULD ARCHEOLOGISTS IN THE FUTURE THINK ABOUT *US*?
THIS GIVES ME AN IDEA FOR THE ***HISTORY HOEDOWN***!
WAY TO GO, LIS...MAKE SOMETHING COOL INTO A CHORE.
NO, IT'LL BE ***FUN***.
IF I WERE A MODERN EGYPTIAN QUEEN, WHAT ***MODERN*** THINGS WOULD I HAVE IN MY BURIAL CHAMBER TO TAKE WITH ME INTO THE NEXT LIFE?
COOTIES.
SERIOUSLY. I'D WANT A COMPUTER, BOOKS, MY SAXOPHONE...
ZZZZZZ... ***BO-RING***.
C'MON, BART...WHAT WOULD ***YOU*** WANT TO TAKE WITH YOU TO THE NEXT LIFE?
NUMBER ONE WITH A BULLET: "***ITCHY AND SCRATCHY***" CARTOONS.

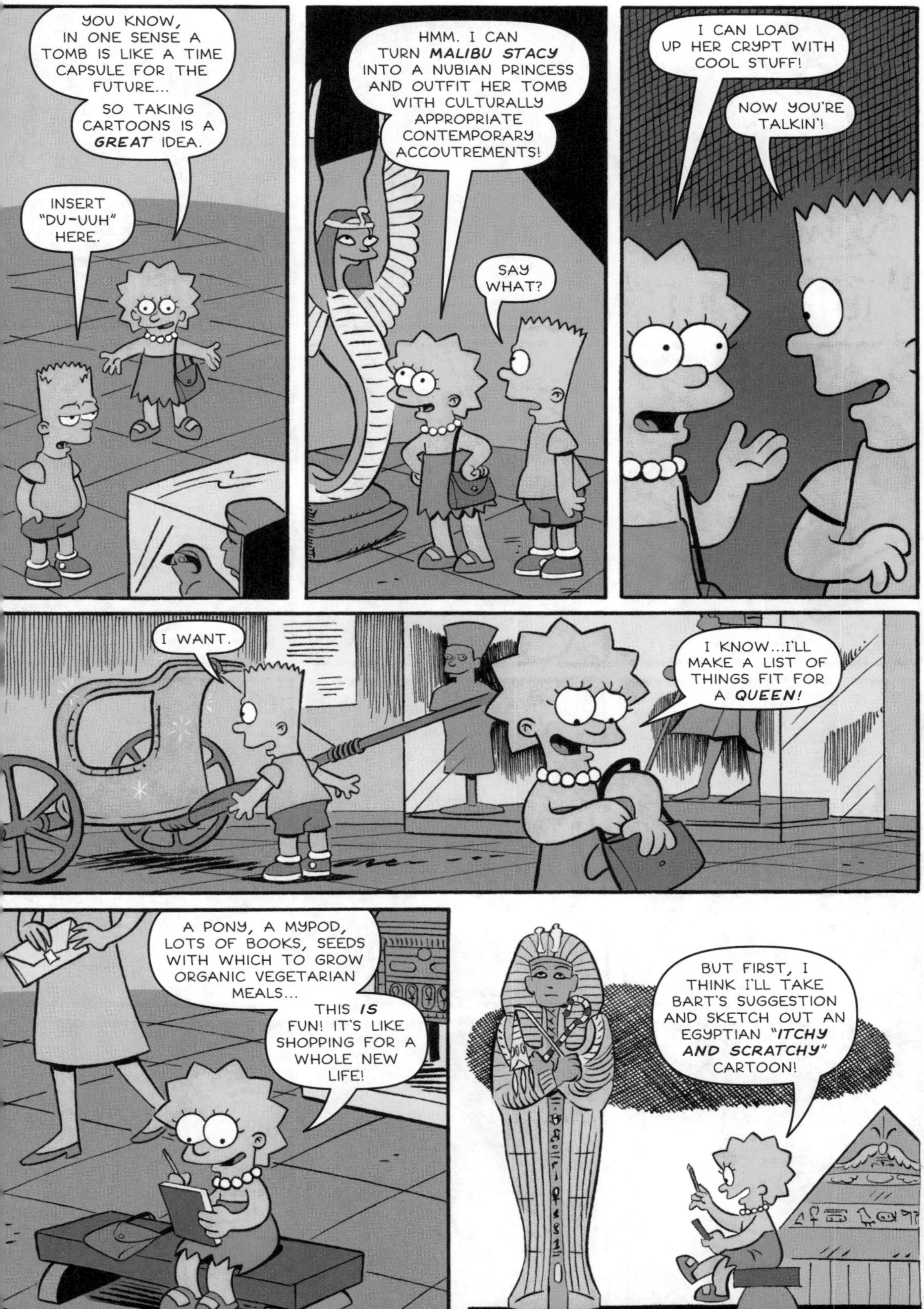
YOU KNOW, IN ONE SENSE A TOMB IS LIKE A TIME CAPSULE FOR THE FUTURE...
SO TAKING CARTOONS IS A GREAT IDEA.
INSERT "DU-UUH" HERE.
HMM. I CAN TURN MALIBU STACY INTO A NUBIAN PRINCESS AND OUTFIT HER TOMB WITH CULTURALLY APPROPRIATE CONTEMPORARY ACCOUTREMENTS!
SAY WHAT?
I CAN LOAD UP HER CRYPT WITH COOL STUFF!
NOW YOU'RE TALKIN'!
I WANT.
I KNOW...I'LL MAKE A LIST OF THINGS FIT FOR A QUEEN!
A PONY, A MYPOD, LOTS OF BOOKS, SEEDS WITH WHICH TO GROW ORGANIC VEGETARIAN MEALS...
THIS IS FUN! IT'S LIKE SHOPPING FOR A WHOLE NEW LIFE!
BUT FIRST, I THINK I'LL TAKE BART'S SUGGESTION AND SKETCH OUT AN EGYPTIAN "ITCHY AND SCRATCHY" CARTOON!

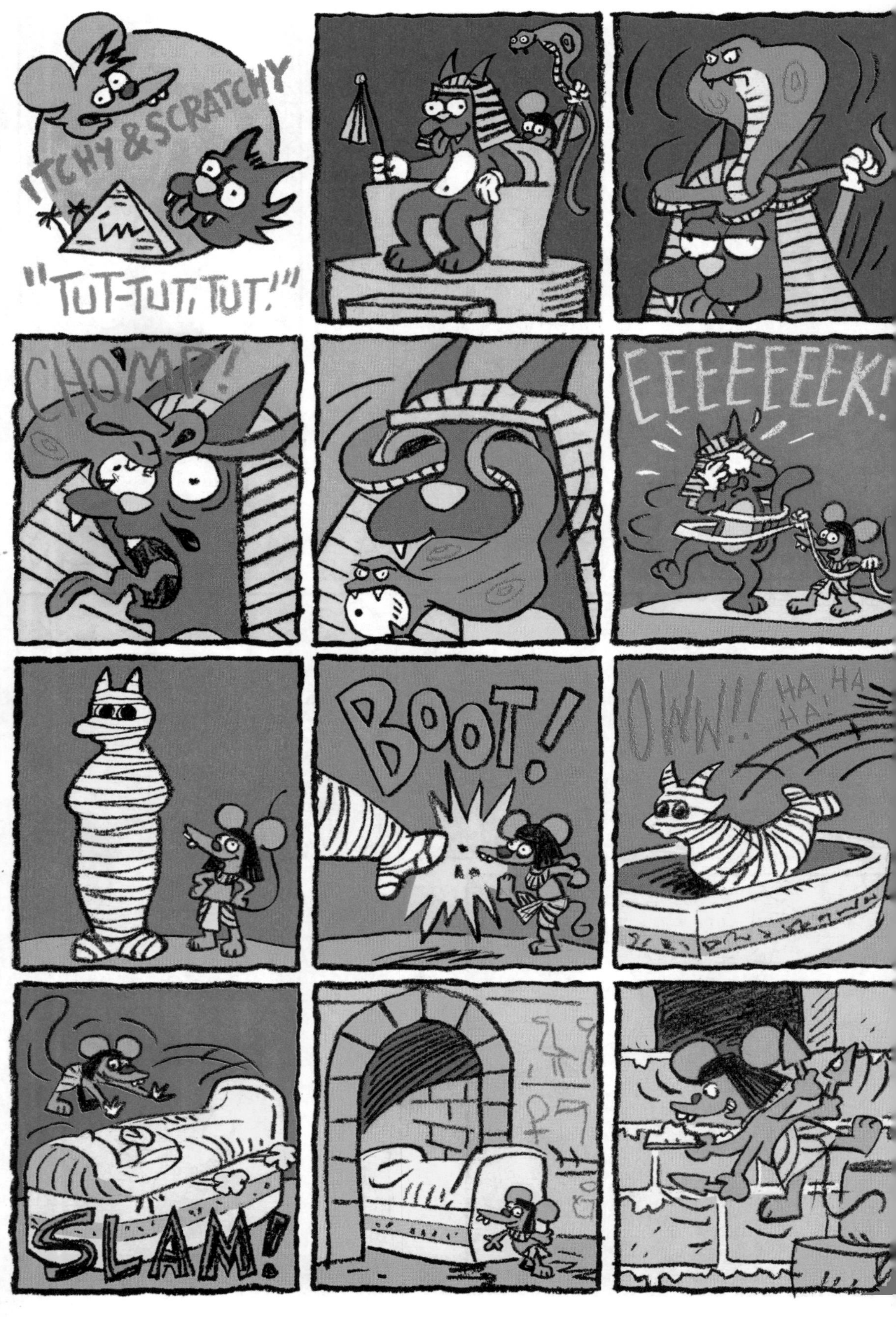

ITCHY & SCRATCHY
IN
"TUT-TUT, TUT!"
CHOMP!
EEEEEEEK!
BOOT!
OWW!!
HA HA HA
SLAM!

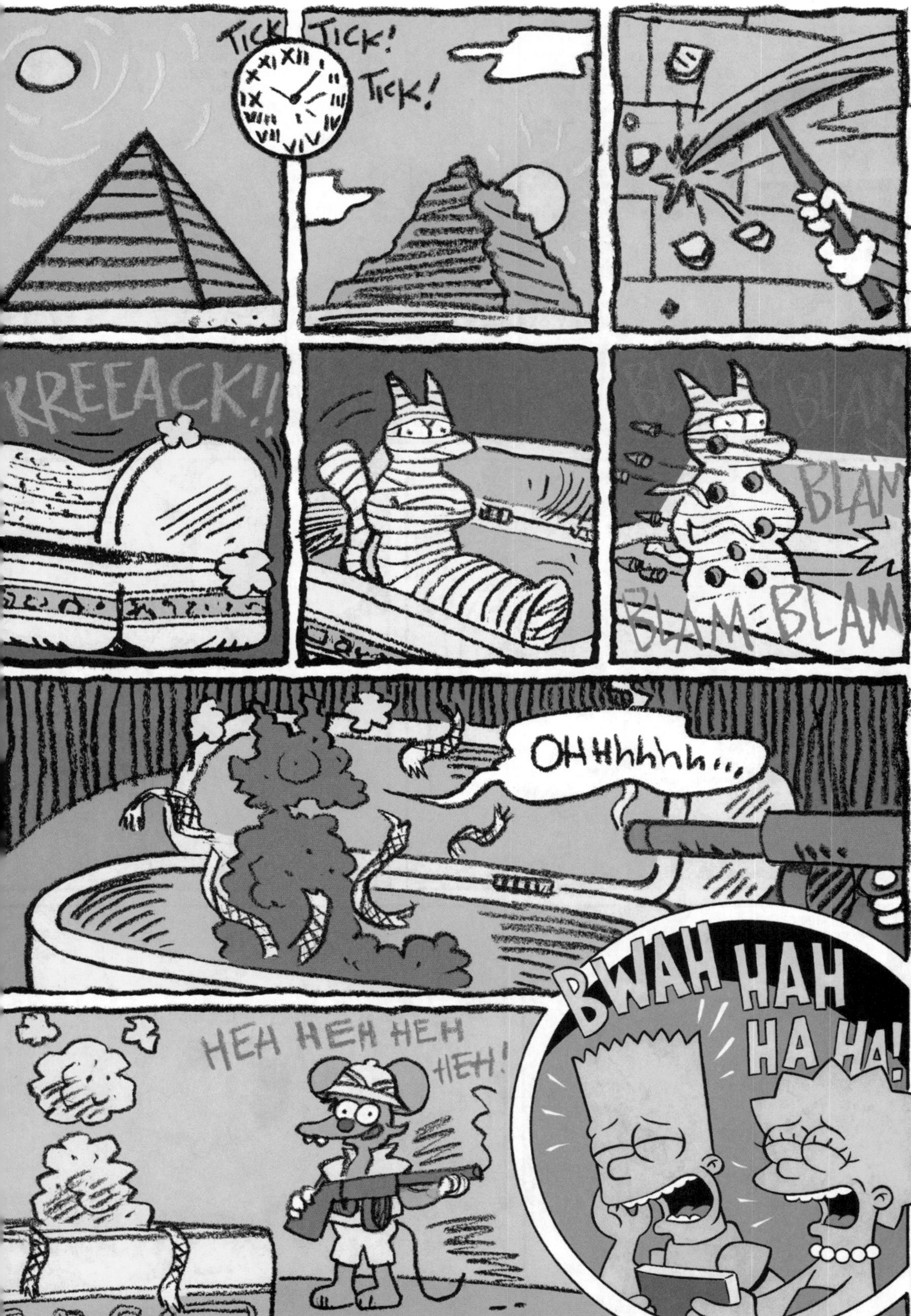
TICK TICK! TICK!
KREEACK!!
BLAM BLAM
BLAM
BLAM BLAM
OHHhhhh...
HEH HEH HEH HEH HEH!
BWAH HAH HAH HA HA!

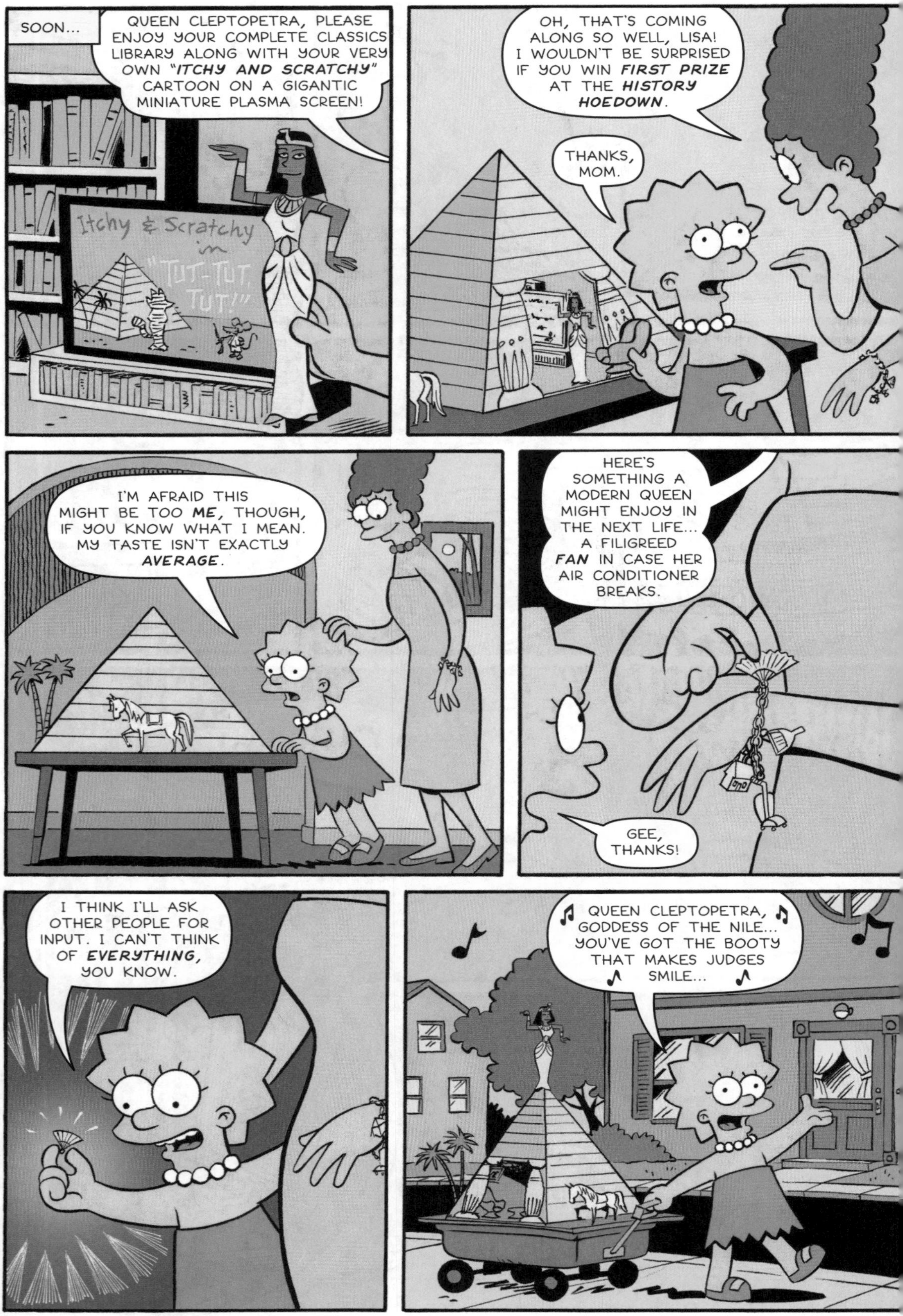
SOON...
QUEEN CLEPTOPETRA, PLEASE ENJOY YOUR COMPLETE CLASSICS LIBRARY ALONG WITH YOUR VERY OWN "ITCHY AND SCRATCHY" CARTOON ON A GIGANTIC MINIATURE PLASMA SCREEN!
Itchy & Scratchy in "TUT-TUT, TUT!"
OH, THAT'S COMING ALONG SO WELL, LISA! I WOULDN'T BE SURPRISED IF YOU WIN FIRST PRIZE AT THE HISTORY HOEDOWN.
THANKS, MOM.
I'M AFRAID THIS MIGHT BE TOO ME, THOUGH, IF YOU KNOW WHAT I MEAN. MY TASTE ISN'T EXACTLY AVERAGE.
HERE'S SOMETHING A MODERN QUEEN MIGHT ENJOY IN THE NEXT LIFE...
A FILIGREED FAN IN CASE HER AIR CONDITIONER BREAKS.
GEE, THANKS!
I THINK I'LL ASK OTHER PEOPLE FOR INPUT. I CAN'T THINK OF EVERYTHING, YOU KNOW.
♪ QUEEN CLEPTOPETRA, ♪ GODDESS OF THE NILE... YOU'VE GOT THE BOOTY THAT MAKES JUDGES ♪ SMILE... ♪

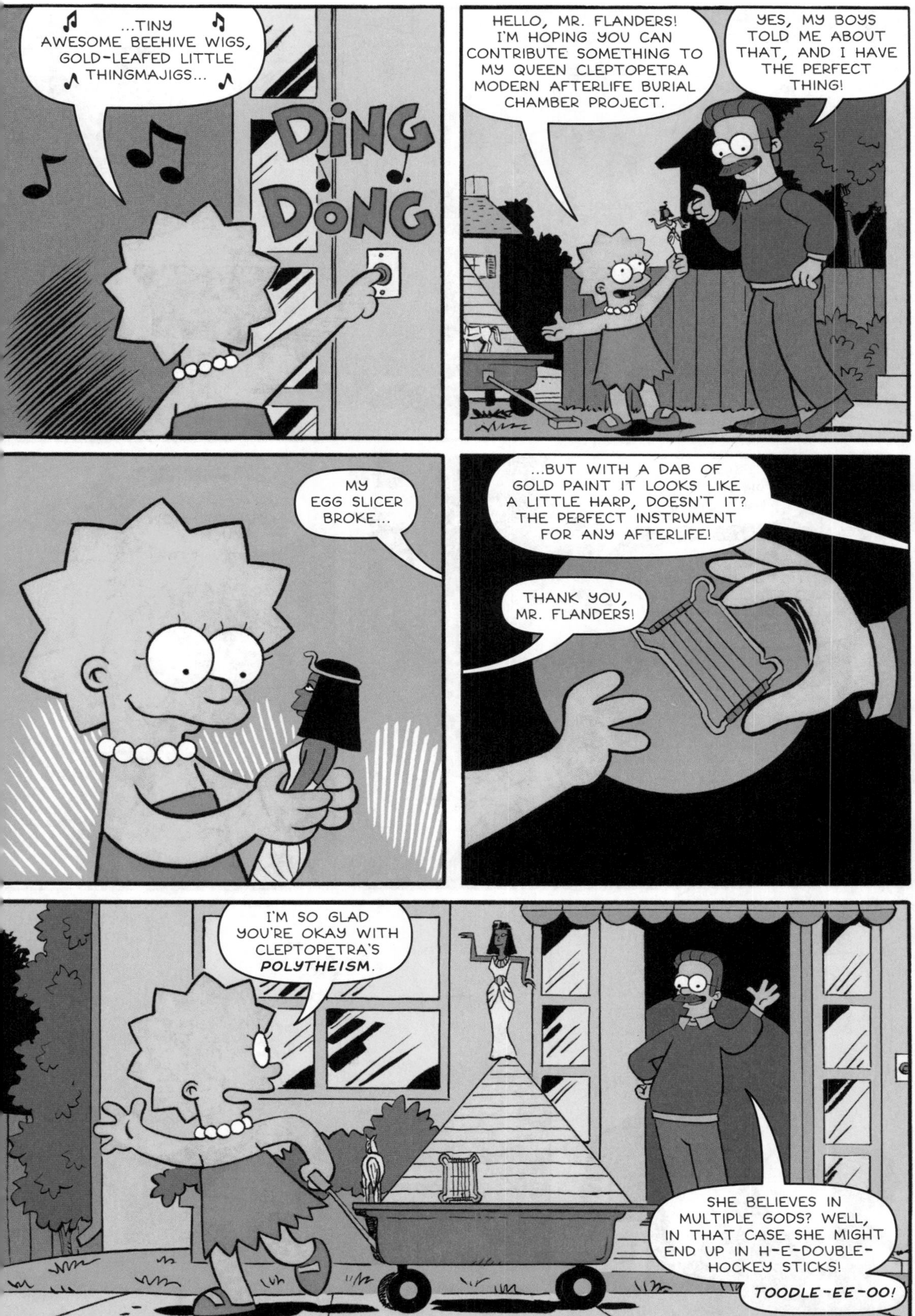
...TINY AWESOME BEEHIVE WIGS, GOLD-LEAFED LITTLE THINGMAJIGS...
DING DONG
HELLO, MR. FLANDERS! I'M HOPING YOU CAN CONTRIBUTE SOMETHING TO MY QUEEN CLEPTOPETRA MODERN AFTERLIFE BURIAL CHAMBER PROJECT.
YES, MY BOYS TOLD ME ABOUT THAT, AND I HAVE THE PERFECT THING!
MY EGG SLICER BROKE...
...BUT WITH A DAB OF GOLD PAINT IT LOOKS LIKE A LITTLE HARP, DOESN'T IT? THE PERFECT INSTRUMENT FOR ANY AFTERLIFE!
THANK YOU, MR. FLANDERS!
I'M SO GLAD YOU'RE OKAY WITH CLEPTOPETRA'S ***POLYTHEISM***.
SHE BELIEVES IN MULTIPLE GODS? WELL, IN THAT CASE SHE MIGHT END UP IN H-E-DOUBLE-HOCKEY STICKS!
TOODLE-EE-OO!

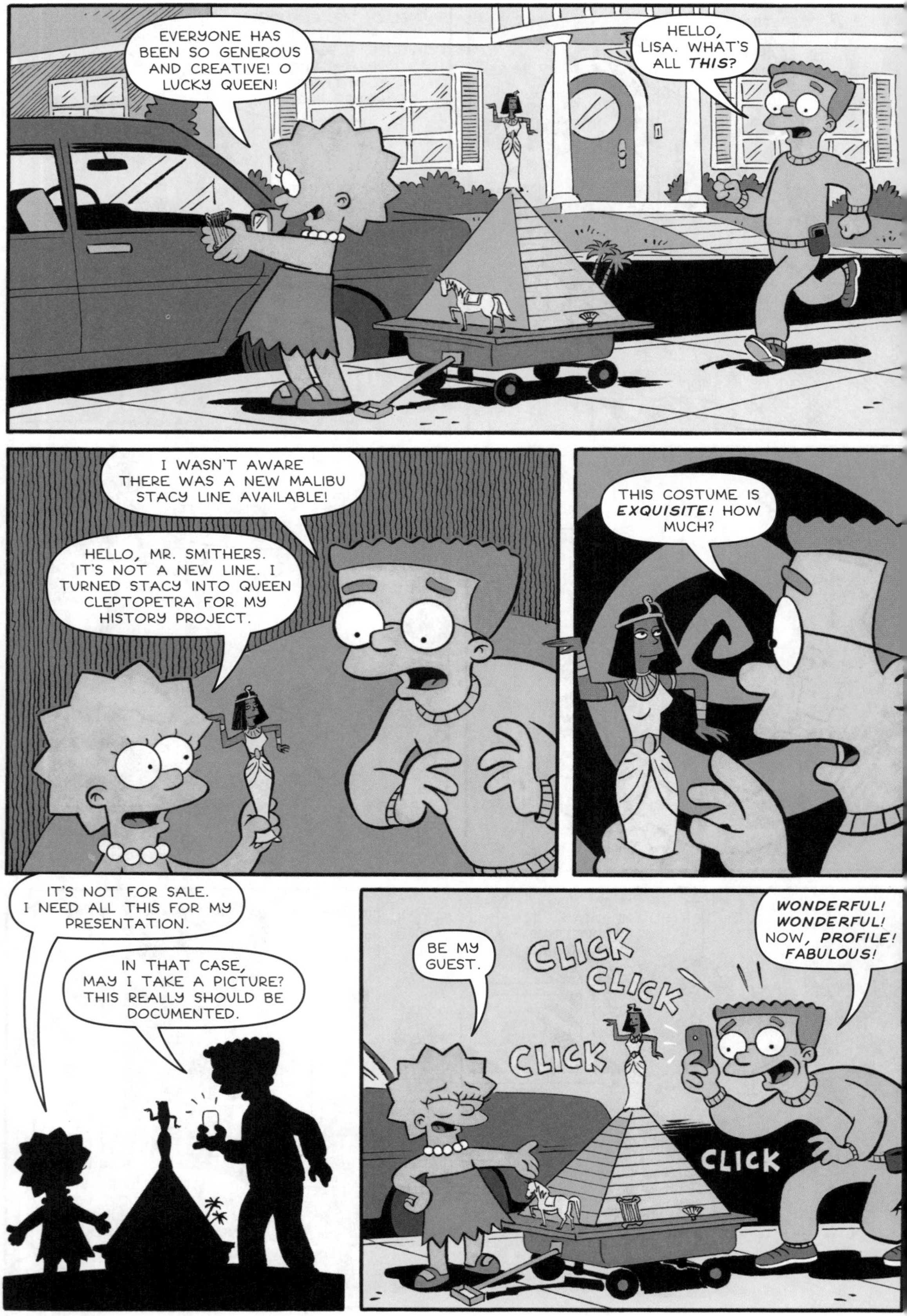
EVERYONE HAS BEEN SO GENEROUS AND CREATIVE! O LUCKY QUEEN!
HELLO, LISA. WHAT'S ALL *THIS*?
I WASN'T AWARE THERE WAS A NEW MALIBU STACY LINE AVAILABLE!
HELLO, MR. SMITHERS. IT'S NOT A NEW LINE. I TURNED STACY INTO QUEEN CLEPTOPETRA FOR MY HISTORY PROJECT.
THIS COSTUME IS *EXQUISITE!* HOW MUCH?
IT'S NOT FOR SALE. I NEED ALL THIS FOR MY PRESENTATION.
IN THAT CASE, MAY I TAKE A PICTURE? THIS REALLY SHOULD BE DOCUMENTED.
BE MY GUEST.
CLICK
CLICK
CLICK
CLICK
WONDERFUL! WONDERFUL! NOW, *PROFILE! FABULOUS!*

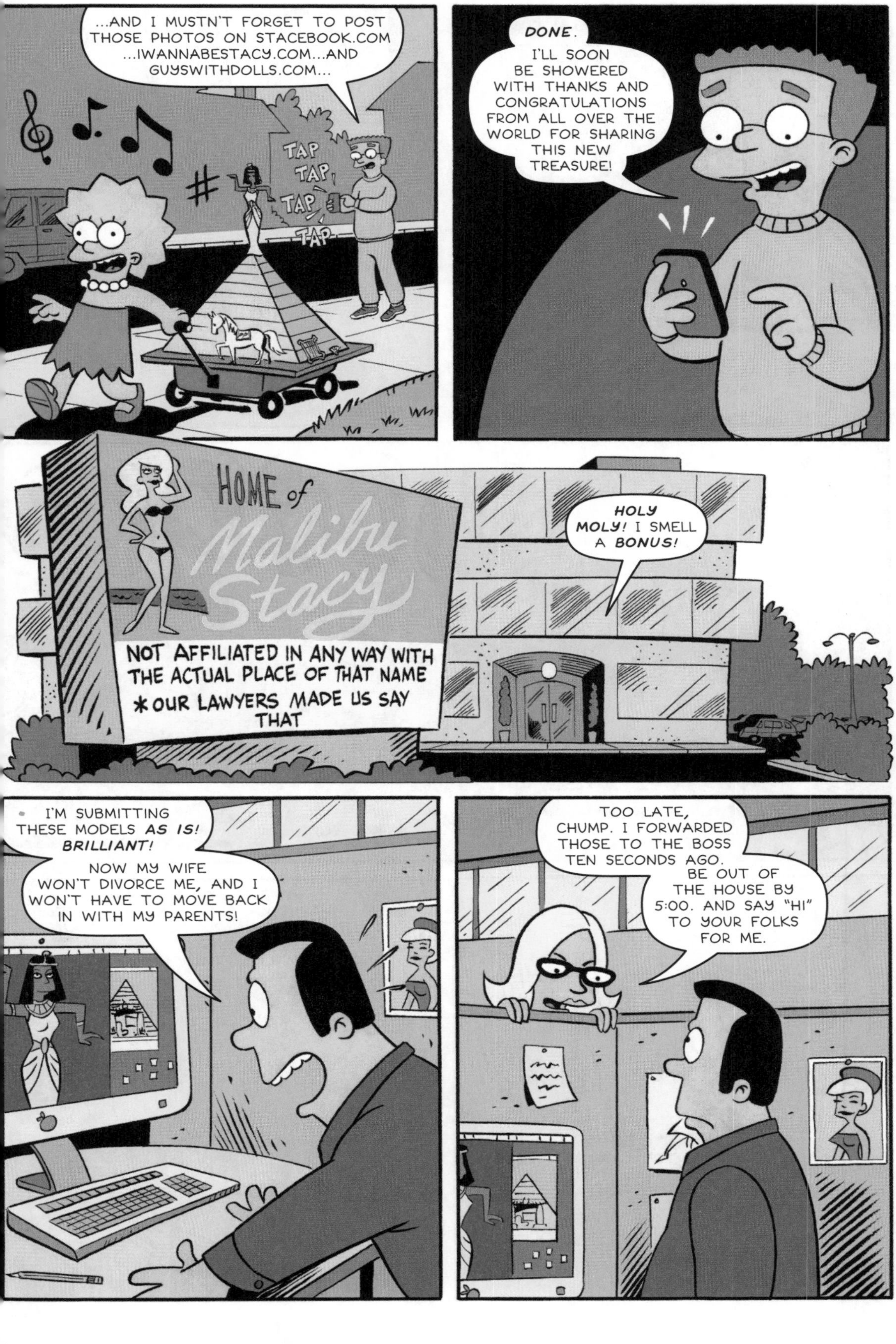

...AND I MUSTN'T FORGET TO POST THOSE PHOTOS ON STACEBOOK.COM ...IWANNABESTACY.COM...AND GUYSWITHDOLLS.COM...
TAP TAP TAP TAP
DONE. I'LL SOON BE SHOWERED WITH THANKS AND CONGRATULATIONS FROM ALL OVER THE WORLD FOR SHARING THIS NEW TREASURE!
HOME of Malibu Stacy
NOT AFFILIATED IN ANY WAY WITH THE ACTUAL PLACE OF THAT NAME
*OUR LAWYERS MADE US SAY THAT
HOLY MOLY! I SMELL A BONUS!
I'M SUBMITTING THESE MODELS AS IS! BRILLIANT!
NOW MY WIFE WON'T DIVORCE ME, AND I WON'T HAVE TO MOVE BACK IN WITH MY PARENTS!
TOO LATE, CHUMP. I FORWARDED THOSE TO THE BOSS TEN SECONDS AGO.
BE OUT OF THE HOUSE BY 5:00. AND SAY "HI" TO YOUR FOLKS FOR ME.

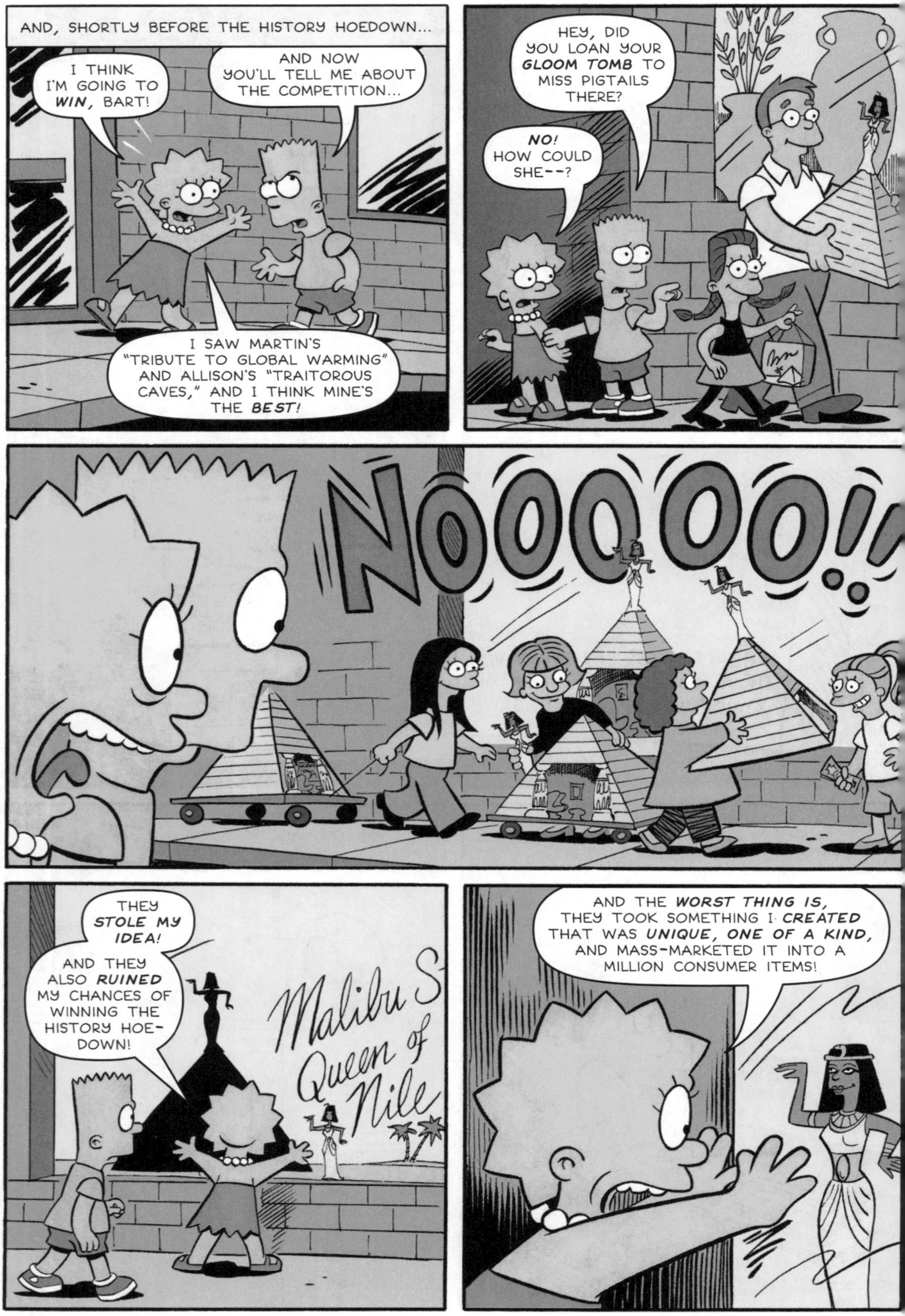
AND, SHORTLY BEFORE THE HISTORY HOEDOWN...
I THINK I'M GOING TO WIN, BART!
AND NOW YOU'LL TELL ME ABOUT THE COMPETITION...
I SAW MARTIN'S "TRIBUTE TO GLOBAL WARMING" AND ALLISON'S "TRAITOROUS CAVES," AND I THINK MINE'S THE BEST!
HEY, DID YOU LOAN YOUR GLOOM TOMB TO MISS PIGTAILS THERE?
NO! HOW COULD SHE--?
NOOOOOO!!
THEY STOLE MY IDEA!
AND THEY ALSO RUINED MY CHANCES OF WINNING THE HISTORY HOE-DOWN!
Malibu S
Queen of Nile
AND THE WORST THING IS, THEY TOOK SOMETHING I CREATED THAT WAS UNIQUE, ONE OF A KIND, AND MASS-MARKETED IT INTO A MILLION CONSUMER ITEMS!

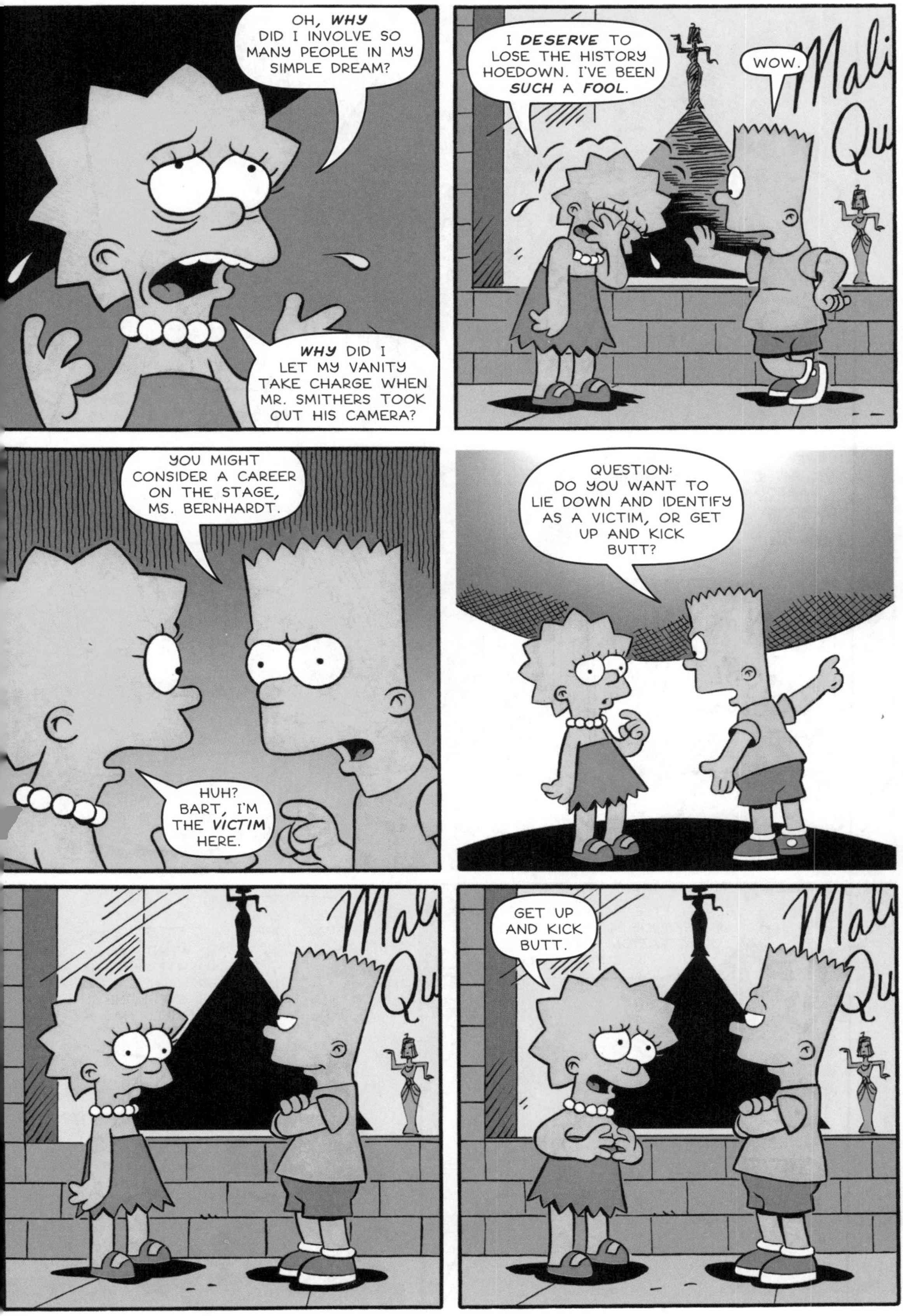
OH, WHY DID I INVOLVE SO MANY PEOPLE IN MY SIMPLE DREAM?
WHY DID I LET MY VANITY TAKE CHARGE WHEN MR. SMITHERS TOOK OUT HIS CAMERA?
I DESERVE TO LOSE THE HISTORY HOEDOWN. I'VE BEEN SUCH A FOOL.
WOW.
YOU MIGHT CONSIDER A CAREER ON THE STAGE, MS. BERNHARDT.
HUH? BART, I'M THE VICTIM HERE.
QUESTION: DO YOU WANT TO LIE DOWN AND IDENTIFY AS A VICTIM, OR GET UP AND KICK BUTT?
GET UP AND KICK BUTT.

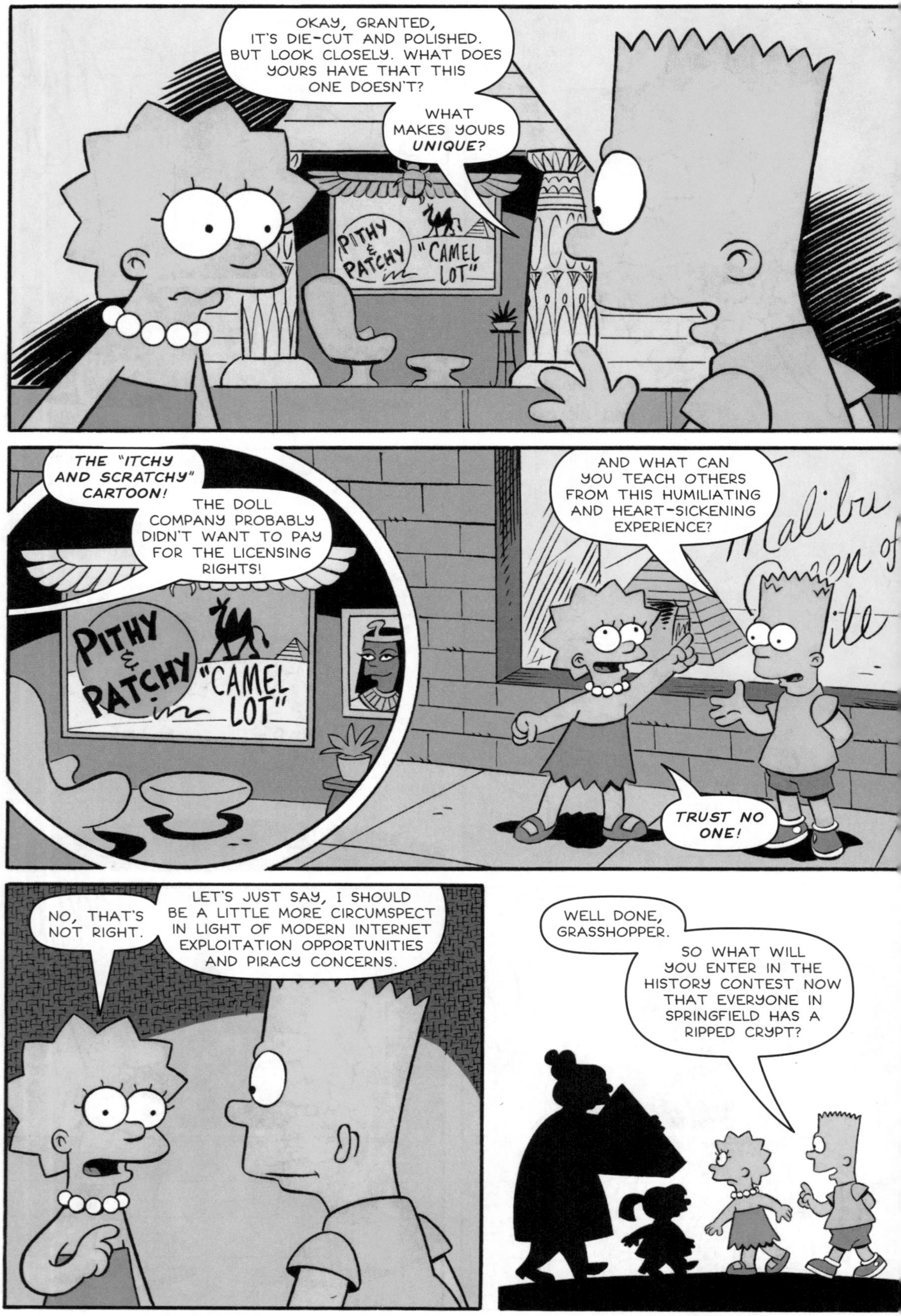
OKAY, GRANTED, IT'S DIE-CUT AND POLISHED. BUT LOOK CLOSELY. WHAT DOES YOURS HAVE THAT THIS ONE DOESN'T?
WHAT MAKES YOURS *UNIQUE*?
PITHY & PATCHY in "CAMEL LOT"
THE "ITCHY AND SCRATCHY" CARTOON!
THE DOLL COMPANY PROBABLY DIDN'T WANT TO PAY FOR THE LICENSING RIGHTS!
PITHY & PATCHY in "CAMEL LOT"
AND WHAT CAN YOU TEACH OTHERS FROM THIS HUMILIATING AND HEART-SICKENING EXPERIENCE?
TRUST NO ONE!
NO, THAT'S NOT RIGHT.
LET'S JUST SAY, I SHOULD BE A LITTLE MORE CIRCUMSPECT IN LIGHT OF MODERN INTERNET EXPLOITATION OPPORTUNITIES AND PIRACY CONCERNS.
WELL DONE, GRASSHOPPER.
SO WHAT WILL YOU ENTER IN THE HISTORY CONTEST NOW THAT EVERYONE IN SPRINGFIELD HAS A RIPPED CRYPT?

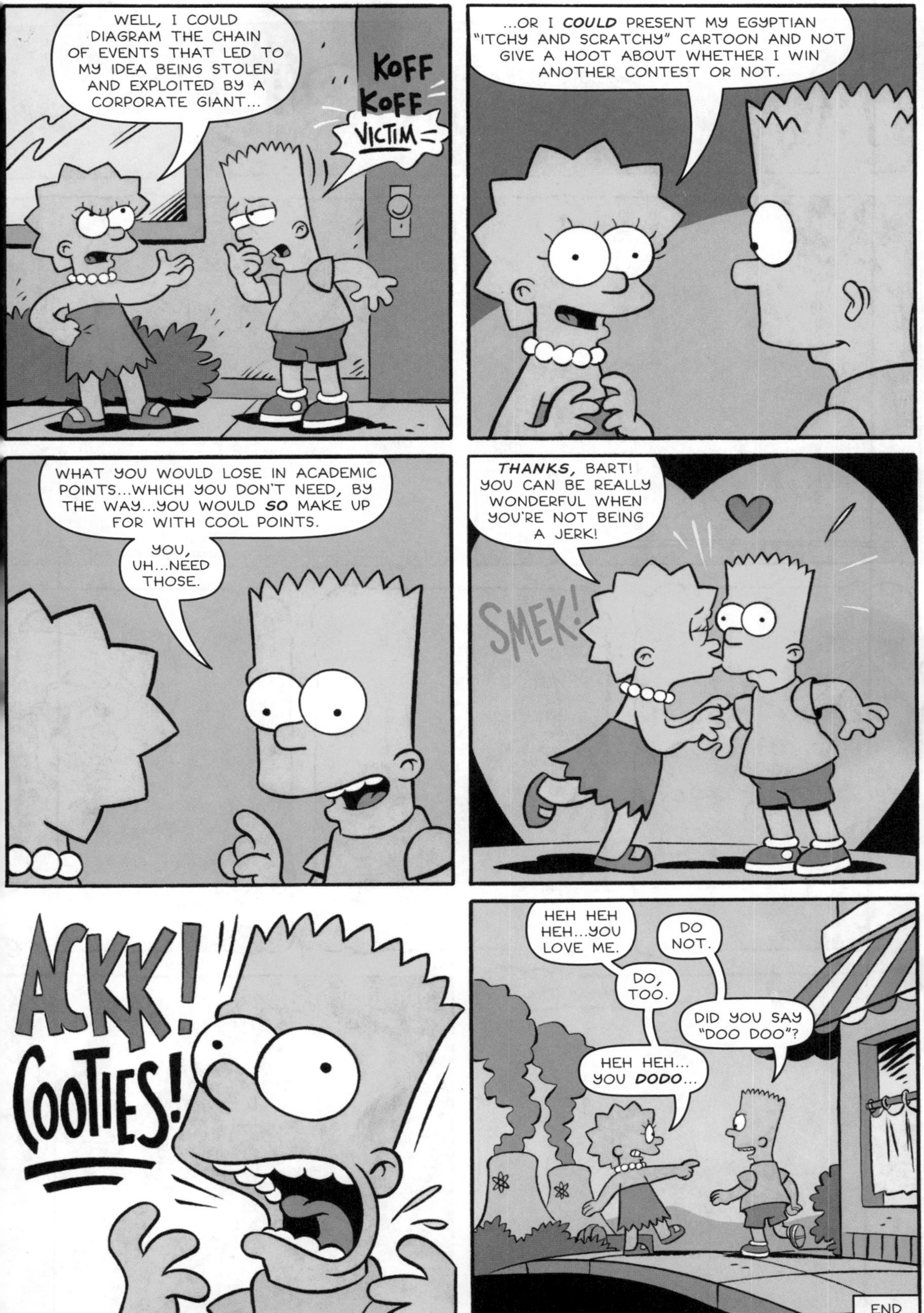
WELL, I COULD DIAGRAM THE CHAIN OF EVENTS THAT LED TO MY IDEA BEING STOLEN AND EXPLOITED BY A CORPORATE GIANT...
KOFF KOFF VICTIM
...OR I COULD PRESENT MY EGYPTIAN "ITCHY AND SCRATCHY" CARTOON AND NOT GIVE A HOOT ABOUT WHETHER I WIN ANOTHER CONTEST OR NOT.
WHAT YOU WOULD LOSE IN ACADEMIC POINTS...WHICH YOU DON'T NEED, BY THE WAY...YOU WOULD SO MAKE UP FOR WITH COOL POINTS.
YOU, UH...NEED THOSE.
THANKS, BART! YOU CAN BE REALLY WONDERFUL WHEN YOU'RE NOT BEING A JERK!
SMEK!
ACKK! COOTIES!
HEH HEH HEH...YOU LOVE ME.
DO NOT.
DO, TOO.
DID YOU SAY "DOO DOO"?
HEH HEH... YOU DODO...
END

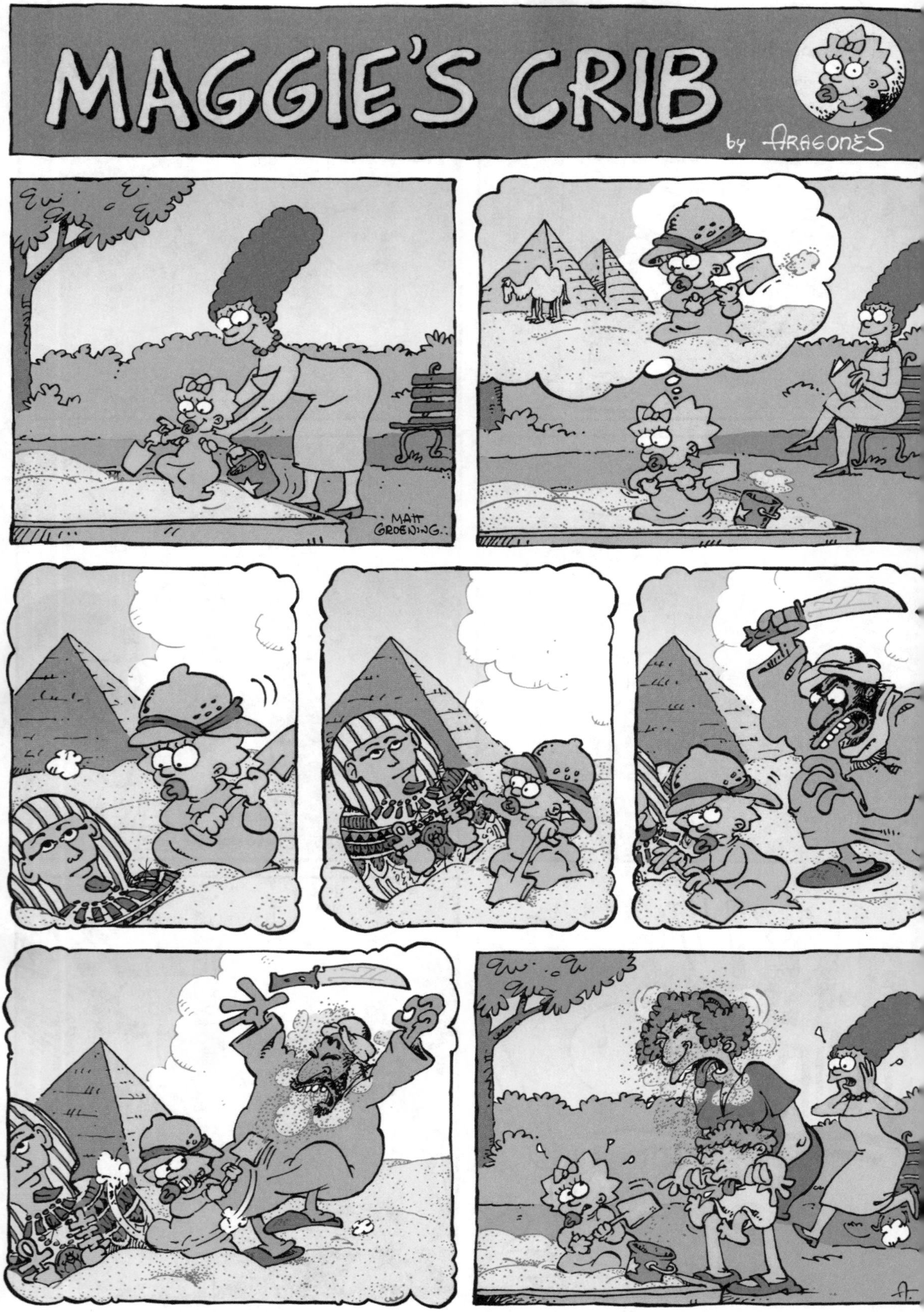
MAGGIE'S CRIB
by ARAGONES
MATT GROENING

SERGIO ARAGONÉS
STORY & ART

ART VILLANUEVA
COLORS

BILL MORRISON
EDITOR

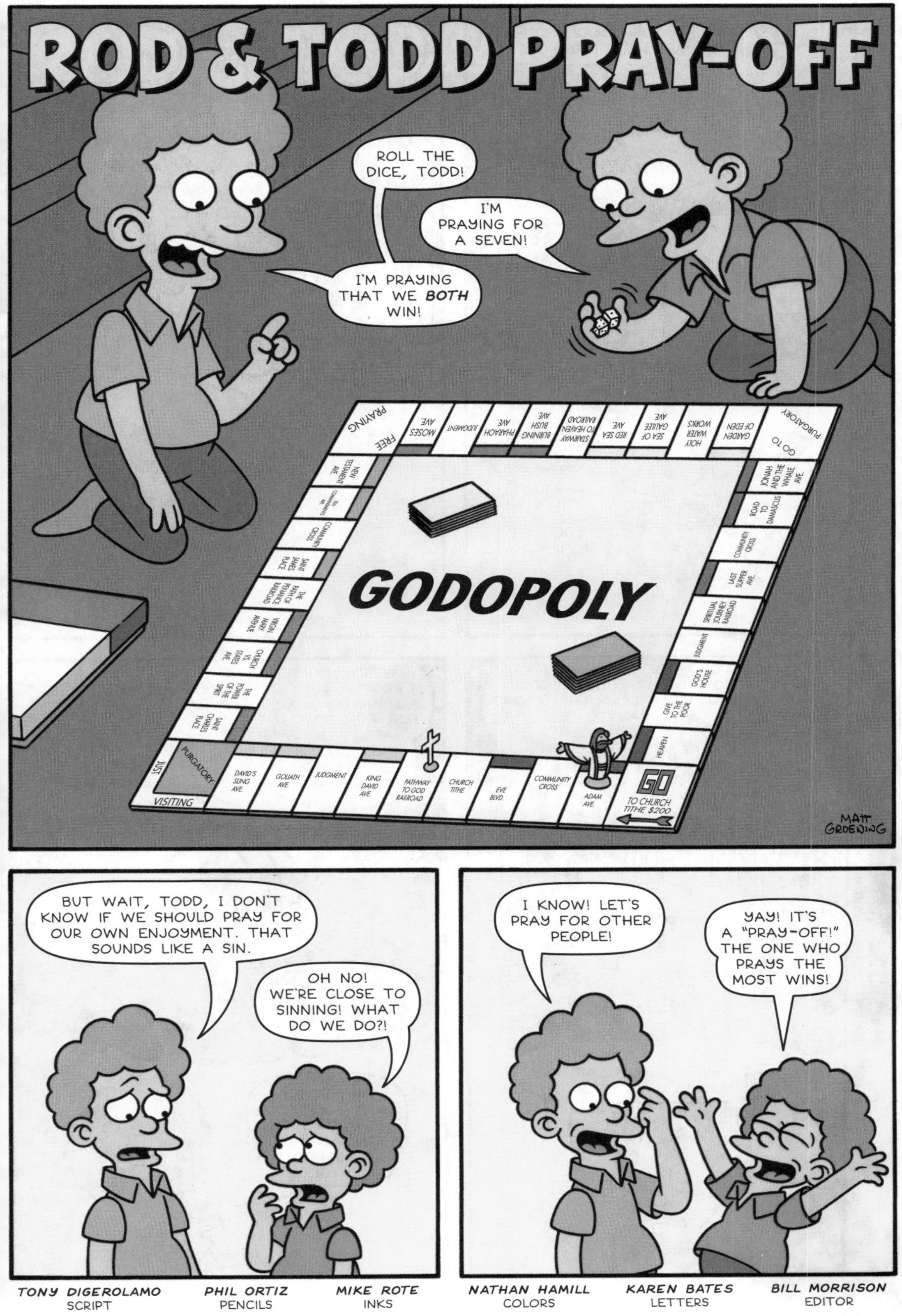
ROD & TODD PRAY-OFF
ROLL THE DICE, TODD!
I'M PRAYING THAT WE BOTH WIN!
I'M PRAYING FOR A SEVEN!
GODOPOLY
GO
TO CHURCH TITHE $200
FREE PRAYING
GO TO PURGATORY
JUST VISITING
PURGATORY
MATT GROENING
BUT WAIT, TODD, I DON'T KNOW IF WE SHOULD PRAY FOR OUR OWN ENJOYMENT. THAT SOUNDS LIKE A SIN.
OH NO! WE'RE CLOSE TO SINNING! WHAT DO WE DO?!
I KNOW! LET'S PRAY FOR OTHER PEOPLE!
YAY! IT'S A "PRAY-OFF!" THE ONE WHO PRAYS THE MOST WINS!

TONY DIGEROLAMO SCRIPT · **PHIL ORTIZ** PENCILS · **MIKE ROTE** INKS · **NATHAN HAMILL** COLORS · **KAREN BATES** LETTERS · **BILL MORRISON** EDITOR

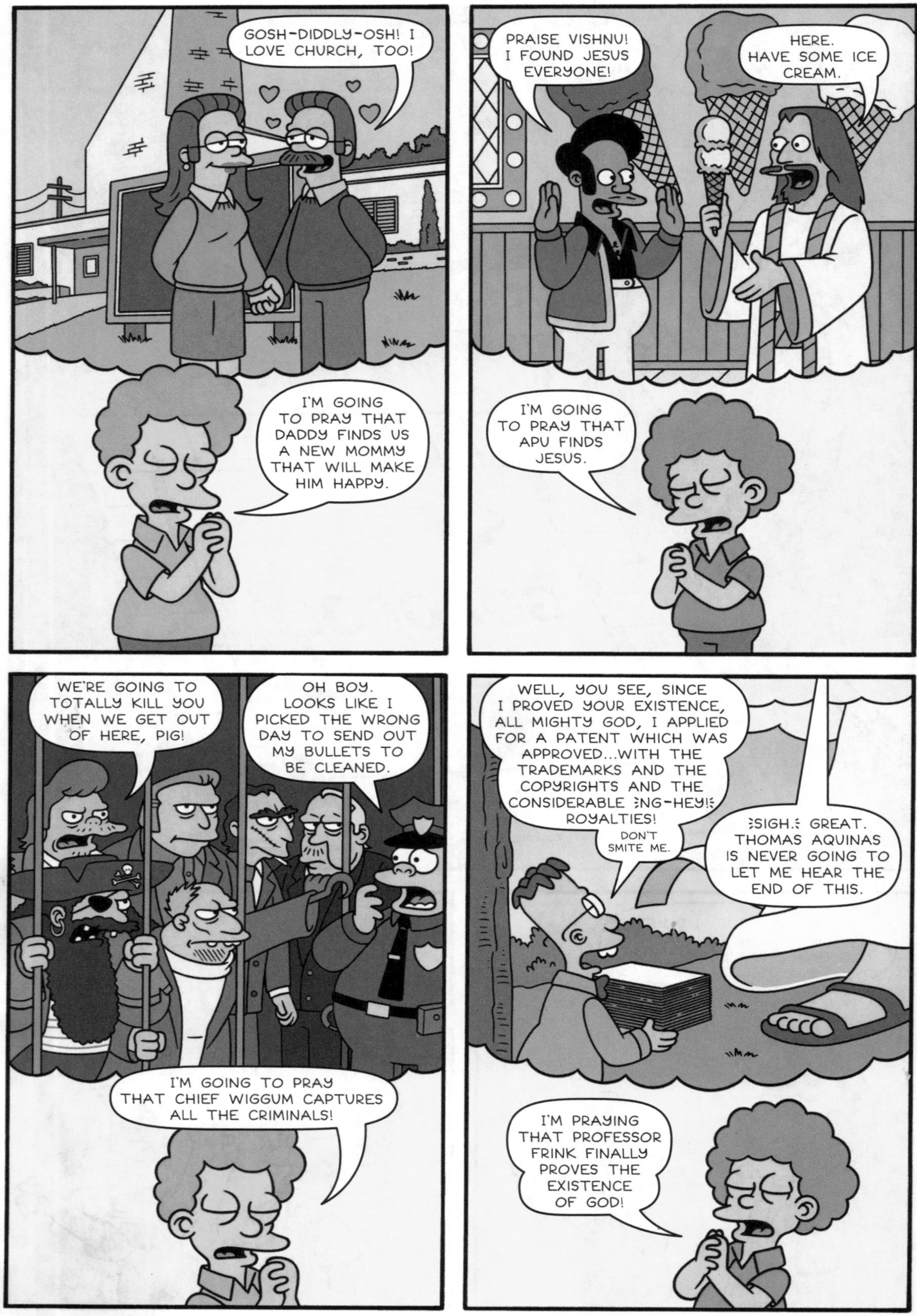
GOSH-DIDDLY-OSH! I LOVE CHURCH, TOO!
I'M GOING TO PRAY THAT DADDY FINDS US A NEW MOMMY THAT WILL MAKE HIM HAPPY.
PRAISE VISHNU! I FOUND JESUS EVERYONE!
HERE. HAVE SOME ICE CREAM.
I'M GOING TO PRAY THAT APU FINDS JESUS.
WE'RE GOING TO TOTALLY KILL YOU WHEN WE GET OUT OF HERE, PIG!
OH BOY. LOOKS LIKE I PICKED THE WRONG DAY TO SEND OUT MY BULLETS TO BE CLEANED.
I'M GOING TO PRAY THAT CHIEF WIGGUM CAPTURES ALL THE CRIMINALS!
WELL, YOU SEE, SINCE I PROVED YOUR EXISTENCE, ALL MIGHTY GOD, I APPLIED FOR A PATENT WHICH WAS APPROVED...WITH THE TRADEMARKS AND THE COPYRIGHTS AND THE CONSIDERABLE :NG-HEY!: ROYALTIES!
DON'T SMITE ME.
:SIGH.: GREAT. THOMAS AQUINAS IS NEVER GOING TO LET ME HEAR THE END OF THIS.
I'M PRAYING THAT PROFESSOR FRINK FINALLY PROVES THE EXISTENCE OF GOD!

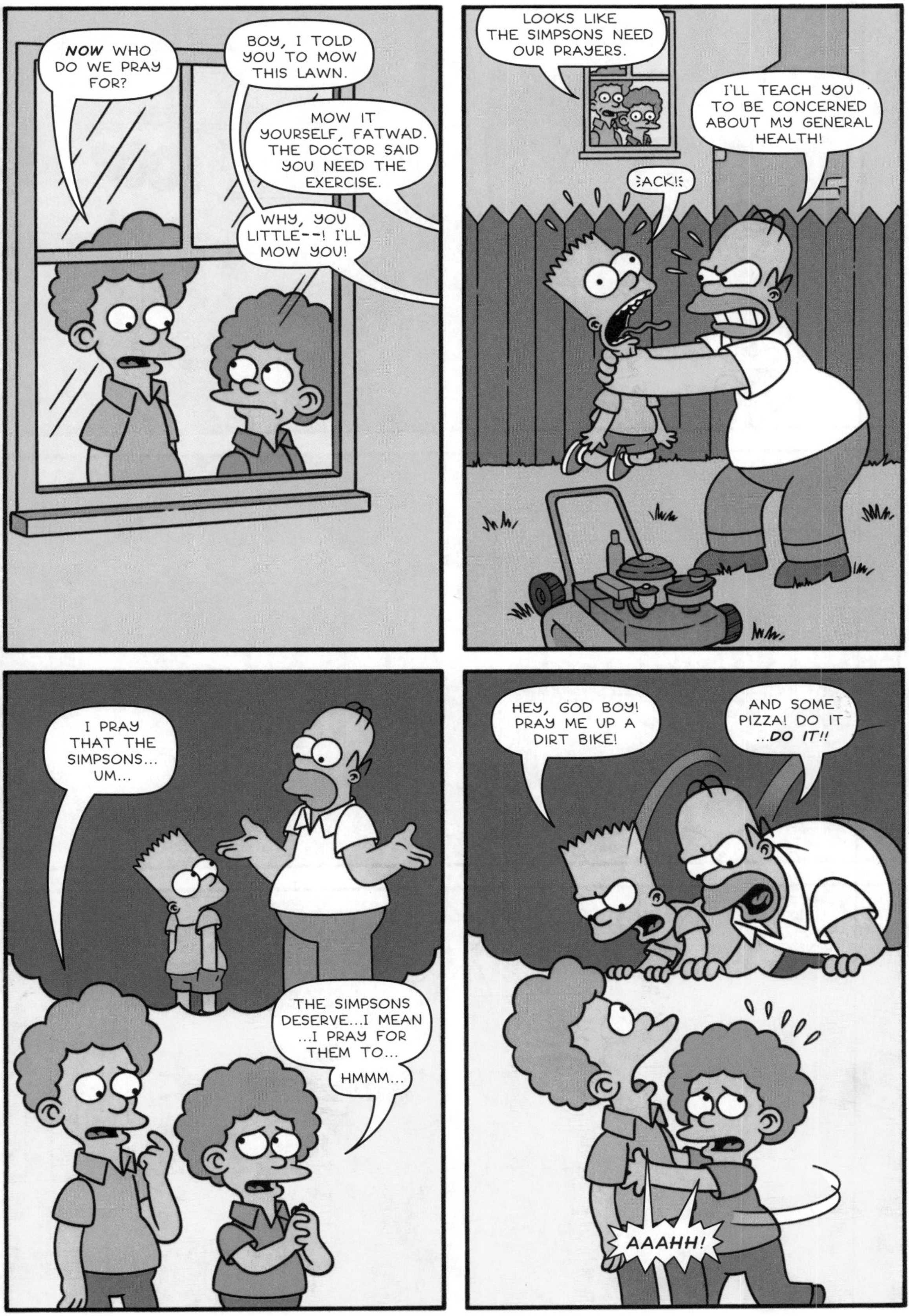

NOW WHO DO WE PRAY FOR?
BOY, I TOLD YOU TO MOW THIS LAWN.
MOW IT YOURSELF, FATWAD. THE DOCTOR SAID YOU NEED THE EXERCISE.
WHY, YOU LITTLE--! I'LL MOW YOU!
LOOKS LIKE THE SIMPSONS NEED OUR PRAYERS.
I'LL TEACH YOU TO BE CONCERNED ABOUT MY GENERAL HEALTH!
ACK!
I PRAY THAT THE SIMPSONS... UM...
THE SIMPSONS DESERVE...I MEAN ...I PRAY FOR THEM TO...
HMMM...
HEY, GOD BOY! PRAY ME UP A DIRT BIKE!
AND SOME PIZZA! DO IT ...DO IT!!
AAAHH!

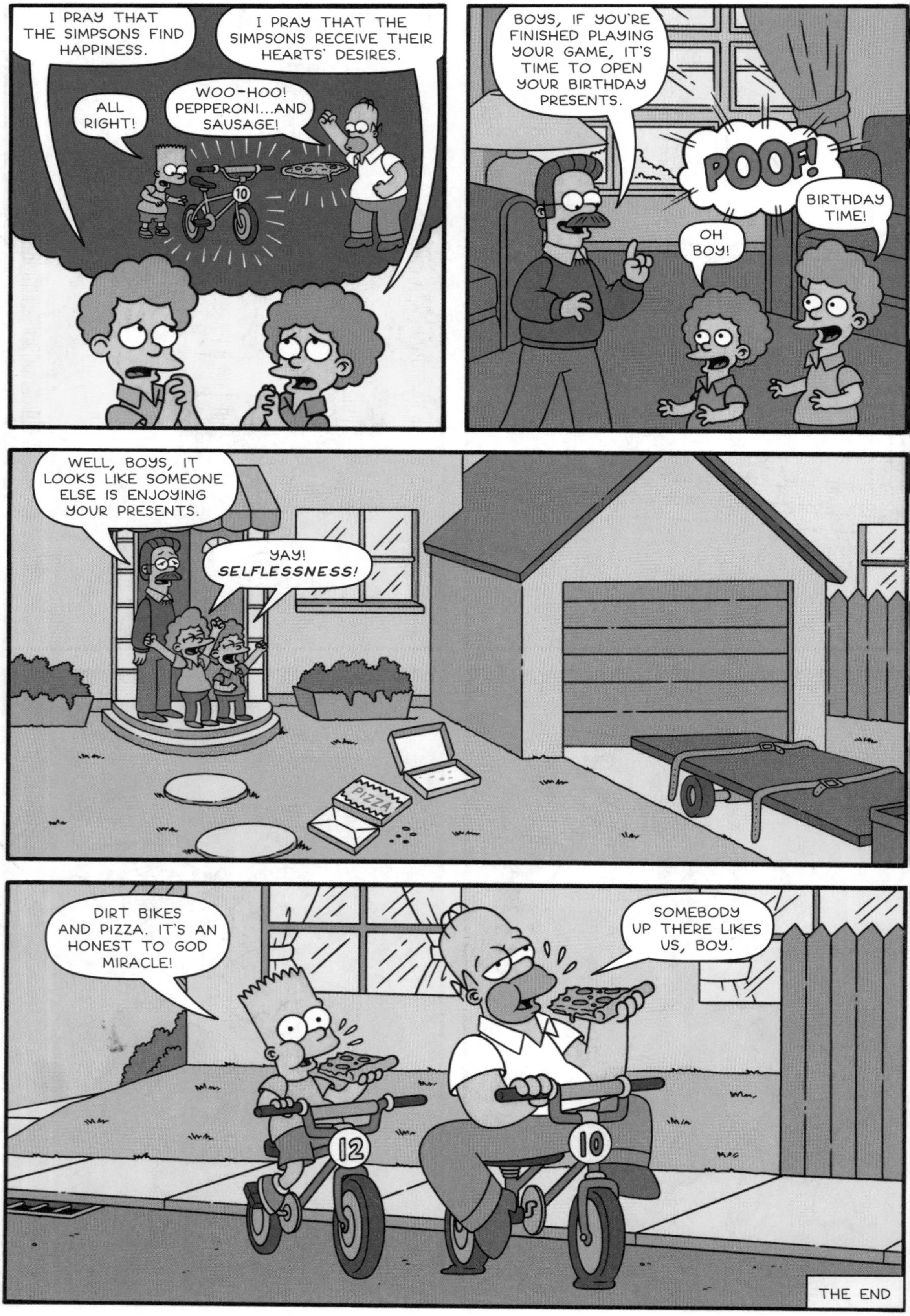
I PRAY THAT THE SIMPSONS FIND HAPPINESS.
I PRAY THAT THE SIMPSONS RECEIVE THEIR HEARTS' DESIRES.
ALL RIGHT!
WOO-HOO! PEPPERONI...AND SAUSAGE!
10
BOYS, IF YOU'RE FINISHED PLAYING YOUR GAME, IT'S TIME TO OPEN YOUR BIRTHDAY PRESENTS.
POOF!
OH BOY!
BIRTHDAY TIME!
WELL, BOYS, IT LOOKS LIKE SOMEONE ELSE IS ENJOYING YOUR PRESENTS.
YAY! *SELFLESSNESS!*
PIZZA
DIRT BIKES AND PIZZA. IT'S AN HONEST TO GOD MIRACLE!
SOMEBODY UP THERE LIKES US, BOY.
12
10
THE END

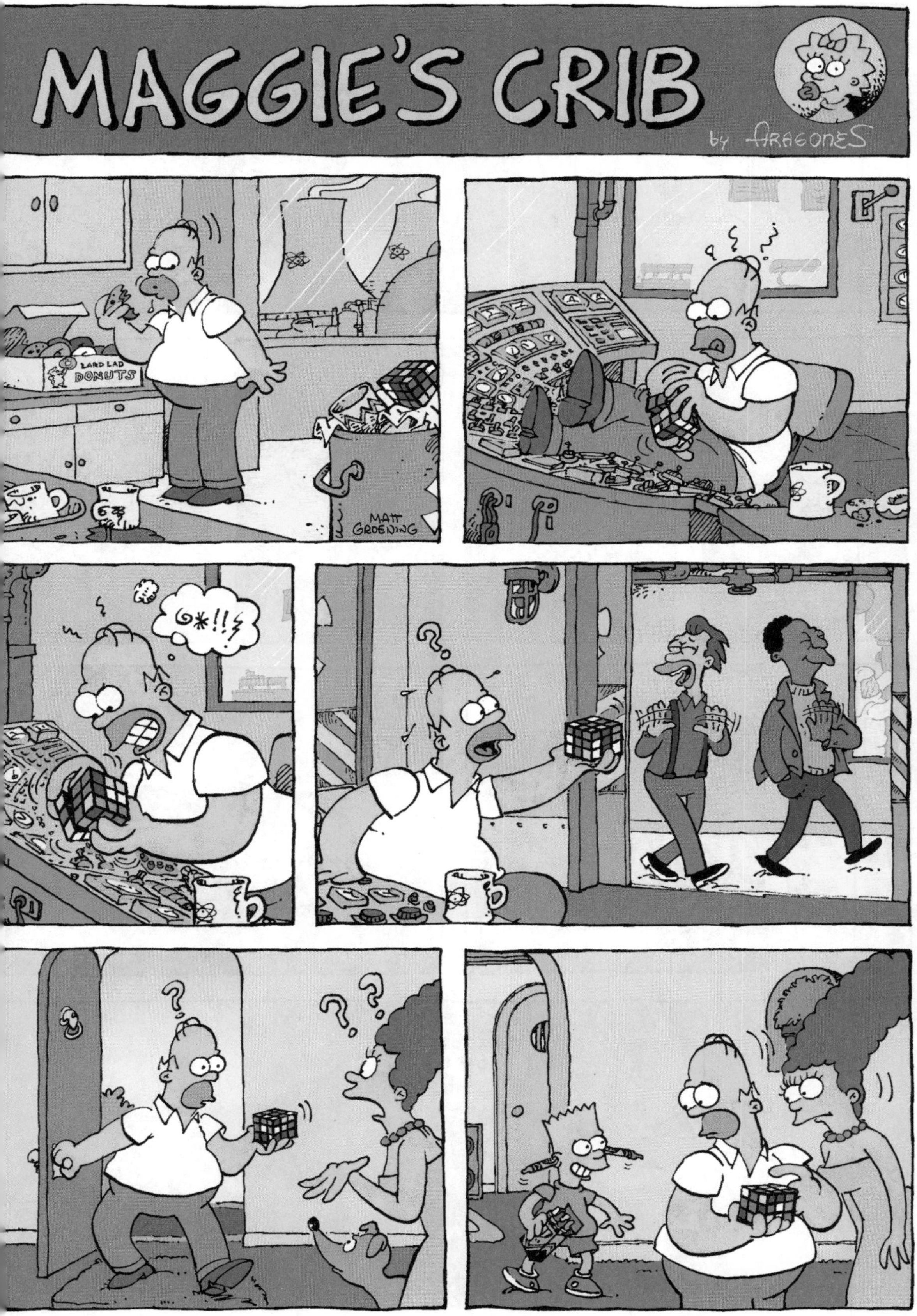
MAGGIE'S CRIB
by ARAGONES
LARD LAD DONUTS
MATT GROENING

SERGIO ARAGONÉS
STORY & ART

ART VILLANUEVA
COLORS

BILL MORRISON
EDITOR

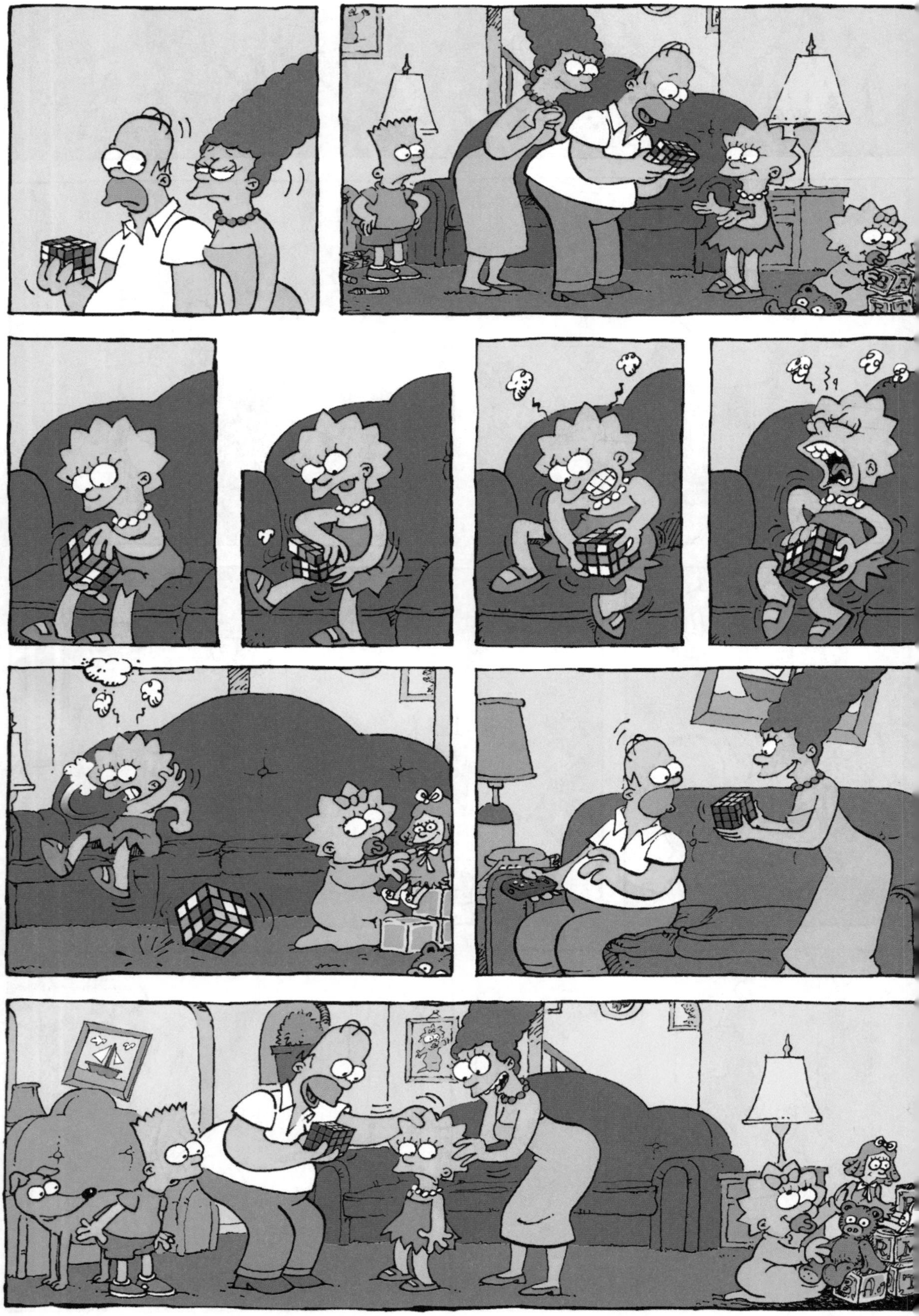

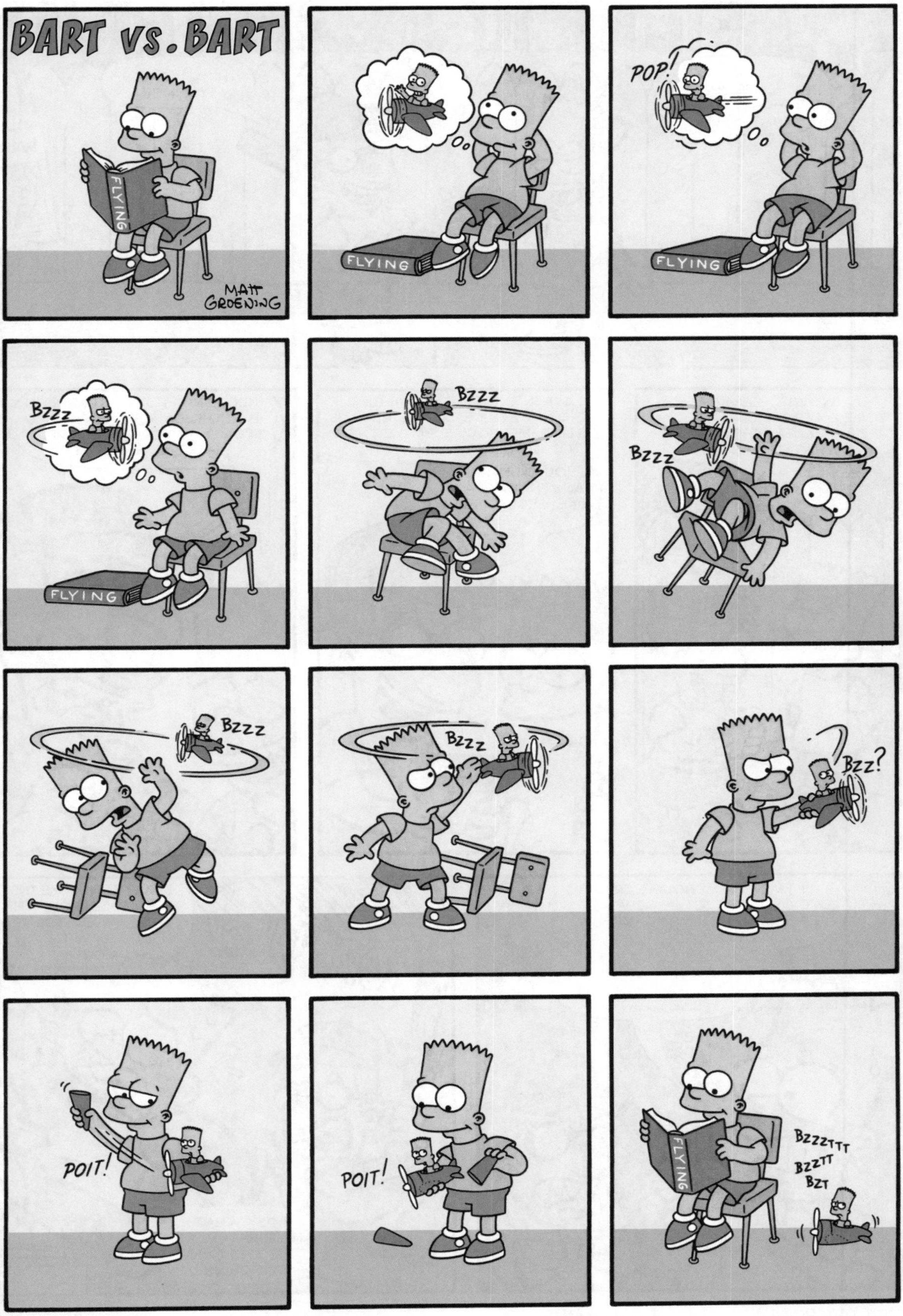
BART VS. BART
MATT GROENING
FLYING
FLYING
POP!
FLYING
BZZZ
FLYING
BZZZ
BZZZ
BZZZ
BZZZ
BZZ?
POIT!
POIT!
FLYING
BZZZTTT
BZZTT
BZT

MARY TRAINOR
STORY

MIKE ROTE
PENCILS & INKS

NATHAN HAMILL
COLORS

BILL MORRISON
EDITOR

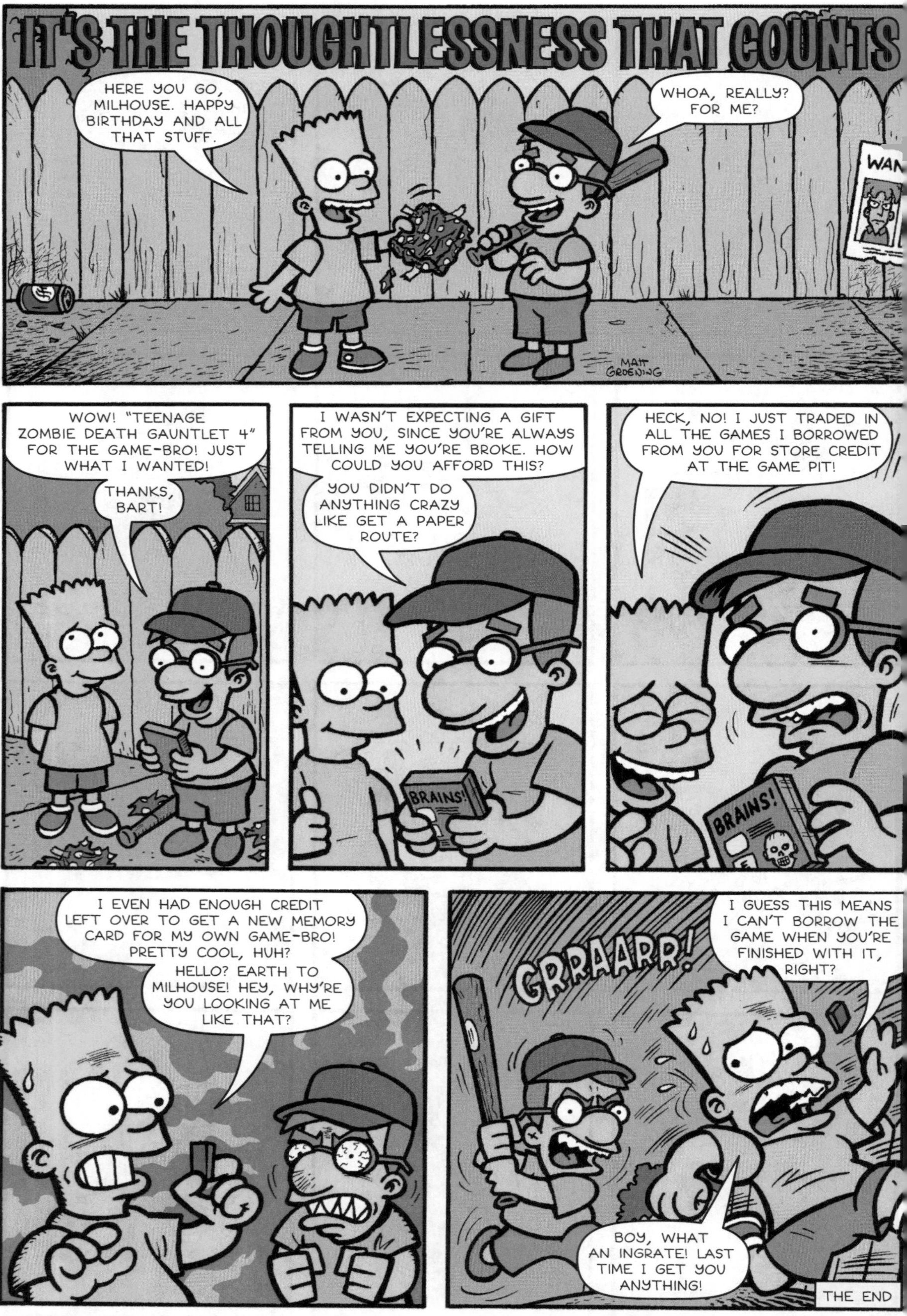
IT'S THE THOUGHTLESSNESS THAT COUNTS
HERE YOU GO, MILHOUSE. HAPPY BIRTHDAY AND ALL THAT STUFF.
WHOA, REALLY? FOR ME?
MATT GROENING
WOW! "TEENAGE ZOMBIE DEATH GAUNTLET 4" FOR THE GAME-BRO! JUST WHAT I WANTED!
THANKS, BART!
I WASN'T EXPECTING A GIFT FROM YOU, SINCE YOU'RE ALWAYS TELLING ME YOU'RE BROKE. HOW COULD YOU AFFORD THIS?
YOU DIDN'T DO ANYTHING CRAZY LIKE GET A PAPER ROUTE?
BRAINS!
HECK, NO! I JUST TRADED IN ALL THE GAMES I BORROWED FROM YOU FOR STORE CREDIT AT THE GAME PIT!
BRAINS!
I EVEN HAD ENOUGH CREDIT LEFT OVER TO GET A NEW MEMORY CARD FOR MY OWN GAME-BRO! PRETTY COOL, HUH?
HELLO? EARTH TO MILHOUSE! HEY, WHY'RE YOU LOOKING AT ME LIKE THAT?
GRRAARR!
I GUESS THIS MEANS I CAN'T BORROW THE GAME WHEN YOU'RE FINISHED WITH IT, RIGHT?
BOY, WHAT AN INGRATE! LAST TIME I GET YOU ANYTHING!
THE END

EVAN DORKIN
STORY & ART

SARAH DYER
COLORS

KAREN BATES
LETTERS

BILL MORRISON
EDITOR

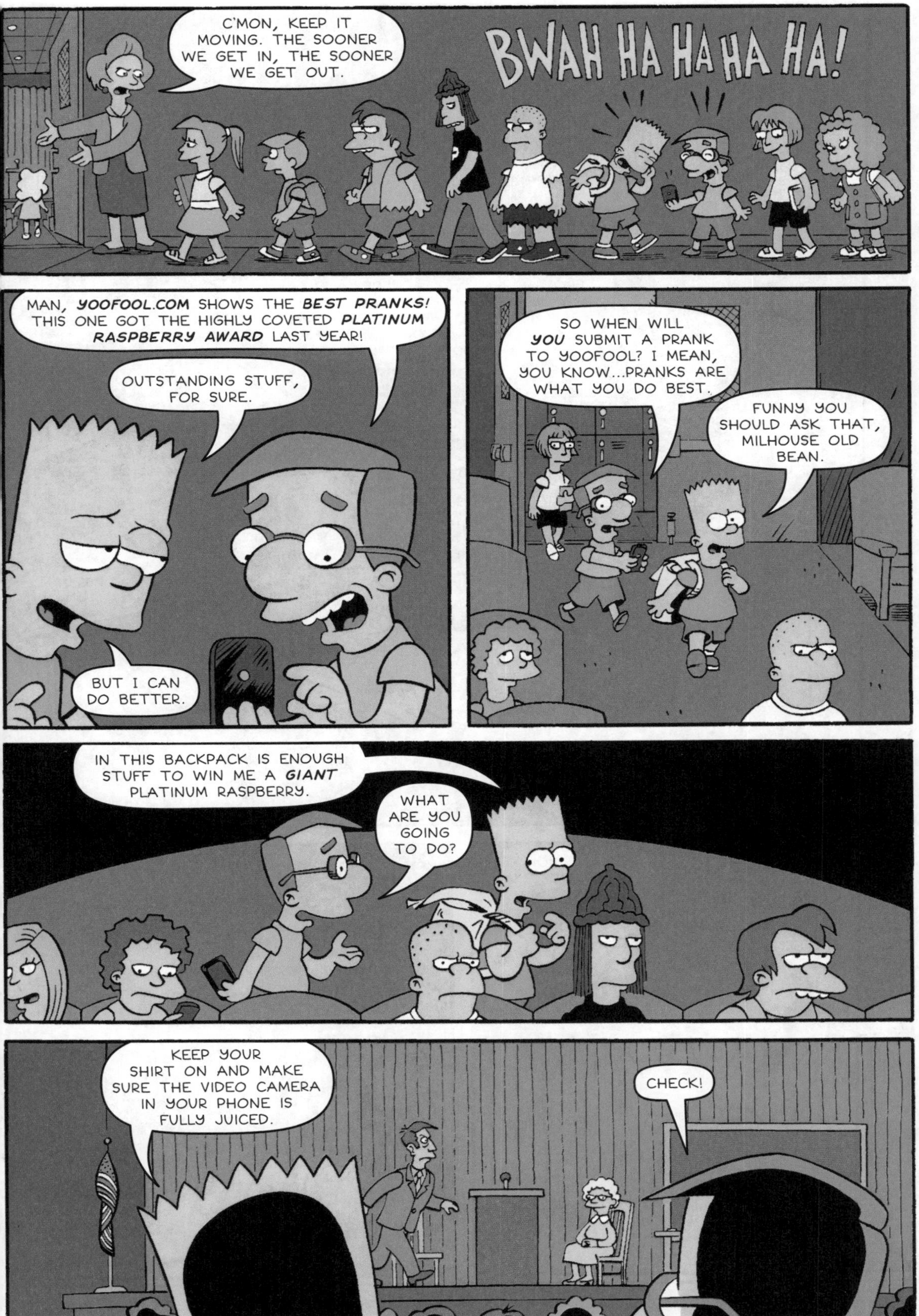
C'MON, KEEP IT MOVING. THE SOONER WE GET IN, THE SOONER WE GET OUT.
BWAH HA HA HA HA!
MAN, YOOFOOL.COM SHOWS THE BEST PRANKS! THIS ONE GOT THE HIGHLY COVETED PLATINUM RASPBERRY AWARD LAST YEAR!
OUTSTANDING STUFF, FOR SURE.
BUT I CAN DO BETTER.
SO WHEN WILL YOU SUBMIT A PRANK TO YOOFOOL? I MEAN, YOU KNOW...PRANKS ARE WHAT YOU DO BEST.
FUNNY YOU SHOULD ASK THAT, MILHOUSE OLD BEAN.
IN THIS BACKPACK IS ENOUGH STUFF TO WIN ME A GIANT PLATINUM RASPBERRY.
WHAT ARE YOU GOING TO DO?
KEEP YOUR SHIRT ON AND MAKE SURE THE VIDEO CAMERA IN YOUR PHONE IS FULLY JUICED.
CHECK!

PRANKS A LOT!

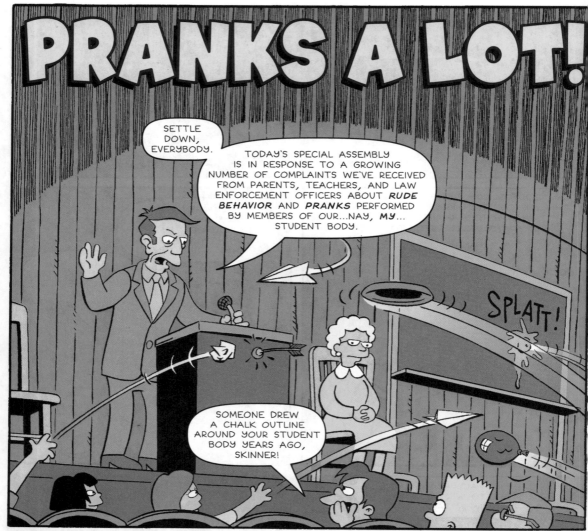

SETTLE DOWN, EVERYBODY.

TODAY'S SPECIAL ASSEMBLY IS IN RESPONSE TO A GROWING NUMBER OF COMPLAINTS WE'VE RECEIVED FROM PARENTS, TEACHERS, AND LAW ENFORCEMENT OFFICERS ABOUT *RUDE BEHAVIOR* AND *PRANKS* PERFORMED BY MEMBERS OF OUR...NAY, *MY*... STUDENT BODY.

SPLATT!

SOMEONE DREW A CHALK OUTLINE AROUND YOUR STUDENT BODY YEARS AGO, SKINNER!

THANK YOU FOR SO *DEFTLY* ILLUSTRATING THE PROBLEM, NELSON.

HEH HEH HEH!

DID HE CALL ME *DEAF*?

WHAT?

MATT GROENING

CAROL LAY
STORY & ART

ART VILLANUEVA
COLORS

KAREN BATES
LETTERS

BILL MORRISON
EDITOR

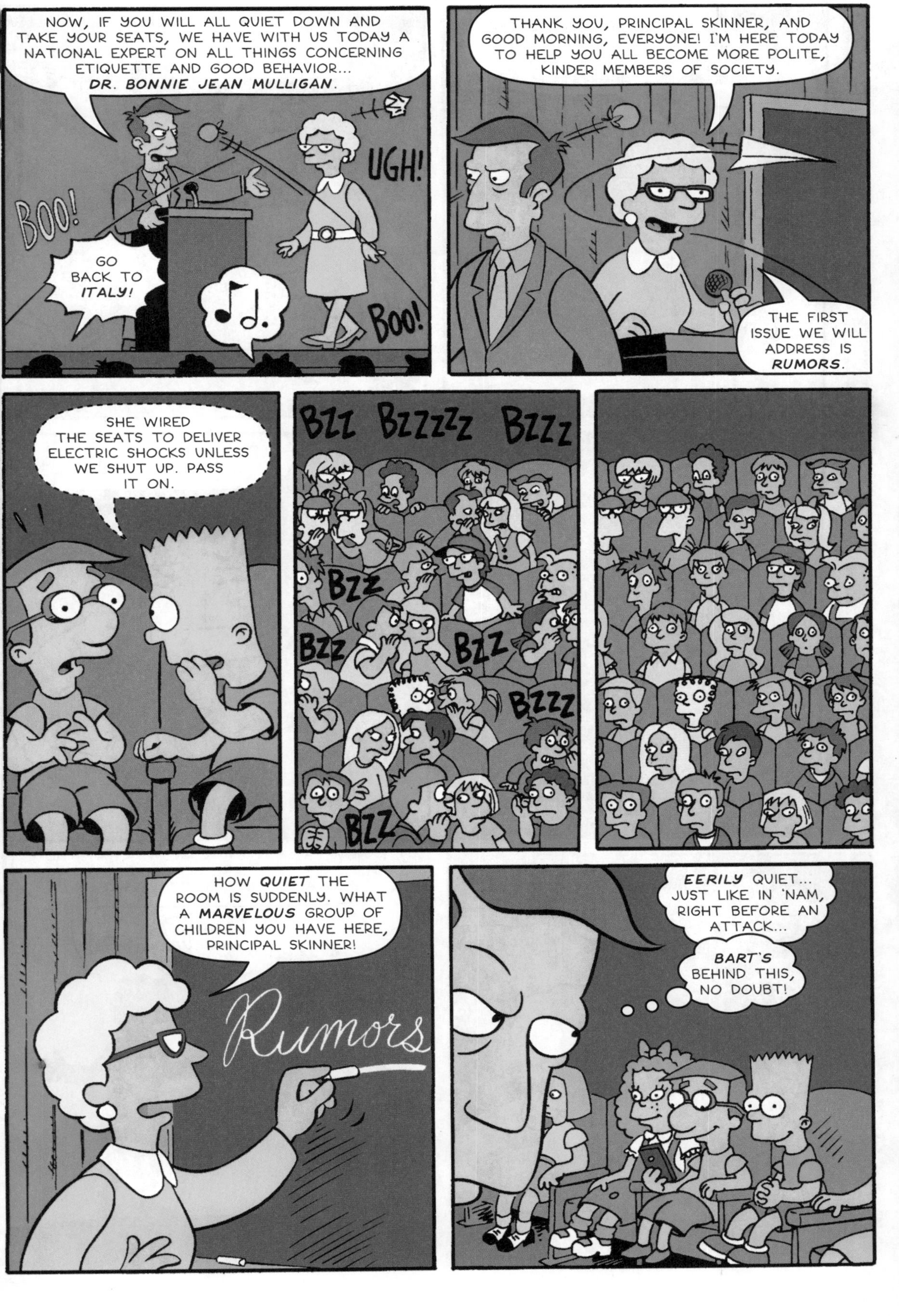
NOW, IF YOU WILL ALL QUIET DOWN AND TAKE YOUR SEATS, WE HAVE WITH US TODAY A NATIONAL EXPERT ON ALL THINGS CONCERNING ETIQUETTE AND GOOD BEHAVIOR... **DR. BONNIE JEAN MULLIGAN**.
UGH!
BOO!
GO BACK TO ***ITALY!***
BOO!
THANK YOU, PRINCIPAL SKINNER, AND GOOD MORNING, EVERYONE! I'M HERE TODAY TO HELP YOU ALL BECOME MORE POLITE, KINDER MEMBERS OF SOCIETY.
THE FIRST ISSUE WE WILL ADDRESS IS ***RUMORS***.
SHE WIRED THE SEATS TO DELIVER ELECTRIC SHOCKS UNLESS WE SHUT UP. PASS IT ON.
BZZ BZZZZZ BZZZ
BZZ
BZZ
BZZ
BZZZ
BZZ
HOW ***QUIET*** THE ROOM IS SUDDENLY. WHAT A ***MARVELOUS*** GROUP OF CHILDREN YOU HAVE HERE, PRINCIPAL SKINNER!
Rumors
EERILY QUIET... JUST LIKE IN 'NAM, RIGHT BEFORE AN ATTACK...
BART'S BEHIND THIS, NO DOUBT!

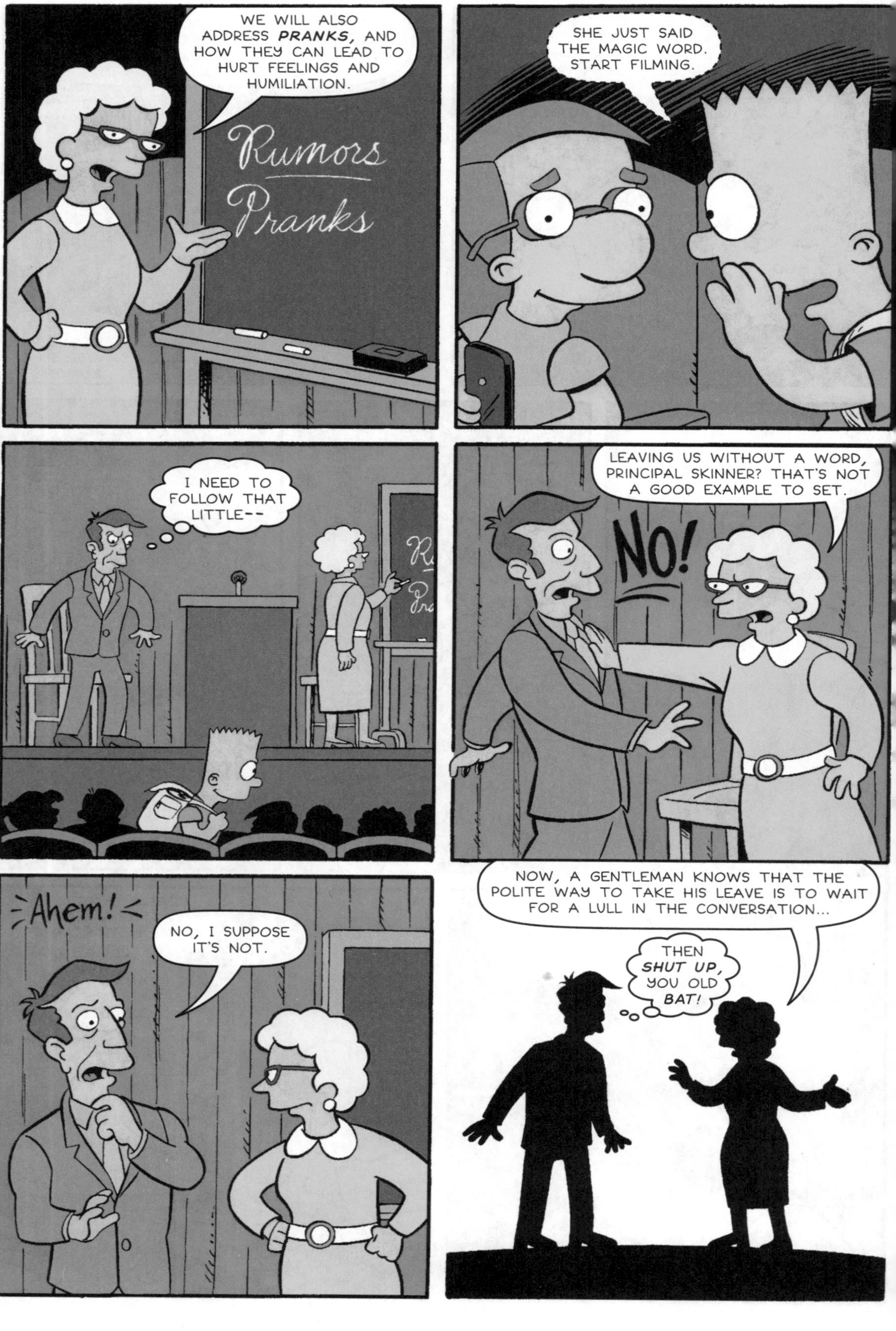
WE WILL ALSO ADDRESS **PRANKS,** AND HOW THEY CAN LEAD TO HURT FEELINGS AND HUMILIATION.
Rumors
Pranks
SHE JUST SAID THE MAGIC WORD. START FILMING.
I NEED TO FOLLOW THAT LITTLE--
LEAVING US WITHOUT A WORD, PRINCIPAL SKINNER? THAT'S NOT A GOOD EXAMPLE TO SET.
NO!
Ahem!
NO, I SUPPOSE IT'S NOT.
NOW, A GENTLEMAN KNOWS THAT THE POLITE WAY TO TAKE HIS LEAVE IS TO WAIT FOR A LULL IN THE CONVERSATION...
THEN **SHUT UP,** YOU OLD **BAT!**

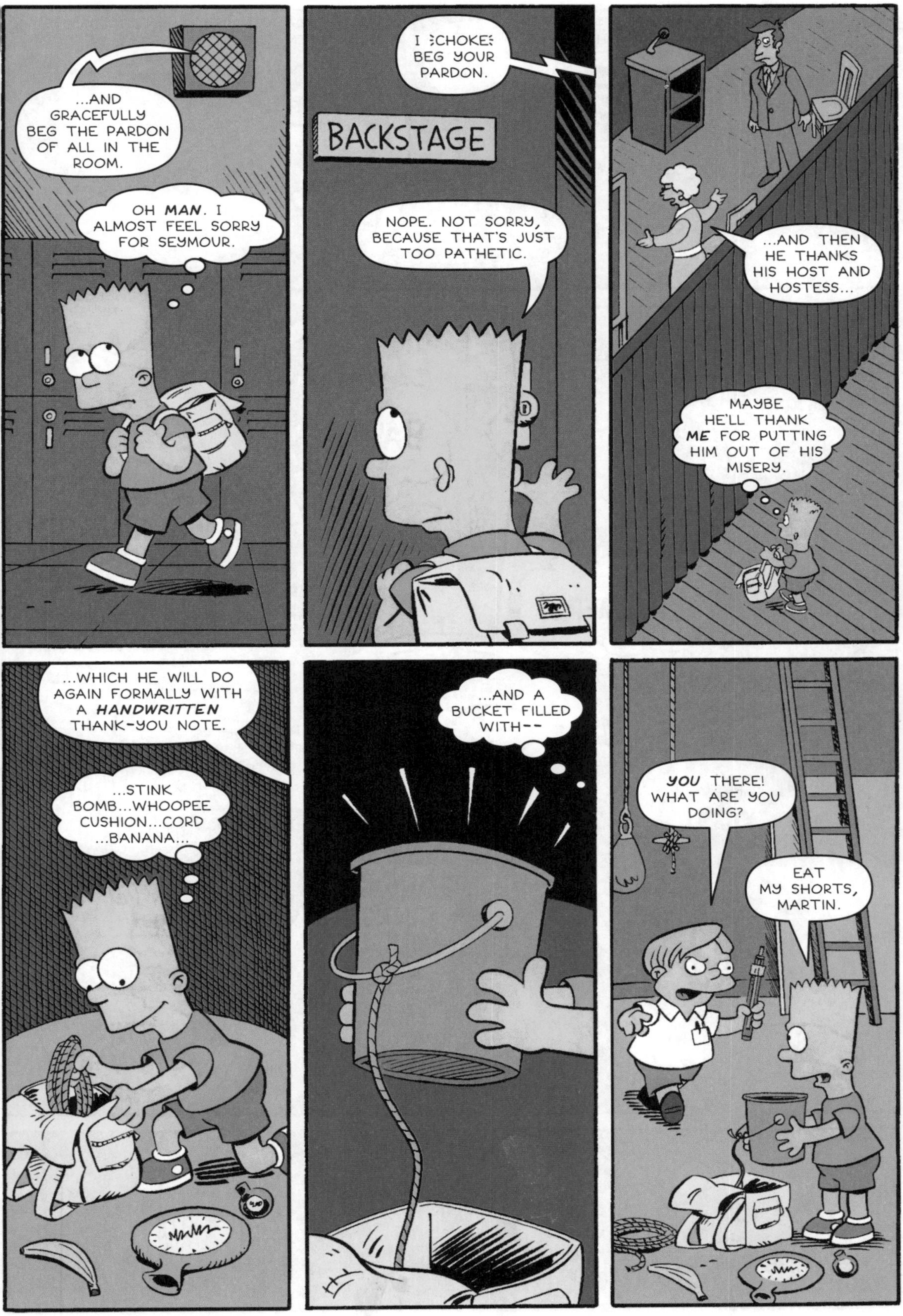
...AND GRACEFULLY BEG THE PARDON OF ALL IN THE ROOM.
OH MAN. I ALMOST FEEL SORRY FOR SEYMOUR.
I :CHOKE: BEG YOUR PARDON.
BACKSTAGE
NOPE. NOT SORRY, BECAUSE THAT'S JUST TOO PATHETIC.
...AND THEN HE THANKS HIS HOST AND HOSTESS...
MAYBE HE'LL THANK ME FOR PUTTING HIM OUT OF HIS MISERY.
...WHICH HE WILL DO AGAIN FORMALLY WITH A HANDWRITTEN THANK-YOU NOTE.
...STINK BOMB...WHOOPEE CUSHION...CORD ...BANANA...
...AND A BUCKET FILLED WITH--
YOU THERE! WHAT ARE YOU DOING?
EAT MY SHORTS, MARTIN.

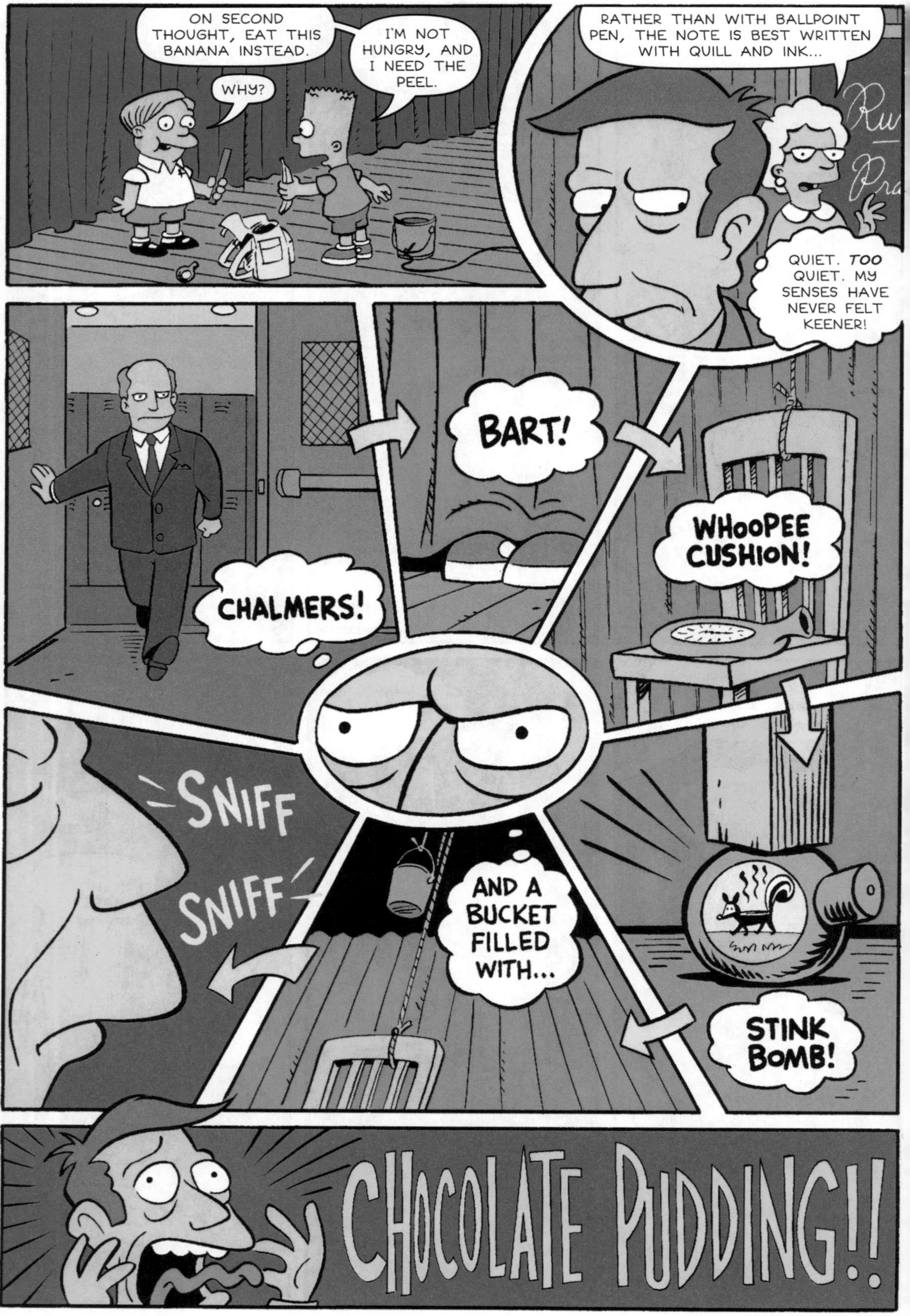

ON SECOND THOUGHT, EAT THIS BANANA INSTEAD.
WHY?
I'M NOT HUNGRY, AND I NEED THE PEEL.
RATHER THAN WITH BALLPOINT PEN, THE NOTE IS BEST WRITTEN WITH QUILL AND INK...
QUIET. TOO QUIET. MY SENSES HAVE NEVER FELT KEENER!
CHALMERS!
BART!
WHOOPEE CUSHION!
SNIFF
SNIFF
AND A BUCKET FILLED WITH...
STINK BOMB!
CHOCOLATE PUDDING!!

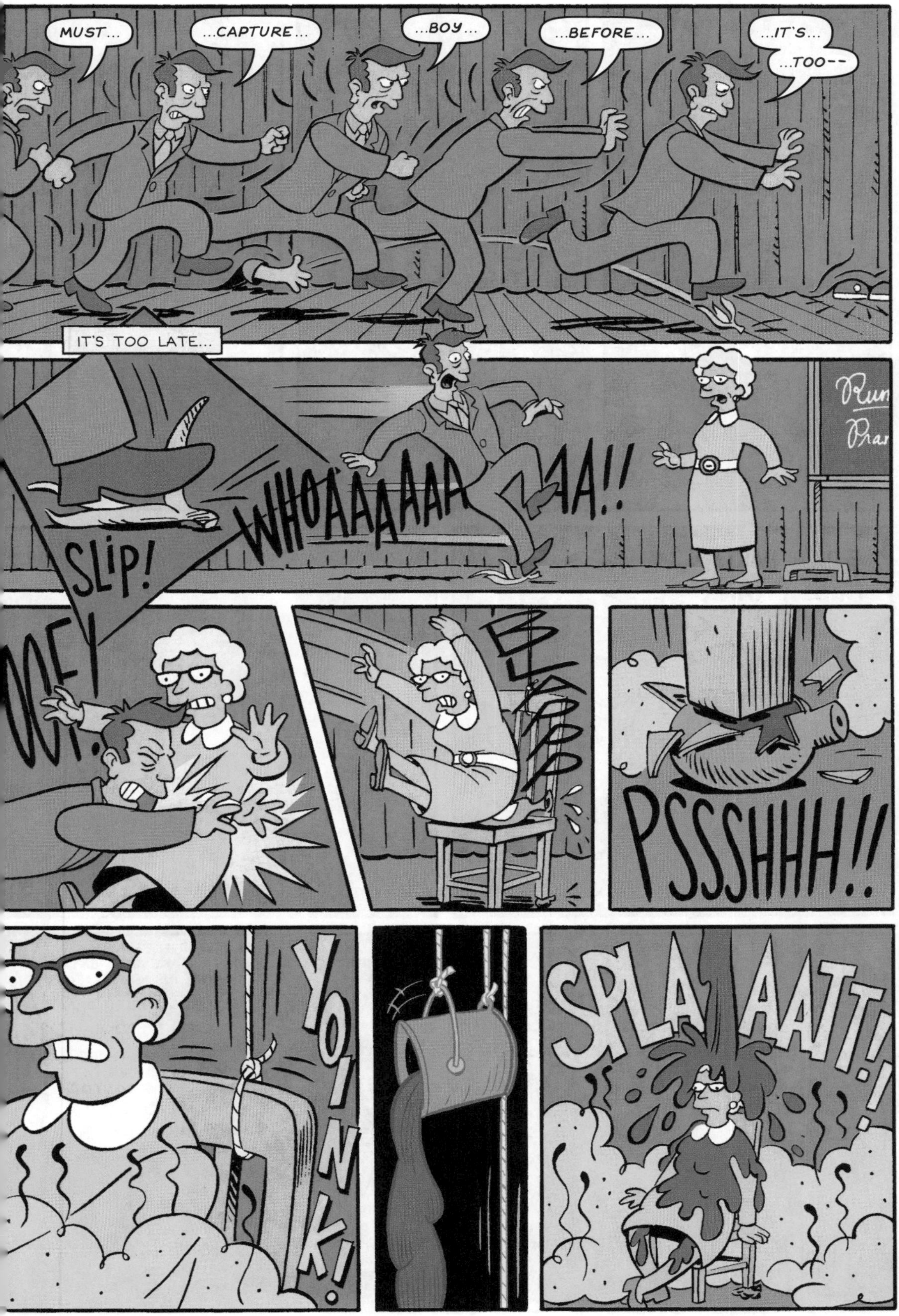
MUST...
...CAPTURE...
...BOY...
...BEFORE...
...IT'S...
...TOO--
IT'S TOO LATE...
SLIP!
WHOAAAAAA
AA!!
PSSSHHH!!
YOINK!
SPLA
AATT!!

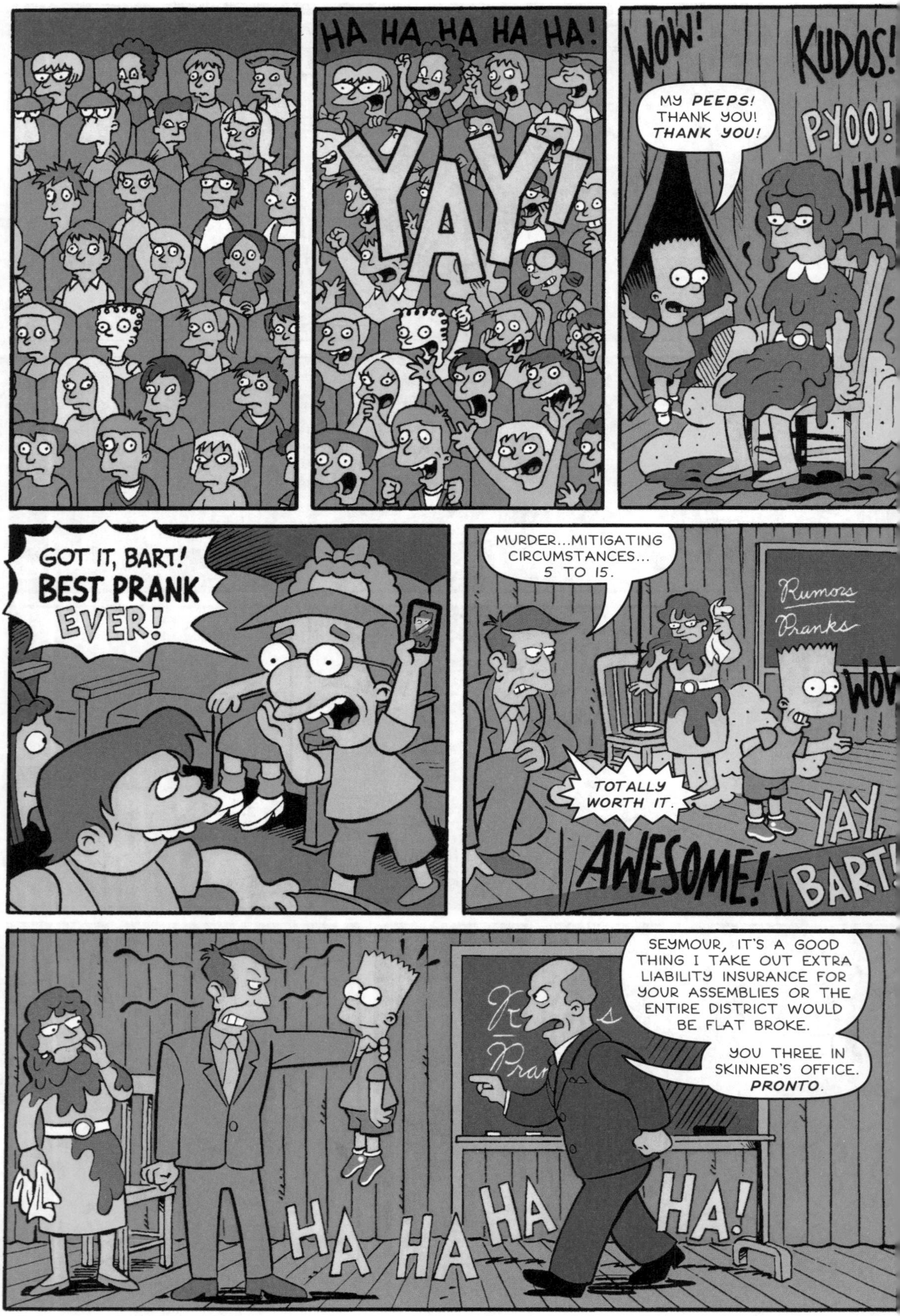

HA HA HA HA HA!
YAY!
WOW!
KUDOS!
MY PEEPS! THANK YOU! THANK YOU!
P-YOO!
GOT IT, BART! BEST PRANK EVER!
MURDER...MITIGATING CIRCUMSTANCES... 5 TO 15.
Rumors
Pranks
TOTALLY WORTH IT.
AWESOME!
YAY, BART!
SEYMOUR, IT'S A GOOD THING I TAKE OUT EXTRA LIABILITY INSURANCE FOR YOUR ASSEMBLIES OR THE ENTIRE DISTRICT WOULD BE FLAT BROKE.
YOU THREE IN SKINNER'S OFFICE. PRONTO.
HA HA HA HA!

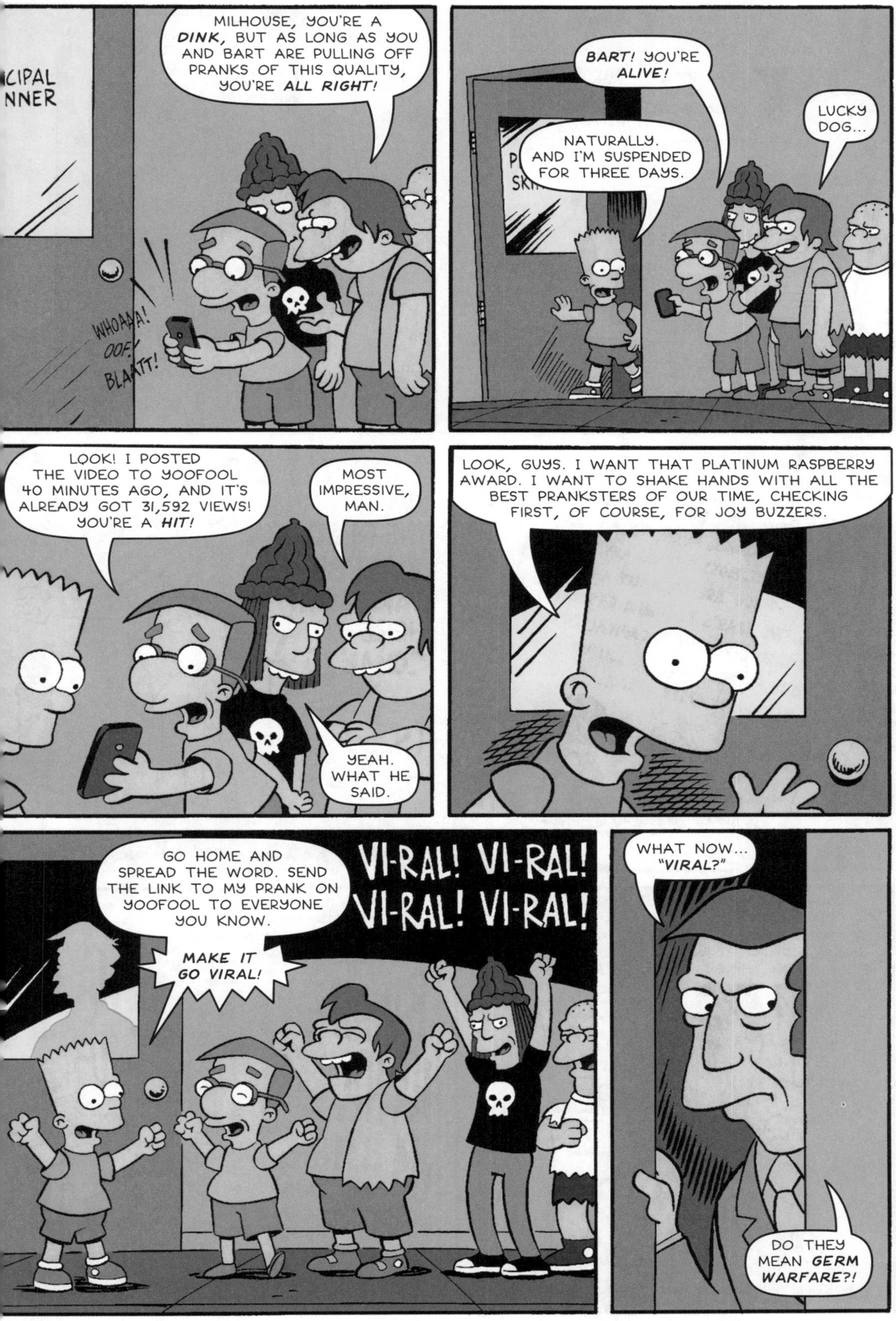
CIPAL
NNER
MILHOUSE, YOU'RE A DINK, BUT AS LONG AS YOU AND BART ARE PULLING OFF PRANKS OF THIS QUALITY, YOU'RE ALL RIGHT!
WHOAAA! OOF! BLAATT!
BART! YOU'RE ALIVE!
NATURALLY. AND I'M SUSPENDED FOR THREE DAYS.
LUCKY DOG...
LOOK! I POSTED THE VIDEO TO YOOFOOL 40 MINUTES AGO, AND IT'S ALREADY GOT 31,592 VIEWS! YOU'RE A HIT!
MOST IMPRESSIVE, MAN.
YEAH. WHAT HE SAID.
LOOK, GUYS. I WANT THAT PLATINUM RASPBERRY AWARD. I WANT TO SHAKE HANDS WITH ALL THE BEST PRANKSTERS OF OUR TIME, CHECKING FIRST, OF COURSE, FOR JOY BUZZERS.
GO HOME AND SPREAD THE WORD. SEND THE LINK TO MY PRANK ON YOOFOOL TO EVERYONE YOU KNOW.
MAKE IT GO VIRAL!
VI-RAL! VI-RAL! VI-RAL! VI-RAL!
WHAT NOW... "VIRAL?"
DO THEY MEAN GERM WARFARE?!

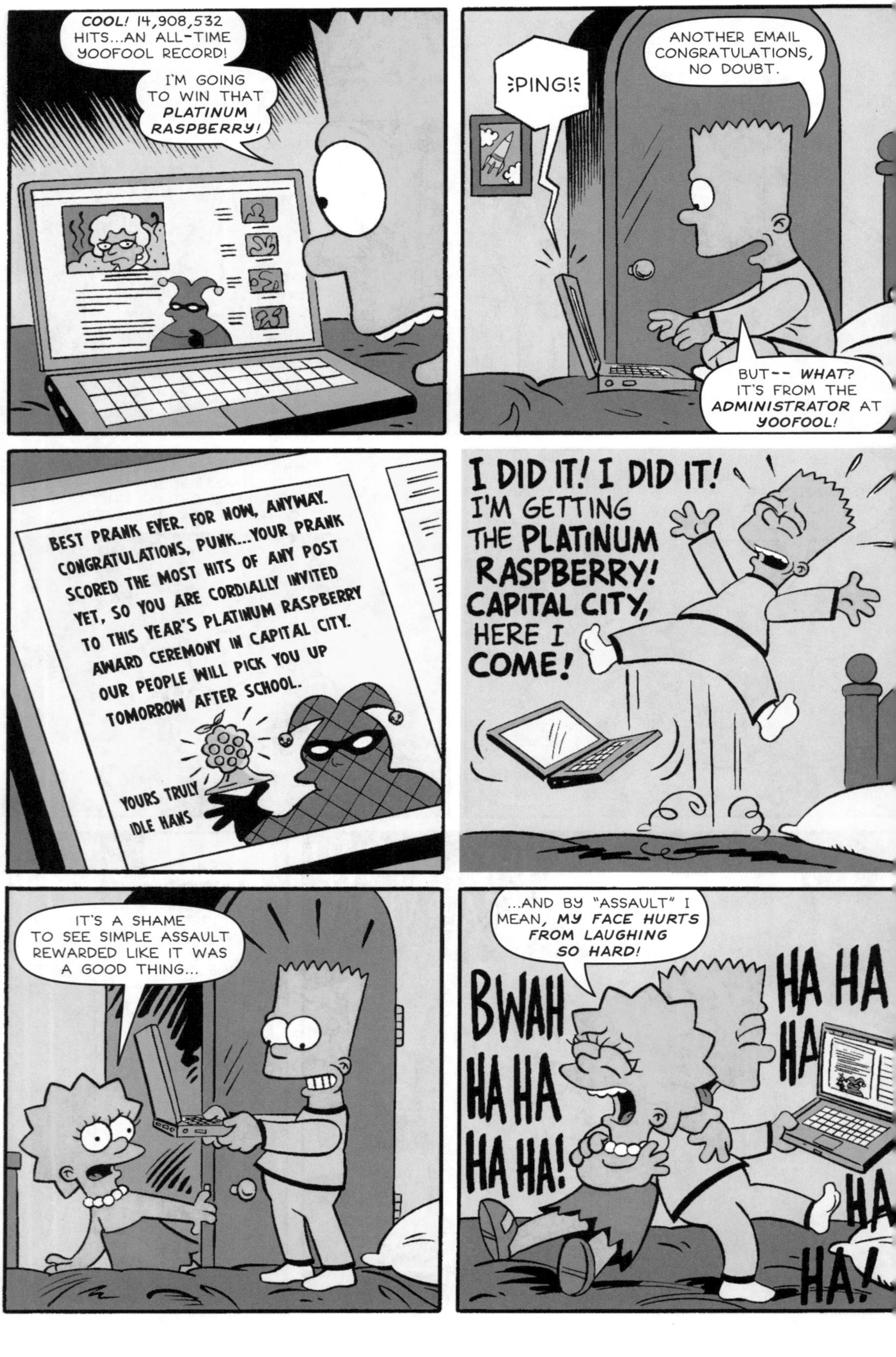
COOL! 14,908,532 HITS...AN ALL-TIME YOOFOOL RECORD!
I'M GOING TO WIN THAT PLATINUM RASPBERRY!
ANOTHER EMAIL CONGRATULATIONS, NO DOUBT.
PING!
BUT-- WHAT? IT'S FROM THE ADMINISTRATOR AT YOOFOOL!
BEST PRANK EVER. FOR NOW, ANYWAY.
CONGRATULATIONS, PUNK...YOUR PRANK SCORED THE MOST HITS OF ANY POST YET, SO YOU ARE CORDIALLY INVITED TO THIS YEAR'S PLATINUM RASPBERRY AWARD CEREMONY IN CAPITAL CITY. OUR PEOPLE WILL PICK YOU UP TOMORROW AFTER SCHOOL.
YOURS TRULY IDLE HANS
I DID IT! I DID IT! I'M GETTING THE PLATINUM RASPBERRY! CAPITAL CITY, HERE I COME!
IT'S A SHAME TO SEE SIMPLE ASSAULT REWARDED LIKE IT WAS A GOOD THING...
...AND BY "ASSAULT" I MEAN, MY FACE HURTS FROM LAUGHING SO HARD!
BWAH HA HA HA HA!
HA HA HA
HA HA!

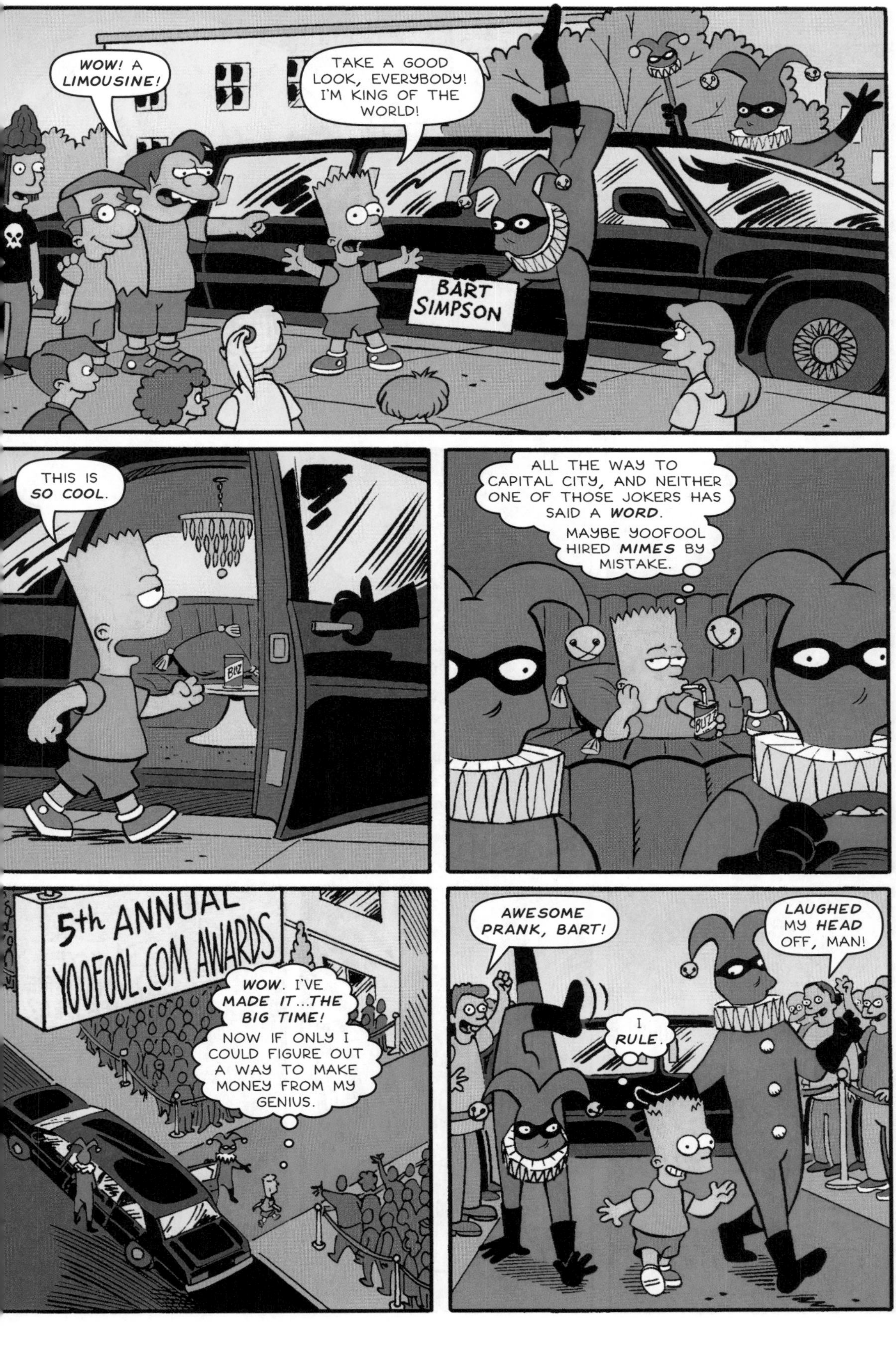
WOW! A LIMOUSINE!
TAKE A GOOD LOOK, EVERYBODY! I'M KING OF THE WORLD!
BART SIMPSON
THIS IS SO COOL.
ALL THE WAY TO CAPITAL CITY, AND NEITHER ONE OF THOSE JOKERS HAS SAID A WORD.
MAYBE YOOFOOL HIRED MIMES BY MISTAKE.
5th ANNUAL YOOFOOL.COM AWARDS
WOW. I'VE MADE IT...THE BIG TIME!
NOW IF ONLY I COULD FIGURE OUT A WAY TO MAKE MONEY FROM MY GENIUS.
AWESOME PRANK, BART!
LAUGHED MY HEAD OFF, MAN!
I RULE.

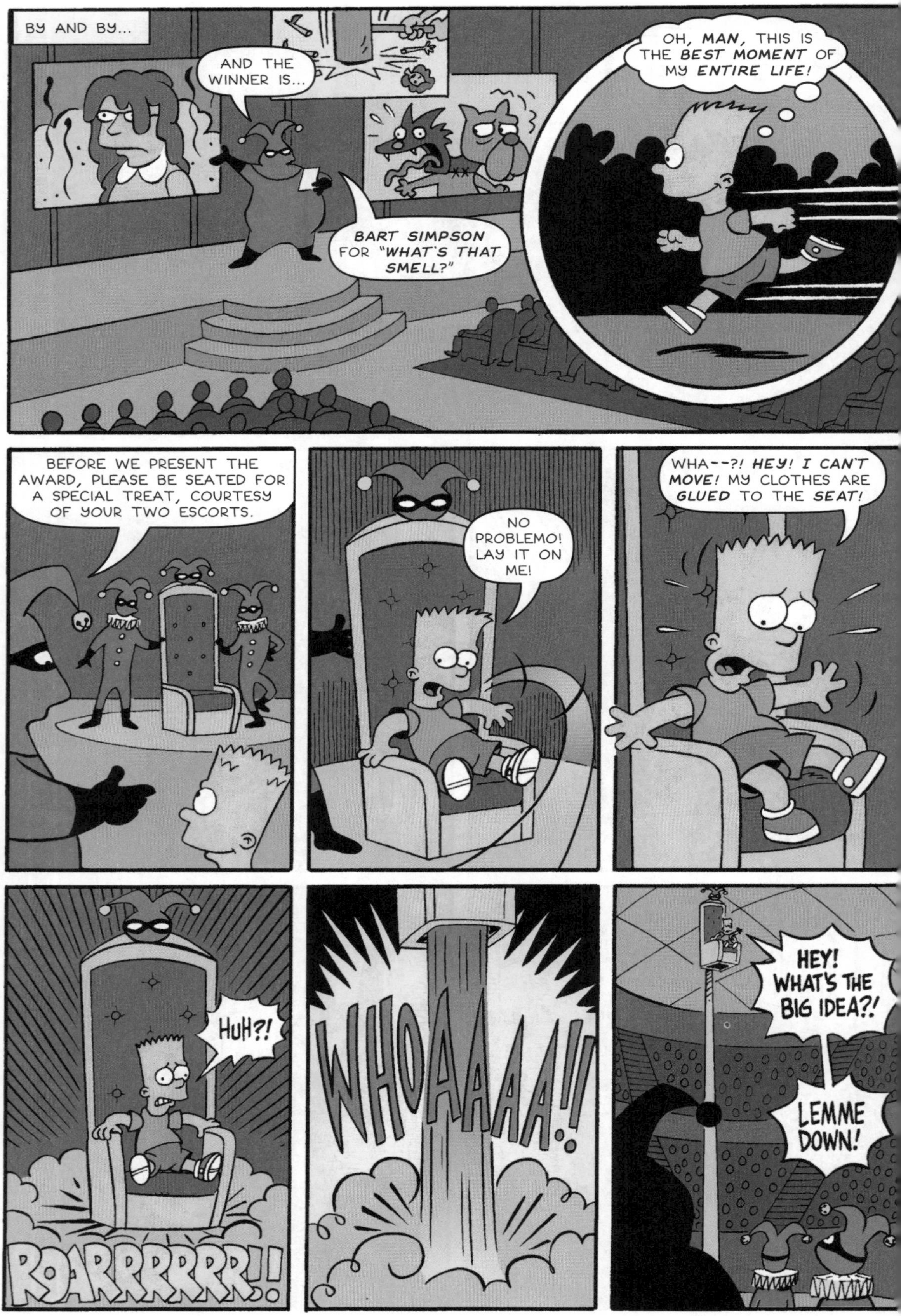

BY AND BY...
AND THE WINNER IS...
BART SIMPSON FOR "WHAT'S THAT SMELL?"
OH, MAN, THIS IS THE BEST MOMENT OF MY ENTIRE LIFE!
BEFORE WE PRESENT THE AWARD, PLEASE BE SEATED FOR A SPECIAL TREAT, COURTESY OF YOUR TWO ESCORTS.
NO PROBLEMO! LAY IT ON ME!
WHA--?! HEY! I CAN'T MOVE! MY CLOTHES ARE GLUED TO THE SEAT!
HUH?!
ROARRRRRR!!
WHOAAAA!!
HEY! WHAT'S THE BIG IDEA?!
LEMME DOWN!

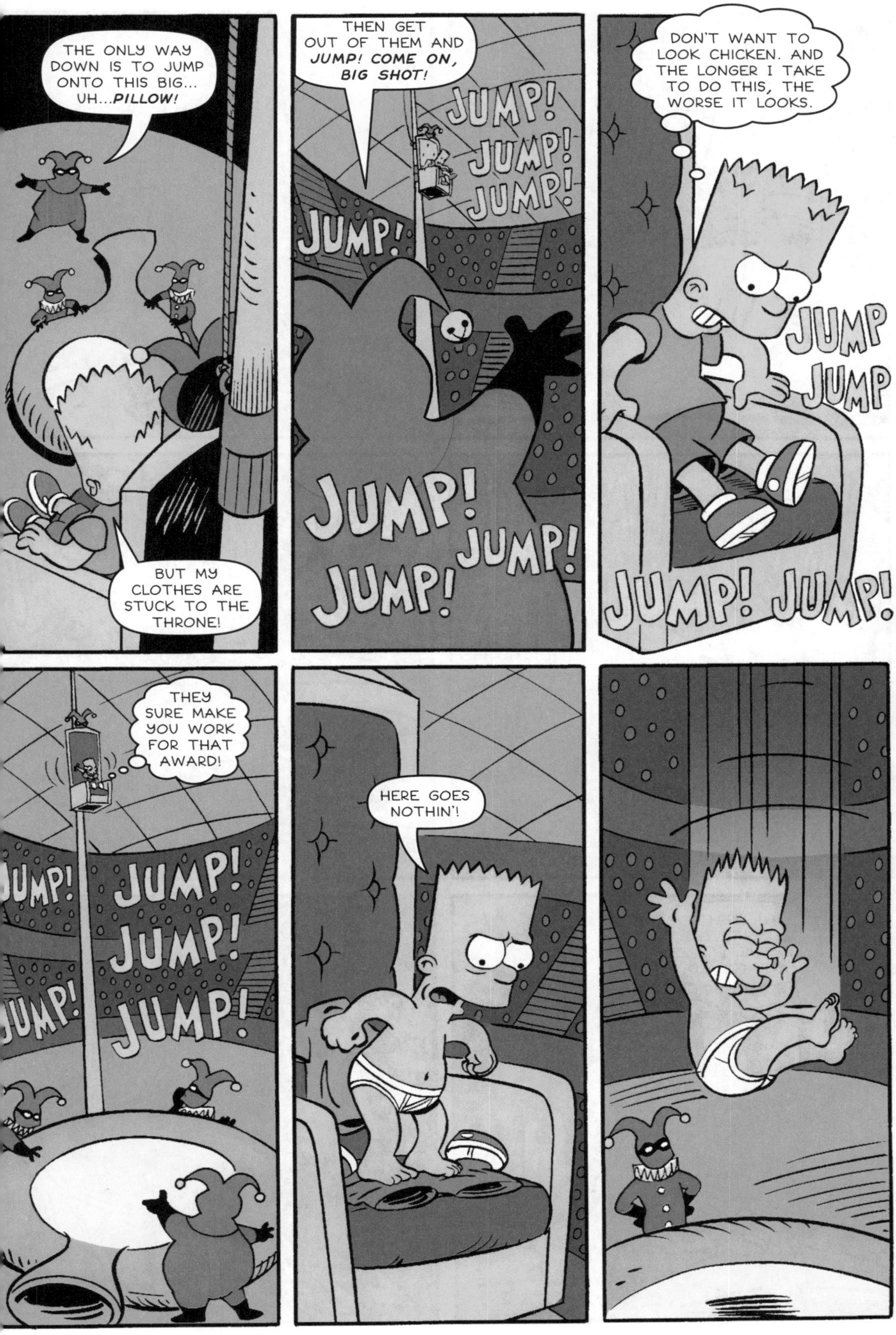
THE ONLY WAY DOWN IS TO JUMP ONTO THIS BIG... UH...*PILLOW!*
BUT MY CLOTHES ARE STUCK TO THE THRONE!
THEN GET OUT OF THEM AND *JUMP! COME ON, BIG SHOT!*
JUMP! JUMP! JUMP!
JUMP!
JUMP! JUMP! JUMP!
DON'T WANT TO LOOK CHICKEN. AND THE LONGER I TAKE TO DO THIS, THE WORSE IT LOOKS.
JUMP JUMP
JUMP! JUMP!
THEY SURE MAKE YOU WORK FOR THAT AWARD!
JUMP! JUMP! JUMP!
HERE GOES NOTHIN'!

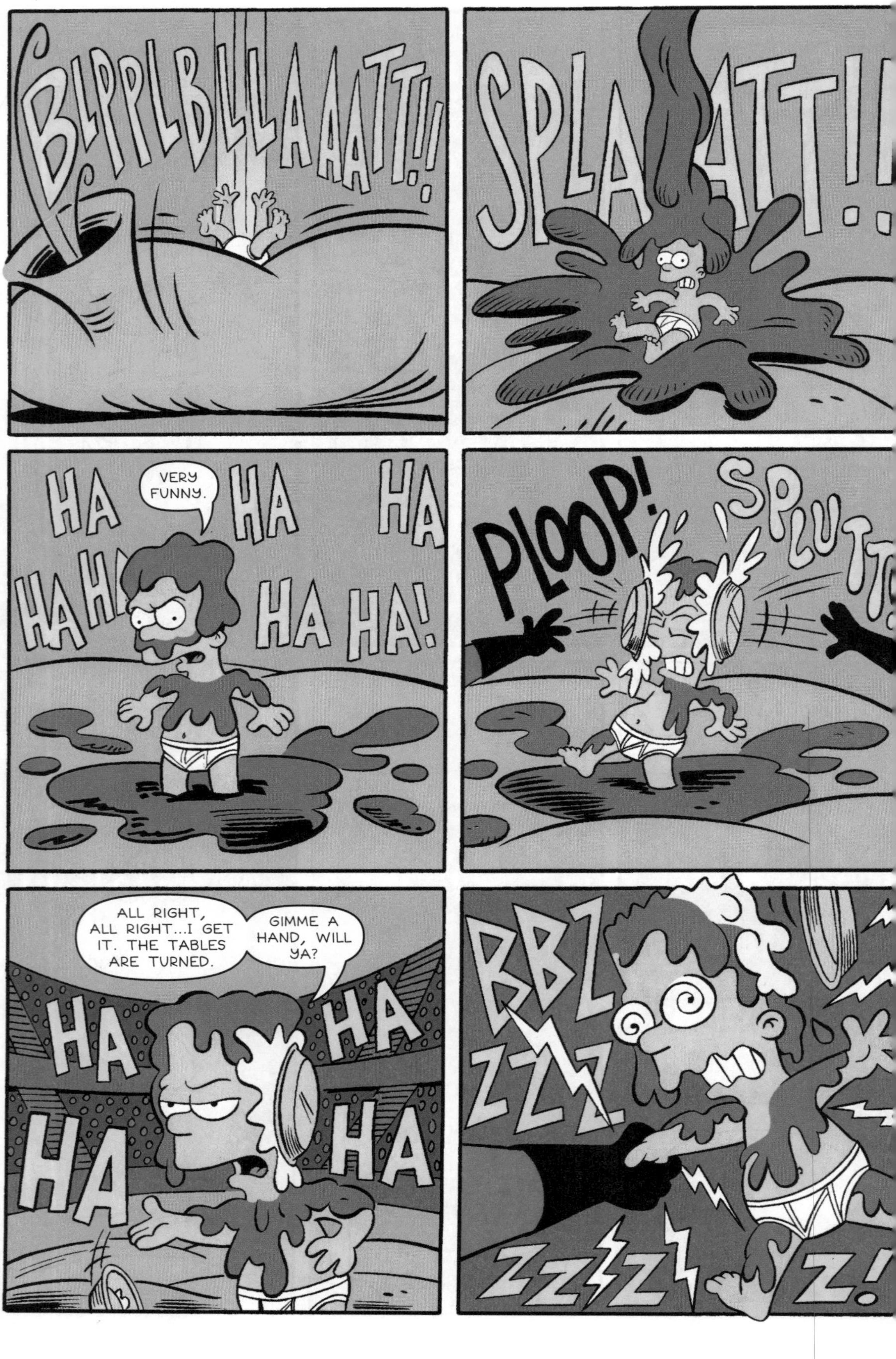
BLPPLBLLAAATT!!!
SPLAATT!!
HA HA HA HA HA HA HA!
VERY FUNNY.
PLOOP!
SPLUTT!
ALL RIGHT, ALL RIGHT...I GET IT. THE TABLES ARE TURNED.
GIMME A HAND, WILL YA?
HA HA HA HA
BBZZZZ
ZZZZ Z!

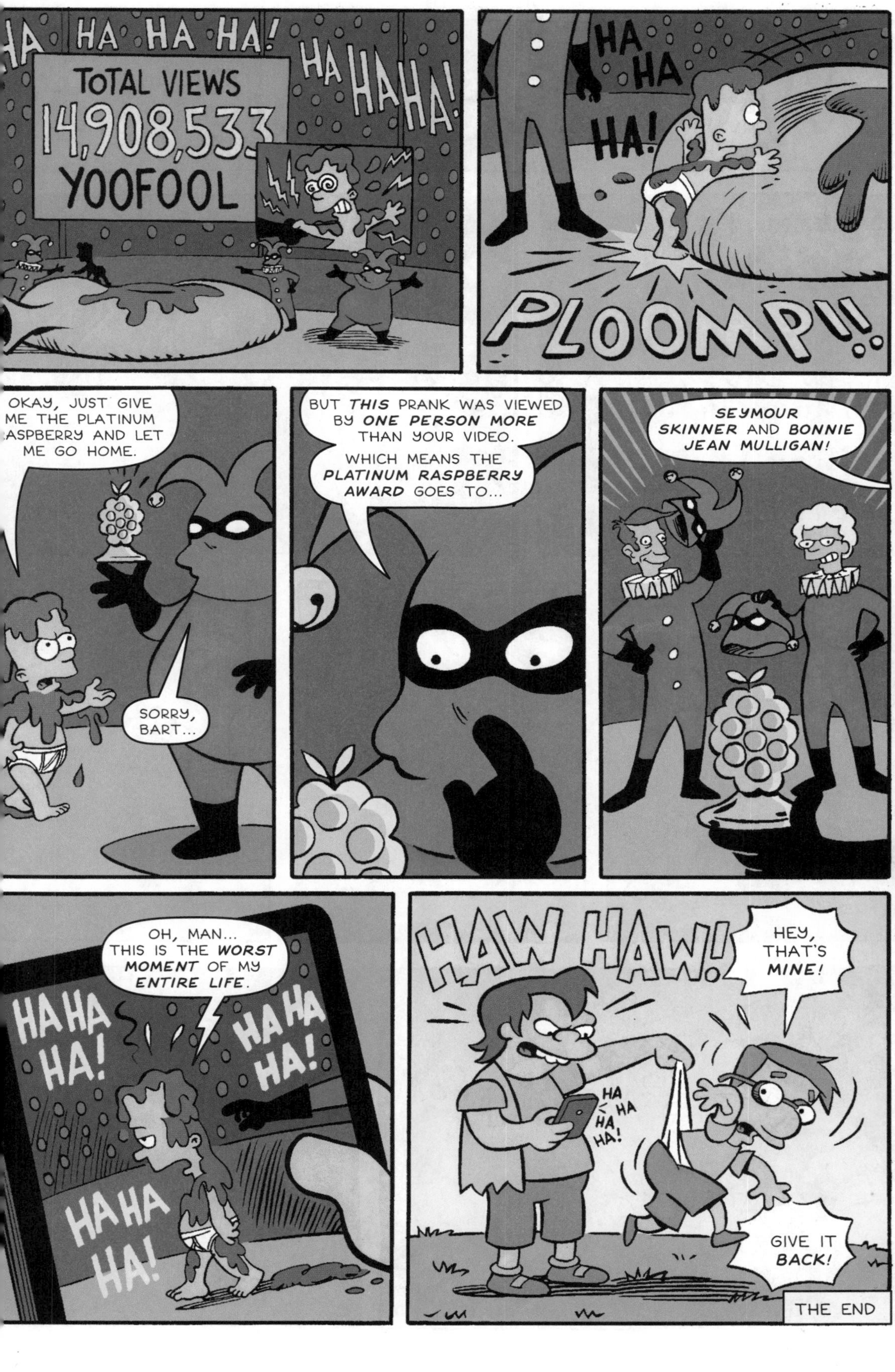
HA HA HA HA!
TOTAL VIEWS
14,908,533
YOOFOOL
HA HA HA!
HA HA
HA!
PLOOMP!!
OKAY, JUST GIVE ME THE PLATINUM RASPBERRY AND LET ME GO HOME.
SORRY, BART...
BUT THIS PRANK WAS VIEWED BY ONE PERSON MORE THAN YOUR VIDEO.
WHICH MEANS THE PLATINUM RASPBERRY AWARD GOES TO...
SEYMOUR SKINNER AND BONNIE JEAN MULLIGAN!
OH, MAN... THIS IS THE WORST MOMENT OF MY ENTIRE LIFE.
HA HA HA!
HA HA HA!
HA HA HA!
HAW HAW!
HEY, THAT'S MINE!
HA HA HA HA!
GIVE IT BACK!
THE END

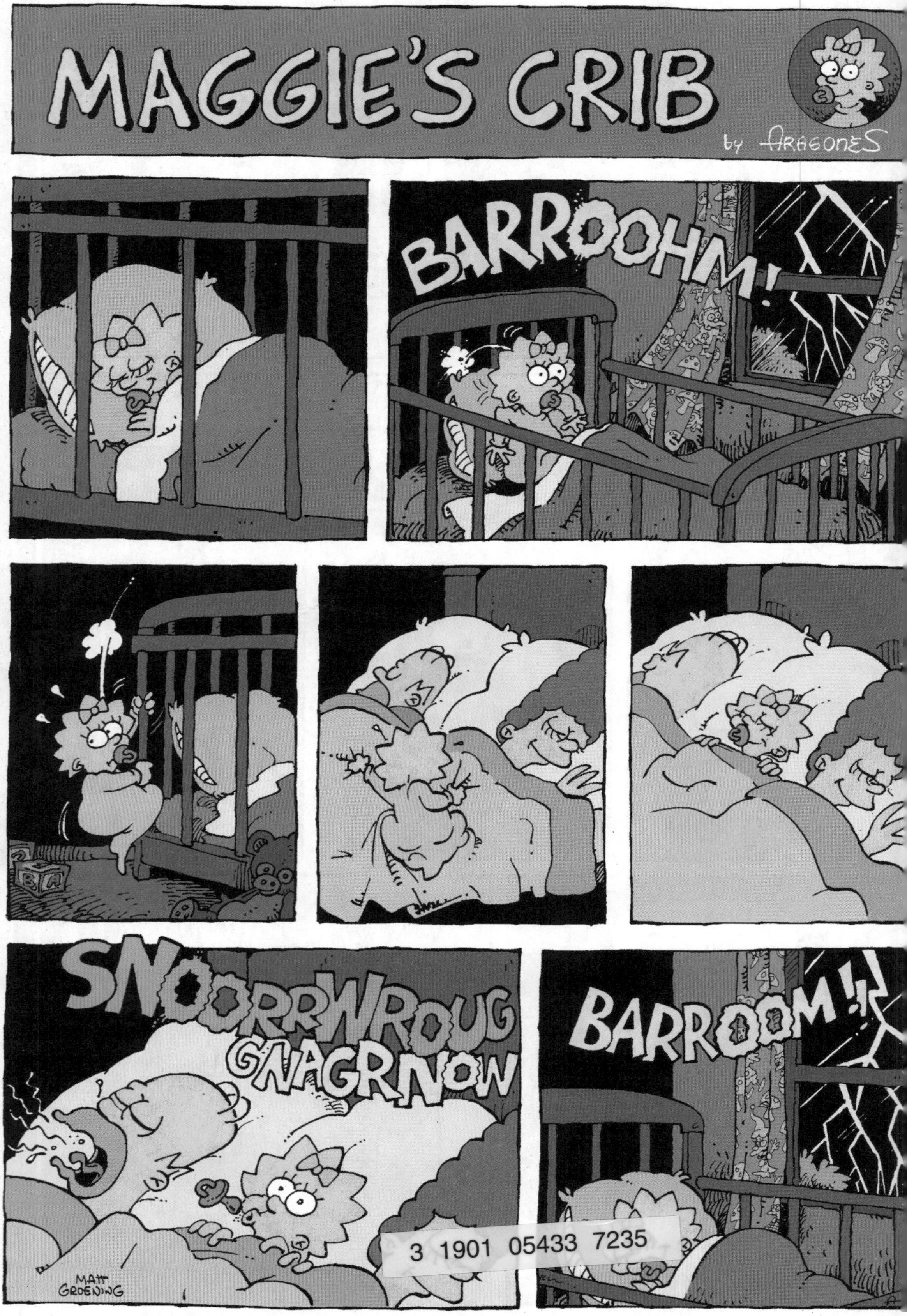
MAGGIE'S CRIB
by ARAGONES
BARROOHM!
SNOORRWROUG
GNAGRNOW
MATT GROENING
BARROOM!!

SERGIO ARAGONÉS STORY & ART

ART VILLANUEVA COLORS

BILL MORRISON EDITOR